"I don't think I fully understood how brave my good friend Tim Hetherington was until reading these pages. Not only does Huffman bring Tim back to life—his brilliant work, his extraordinary vision—but he also leads us through some of the most harrowing combat of our generation. His description of the siege of Misrata should be read by anyone who imagines they understand war—or courage, or fear. For all my time as a war reporter, I don't think I fully understood those things until reading Huffman's incredible book."   —Sebastian Junger

"Celebrate[s] Tim Hetherington's life . . . focusing on Tim's relationship with his work . . . recount[s] his last days in Libya in excruciating detail."
                                                            —Peter van Agtmael, *TIME*

"[*Here I Am*] captures the unflinching life of war photographer Tim Hetherington. . . . Huffman re-creates the suspense of battle, the tension between competing photographers who, by nature, are judgmental of one another's approach to depicting war; he builds detailed characters of Libyan ambulance drivers, fighters, and commanders as successfully as he depicts the contentious clique of photographers."   —Lynsey Addario, Daily Beast

"A powerfully written biography . . . titled *Here I Am* in reference to a moment that Hetherington finds himself in his own viewfinder, reflected back in a mirror. This is poignant imagery and metaphor for the entire body of this extraordinary artist and humanist's life."   —Huffington Post

"In stark, unsentimental words, Huffman shows how the bold and ambitious Hetherington was drawn past even his own inner psychological boundary. . . . Gut-wrenching as his story is, it's an inspirational one that is especially significant in this era of media downsizing and of sanitized, corporate-driven journalism."   —Tom Henry, *Minneapolis Star Tribune*

"A tale worth telling, a look into a world of violence and chaos few could understand."   —Joe Rogers, *Jackson Clarion-Ledger*

"Huffman recounts Hetherington's career in chapters that expand on the many conflicts the photographer covered: The Liberian civil war; the genocide in Sudan . . . the American occupation of Afghanistan . . . and succeeds in immersing us in Hetherington's daily reality while in conflict zones. . . . Many excellent interviews with friends and colleagues add a personal dimension to the photographer's extraordinary life."

—Michael Meyer, *Columbia Journalism Review*

"Huffman takes readers into the midst of some dangerous and gruesome battle zones that Hetherington recorded. The book is part biography and part war chronicle, but it is also a skillfully constructed eulogy, in which Huffman allows many of Hetherington's friends and colleagues to reminisce about a fallen comrade. . . . By deftly combining such personal memories with vivid descriptions of battle zones, Huffman makes *Here I Am* a must-read as a uniquely constructed memoriam."   —Joseph Hnatiuk, *Winnipeg Free Press*

"Compelling . . . Huffman details Hetherington's early career, friendships, and experiences with rebels in Africa, and influences and aesthetic struggles. . . . and offers perspectives from firsthand sources to unveil the heroism and errors of his final days."   —*Publishers Weekly*

"Huffman recounts the career arc of British-born and -educated Hetherington while simultaneously providing insights into the mentality of war photographers during the past century. . . . A first-rate biographical portrait that also deserves accolades for its insights into the minds of adventure-seeking photographers."   —*Kirkus Reviews*

"Huffman details the life of a man who wasn't satisfied to record images but wanted to understand the causes behind the war, the histories of conflict, and the individuals—many, adolescents—caught in the horror and drama of war. Through Hetherington's extraordinary life, Huffman explores a dangerous profession and how one man pursued it with his own personal twist."

—*Booklist*

HERE I AM

The Story of Tim Hetherington,
War Photographer

Alan Huffman

Grove Press
New York

Published simultaneously in Canada
Printed in the United States of America

ISBN: 978-0-8021-2091-5
eISBN: 978-0-8021-9366-7

Grove Press
an imprint of Grove/Atlantic, Inc.
154 West 14th Street
New York, NY 10011

Distributed by Publishers Group West

www.groveatlantic.com

14 15 16 17   10 9 8 7 6 5 4 3 2 1

CONTENTS

CONTENTS

1

MISRATA, LIBYA,
APRIL 20, 2011

The walls of the old al-Beyt Beytik furniture store were riddled with holes from mortar and machine-gun fire. Some were the size of the wounds they were intended to inflict. Others were as big as picture windows. In a back room on the third floor the ragged openings framed views of the war zone outside: a distant, solitary figure with a Kalashnikov, silhouetted on Tripoli Street; a burned-out car at the base of a towering palm; a shot-up Pepsi billboard. Viewed as a whole, they evoked a nightmare gallery, showcasing images of war that could get you killed if you stared at them too long.

In late afternoon, sunlight streamed through the holes, illuminating smoke-blackened walls, floors littered with bullet casings, and, in one corner, the rumpled sleeping bags of the Gaddafi snipers. The snipers had shot through the holes at anyone who passed through their field of vision below—mostly young men in head scarves, combat helmets, or baseball caps who darted across Tripoli Street or swerved through intersections in trucks with shattered windshields.

At a little before 4:30 p.m. on the day the snipers were finally killed, the frozen images framed by the holes in the front of the building were suddenly set in motion. A tall, handsome man sprinted past on the sidewalk below, gripping a camera in his left hand, holding the strap of his rucksack with the other to keep it from bouncing as he ran. A few seconds later there was an explosion.

Tripoli Street, like most streets in Misrata, was lined with bombed-out buildings. Earlier in the day, al-Beyt Beytik had been the scene of a firefight between the snipers and perhaps thirty rebels who had fought from room to room with weapons designed for longer-range combat—automatic rifles and grenades. The result was like an ATF raid on a serial killer's holdout but with interested spectators and a retinue of photographers who filmed the action on Flip cams and iPhones. Some of the rebels laughed and smoked cigarettes. One arrived with a handful of bottle rockets, grinning as he sang "Happy Birthday." In one of the photographer's videos someone laughs nervously offscreen.

At one point in the video one of the rebels balances a piece of broken mirror on a section of angle iron and extends it through a doorway to reveal the snipers hiding around the corner. Behind him, Tim Hetherington peers through his camera at the reflection and is heard to say of the hidden snipers, "One is dead. They're under the beds." A bearded man in a headscarf steps forward and begins firing his Kalashnikov around the corner. It is unclear if he hits anyone but he keeps firing.

Hetherington and the other photographers crowd behind him in the hallway, with perhaps a dozen rebels and a few onlookers. When the first gunman steps back, another takes his place and begins firing blindly into the room. The metallic snap of bullets echoes through the building. The rebels chatter in Arabic. Hetherington says, "Fucking hell." Someone else says, "Oh, my God." Eventually the rebels set a

2

couple of car tires on fire and roll them into the snipers' room, hoping to smoke them out.

Al-Beyt Beytik stands a block from where Tripoli Street crosses a bypass known as the Coastal Road on a long bridge that leads toward the capital, about 120 miles to the west. For the past two months Tripoli Street had been a linear battlefield, starting at the center of Misrata and lurching toward the bridge, as the city was besieged by the army of Muammar Gaddafi, bent on stopping the westward advance of the Libyan uprising toward Tripoli. The siege of Misrata, which had brought everyone to al-Beyt Beytik that day, was the climax of the first Arab Spring uprising to escalate into a full-scale war. Misrata, a Mediterranean port of about 300,000 people, was surrounded, and the government forces had positioned snipers—many of them mercenaries—in all of the tallest buildings. Among the mercenaries, it was said, were a group of Colombian women with particularly deadly aim.

Aside from occasional NATO air strikes, Misrata's only defense came from the kind of men who shot up the interior of al-Beyt Beytik that day—local rebels with little or no military training, people who before the war had been truck drivers, salesmen, artists, office workers, laborers, lawyers, students, or unemployed. In the beginning most did not have guns. Some had arrived on the front lines armed with knives or steel rods. Over time, they managed to ambush and kill a few Gaddafi soldiers and steal their guns, which they used to kill others, acquiring more guns in the process. Meanwhile, weapons and ammunition were being smuggled into the port aboard fishing boats, so that by April 20, 2011, the day they attacked the furniture store, most of the rebels had guns, though not everyone knew how to use one.

That afternoon, as Hetherington sprinted past al-Beyt Beytik, a few dozen rebels and a small group of photographers lingered on Tripoli Street, waiting for what came next, which turned out to be a mortar blast, after a long, relatively quiet period. The bomb exploded on the sidewalk in front of an auto repair garage, scoring the pavement in a star-shaped pattern, sending smoke, dust, and shrapnel into the group of people who stood—or, in Hetherington's case, ran—nearby. As the smoke cleared, a Spanish photographer watching from across the street saw perhaps ten bodies strewn about and people sprinting for cover. Soon a few cars and trucks emerged from hiding places and sped away. A few vehicles stopped and rebels leaped out and began loading the injured into them to take them to al-Hekma, the city's only functioning hospital. The photographer across the street, whose name was Guillermo Cervera, snapped three pictures of the aftermath of the explosion with his iPhone, then ran to help. At the scene of the explosion he flagged down a car and pushed two of the photographers, one of whom was bleeding from his chest, into the backseat. The car then sped away. Next Cervera helped two rebels load Hetherington and a second photographer, an American named Chris Hondros, into the bed of a black pickup truck, after which the rebels jumped into the front seat, Cervera climbed into the bed with his injured friends, and they drove away, down the sidewalk and into an alley to a side street that went north from Tripoli Street toward al-Hekma. Hetherington was bleeding profusely from a small wound at the top of his right leg. Hondros, who still wore his combat helmet, was unconscious and had an ugly gash in his forehead.

Where the alley emptied into the side street, the driver saw an ambulance and stopped. After a quick and frenzied discussion, the decision was made to transfer Hondros, who was at the back of the bed with his feet hanging off, to the ambulance. He was the easiest to get out. While the transfer was taking place, Cervera took a photo of Hetherington lying on his back in the bed of the truck, propped against ammunition boxes. Then everyone got back in the truck and the driver tore off down the sandy street in a cloud of dust. As they sped toward al-Hekma, Hetherington began to lose consciousness due to loss of blood. Cervera took his hand in his own and spoke to him soothingly, trying to keep him awake.

The streets passed between walled residential compounds that had been subjected to frequent shelling and sniper fire so that the routes were full of obstacles—downed power lines, destroyed cars and trucks, the rubble of collapsed walls. Everyone other than the fighters was long gone. The pickup and the ambulance behind it rarely slowed, though at one point the truck's driver had to jam on his brakes and swerve to avoid colliding with a car full of rebels that appeared out of a blind side street. Eventually—it felt to everyone like an eternity—the warren of sandy streets led to a paved road, which in turn led to a series of checkpoints that the rebels quickly waved the vehicles through, across several roundabouts and, finally, to the avenue that led to al-Hekma. On the final stretch there was a series of speed bumps, which jostled the injured men. Some fifteen minutes had passed by the time the pickup and the ambulance careened into the narrow driveway of the small hospital, where a tent had been set up in the parking lot as an emergency room.

Alerted over the radio that two more Western photographers were on the way to the hospital, a group of rebels, nurses, and doctors rushed out to meet the vehicles. They pulled Hetherington from the bed of the truck, loaded him onto a gurney, and hurried with him into the tent. Others removed the stretcher on which Hondros lay and rushed him into the main hospital, to the small ICU.

Inside the tent were the other two photographers who had been injured in the attack—an American, Michael Christopher Brown, who was one of the men Cervera had pushed into the car, and a Brit, Guy Martin, who had been transported in another pickup truck. There were also perhaps six injured rebels, some with equally grave injuries, though they would not be mentioned in later news accounts. At least three rebels were dead, or soon would be. Hetherington had by now

lost consciousness, and was possibly dead, but for ten or fifteen minutes a group of Italian and Libyan doctors pushed violently against his
chest, trying to resuscitate him. A rebel photographer named Mohammed al-Zawwam filmed the scene with his video camera, pushing his
way through the crowd, now and then bumping into someone so that
his footage veers wildly from the men on the gurneys to the floor to
the back of someone's head. At the point where he comes upon Hetherington, we hear him say, off camera, "Tim," in surprise and recogni-
tion. He then focuses on Hetherington's body for a long moment and
zooms in on his face, close enough to pick up the stubble on his chin.

As al-Zawwam filmed, a Brazilian photographer with a dark,
manicured beard, whose hair was trimmed into a kind of soccer mul-
let, observed him getting in the way of the doctors and nurses and
kicked him. A moment later, the Brazilian, whose name was André
Liohn, saw Cervera standing off to the side and said, angrily, "I told
you, you shouldn't have been there." Liohn would later post a message on his Facebook page that said, "Sad news. Tim Hetherington
has died just now in the Misrata hospital when covering the frontline,
Chris Hondros is in a serious state."

2
FROM ENGLAND

In the summer of 2003 a Liberian rebel named Black Diamond was roaming the remote garrison of Tubmanburg, Liberia, when she saw Tim Hetherington sitting on the balcony of a house that belonged to her leader, General Cobra. At the time, the West African nation was in the midst of its second civil war in a little more than a decade, and Black Diamond was in charge of a group of female fighters. Her life had an ecclesiastical aspect. She had joined the rebels after being raped at seventeen by government soldiers who had killed her parents, and she was known as a relentless, fearsome fighter. Later in the summer she would be featured in a BBC report called "Liberia's Women Killers" for which she posed with a pistol and an AK-47. She was rumored to have castrated enemy soldiers, though she declined to publicly verify or deny the claims. Her exploits eventually became so notorious that some Liberians thought she was a myth.

In that context, the arrival of a tall, handsome, stranger, a white man who seemed to be having a good time, struck her as odd. Black Diamond had heard that two white men were scheduled to arrive in Tubmanburg to film the rebels during their assault on the Liberian capital, Monrovia, but by the time the journalist Sebastian Junger interviewed her in 2011 for a documentary film about Hetherington's life, after he'd been killed in the North African nation of Libya, she had transformed Hetherington into something of a legend, an apparition. In the lilting patois of Liberian English, she said her first thought was, "Wow, what a strange guy . . . what a handsome man doing in the lion den?"

Black Diamond and her female compatriots, including many who had likewise been raped by government soldiers, were part of a rebel group known as LURD, which stood for Liberians United for Reconciliation and Democracy, a lofty name that belied a violent history in a place long noted for violence. Hetherington and the filmmaker James Brabazon had traveled to Liberia to accompany LURD during its second assault on Monrovia. Junger would later become a friend and professional collaborator of Hetherington's and, in the summer of 2003, had been reporting on the war from inside Monrovia, on the other side.

Hetherington stood out in a crowd, and his appearance unsettled Black Diamond, she said. She was unsure why such a man would give up a comfortable life to put himself at risk in someone else's civil war. During his eight years as a photographer covering numerous wars, conflict zones, and other places of human disaster, which began that summer in Liberia, Hetherington would ponder the question himself. It seemed at times as if war photographers were vultures and, at others, part of the conscience of the world. Going back and forth between war zones and the comforts of home tended to make such photographers perennial outsiders.

The simple answer is that a war photographer is someone who makes his living photographing wars—someone like Robert Capa or Larry Burrows, who put their lives at risk to illuminate what was happening in the world's dark and violent recesses, and meanwhile brought high drama to the mass media. Hetherington was among the best known photographers covering war at the time of his death, but his interests extended beyond what journalists call "bang-bang" photos. Often his war photographs are not of combat itself but of faces and telling details about the people caught up in the conflict. He tended to immerse himself in their world, and to stay there longer than most of his peers, who tended to show up, snap dramatic photos, and move on. Wherever Hetherington was, he was always *there*. He preferred to describe himself as a maker of images, someone who told stories through a variety of media, including still photography, video, and written narratives, and he saw himself as an artist with a strong humanitarian bent. His aim, as he later put it, was to try to explain the world to the world. As it happened, there was no better place to do that—to show what mattered—than in a war zone.

The nexus of conflict photography as a journalistic discipline was, in fact, art, though its original intent was more about military strategy than the kind of storytelling that characterized Hetherington's career. The earliest precedent for war photography is generally considered to be the work of a Dutch painter named Willem van de Velde the Elder, who in 1666 rowed out in a small boat to sketch an encounter between the Dutch and British navies during what was known as the Four Days Battle. Van de Velde later used his drawings as the basis for heroic oil paintings, as well as to acquire a commission from the British government to sketch naval battles for official review. Numerous other painters followed suit in subsequent wars. The British war photographer Roger Fenton also started out as a painter in the mid-nineteenth century. After visiting an exhibition of photography in London in 1851, he studied photography for two years, then got an assignment to cover the Crimean War, also for England and, again, for official, strategic purposes. In the United States the painter Mathew Brady started photographing in the 1840s and later became famous for his photos of the

American Civil War, including graphic images of corpses, which was a new phenomenon that brought home the reality of war in a less stylized, sanitized format. Both Brady and Fenton were limited in their choice of subjects by the slowness and awkwardness of their equipment; because of the necessary length of exposure times subjects had to be still, which meant that they primarily photographed landscapes, buildings, and people who were posed, much as they would have been for a painter. As a result, the first photographic images of war were, like many of Hetherington's own combat portraits, carefully framed and comparatively static. Their subjects—the live ones, at least—had time to think about how they were being recorded and tended to consciously play the role. So did Fenton and Brady, who in some cases staged their photos.

War photographers hit their stride during World War II, and by then most had their own agendas—to share the drama with the public. Among the first well-known war photographers was Robert Capa, who covered the Spanish Civil War, World War II, and the First Indochina War, where in 1954 he was killed by a landmine. The role of war photographers became pivotal during the Vietnam War, when photographers such as Burrows—another Brit who, like Capa and Hetherington, died at war—brought home powerful images that not only entertained the public but illustrated precisely and on an intimate level what was at stake in war.

At the time Hetherington traveled to Libya to cover that country's 2011 revolution, technology had enabled instant media coverage via satellite uplinks and websites, which further amplified the demand for war images, as well as the risks associated with producing them. But in the summer of 2003, when Hetherington and Brabazon arrived in Liberia, video was just coming to the fore as a critical component of war coverage. So in addition to his video cameras Hetherington carried comparatively antiquated still cameras that were more suited to

10

studio work; the combination enabled him to cover the conflict both on the cutting edge of journalism and in the creative, timeless style of an artist.

As Hetherington's career unfolded, most people described him as a war photographer, but he said he had "no interest in photography, per se." Instead, he was interested in the power of images—photographs, films, drawings, paintings, fly posters glued to utility poles, spray-painted graffiti—to spark dialogue about what was happening in the world. Photography was the primary tool at his disposal, and it gave him an outlet for both his creative and his humanitarian interests. It also provided a potential means for exorcising internal demons that he never fully described other than as "a destructive tendency inside myself." War photography required a certain remove, a personal distancing from the core conflict that counterbalanced the photographer's physical proximity. Yet as Hetherington told one interviewer, "I think the important thing for me is to connect with real people, to document them in these extreme circumstances, where there aren't any kind of neat solutions, where you can't put any kind of neat guidelines and say this is what it's about, or this is what it's about." He wanted to show what was happening to people beyond the firing of weapons.

Timothy Alistair Hetherington was born in Birkenhead, near Liverpool, in 1970, to a family of comfortable means—father Alistair, mother Judith, brother Guy, and sister Victoria. As a boy he had a notably inquisitive mind and showed talent as an artist. At age ten his parents enrolled him in a private boarding school run by Jesuits known as Lancashire Benedictine, at Stonyhurst College, where he was appalled by the frequent bullying and use of corporal punishment, as he later told Junger. He learned to loathe conflict yet over time felt compelled to understand it; he became, in Junger's words, a "bright spirit drawn to dark places." At his religious confirmation, Hetherington added a third name, Telemachus, after a central character in Homer's *Odyssey*,

11

the son of the Greek god Odysseus who searches for news about his father while he was at war; Telemachus was also the name of a saint who was stoned to death in a Roman amphitheater after trying to halt a gladiator fight.

Early on, Hetherington had ideas of becoming a writer and studied English literature and the classics at Lady Margaret Hall, a college of Oxford University. After graduating in 1992, he used a £5,000 bequest from his grandmother to travel for two years in India, China, and Tibet, feeding his curiosity about the lives of people in unfamiliar circumstances. His family rarely heard from him during his travels, receiving only a handful of faxes, until he showed up back in England, a patient of the London School of Tropical Medicine, suffering from a host of tropical diseases. After being hospitalized for about a month he took a minor editing job, which he found unsatisfying, and then made the decision to study photography. He later said he'd had an epiphany after returning from India, which led him to want to "make images." He was profoundly influenced by the 1983 film *Sans Soleil*, directed by Chris Marker, which showed how powerful film, still photos, and a combination of the two could be. "That film was a real turning point," he said.

Because photography was easier to get into on his own than film, Hetherington began taking night courses in the discipline while working at various jobs, and eventually he enrolled full-time in photojournalism graduate school at Cardiff University in Wales. There, he was known as a driven student who attracted attention when he walked into a room—he was tall, good-looking, and affable and had a keen sense of humor, could party with the best of them, and sported a mass of long dreadlocks that he often tucked inside an oversized skullcap. He showed particular interest in photographing sports and health stories and had a tendency to immerse himself in his subjects: a photo essay about people who suffered from Alzheimer's and dementia required him to spend long hours for several days at an adult day care center. When he set out to do a photo essay on youth violence, he hung out at the emergency room at a Cardiff hospital—this in an era when a photographer could do such things without privacy restrictions—to observe when young men arrived whose injuries had resulted from fights. He was also exploring multimedia, a fairly new concept at the time. When Stephen Mayes, an external examiner of student projects at Cardiff (and later a friend of Hetherington's), reviewed his work he was "blown away," he said. It was powerful, original, and pushed the limits of conventional photography. Hetherington's final class project at Cardiff, in 1997, was an essay on alcohol-related violence, as observed in a hospital emergency room. Afterward, he began getting freelance photography jobs around London, shooting for the *Big Issue,* a magazine sold by homeless people, and the *Independent* newspaper. He was comfortable moving freely between very different worlds. At Oxford he had attended formal dining clubs in white tie and waistcoat; at Cardiff, he was the dreadlocked guy; now he was exploring every facet of the world around him for whatever publication would pay him to do so.

Then, in 1999, he began to find his focus while covering the Millennium Stars, a Liberian soccer team that was touring the UK. The team members were former combatants in the first Liberian civil war, which had ended three years before. Hetherington had called the trip's sponsor to see if he could arrange a ride on the tour bus. He was told the team was looking for someone to film them back in Liberia. "And that's how it all began," Hetherington later said. In exchange for filming, his expenses—for travel, film, and lodging—were covered but little else. The journey proved worthwhile. His photos were picked up by several magazines, and along the way he fell in love with West Africa and began following what was happening in the region more closely. "When I went to Liberia, it just blew me away," he said. "I'd never experienced a country like that before in my life."

From Liberia he traveled to neighboring Sierra Leone, which was experiencing its own civil war, also to photograph soccer players. Soccer was one of the few pastimes that people in war-ravaged nations such as Liberia and Sierra Leone could take joy in. Though it provided a needed diversion, Hetherington said of a later photo essay on the subject that it was a story about war "disguised as sport." Hetherington did not directly experience combat but he felt its presence in Sierra Leone, as he had in Liberia. He shot a series of portraits of people who had been blinded by rebels and came upon a choir of blind students who inspired him to arrange a UK tour for them. The choir members, mostly children (though there were a few adults), had been blinded by childhood diseases or by torture and abuse during the civil war. Hetherington abhorred the inhumanity of war yet was attracted to understanding its origins and ramifications. In helping to arrange the blind choir's tour of the UK he hoped to show the impact of the West African wars and, in turn, expose the students to the outside world.

He happened upon the Milton Margai School in Freetown, Sierra Leone, and saw parallels between the school's blind choir and the Millennium Stars, because both involved young people dealing with handicaps or other hardships induced by war. Both of the underlying wars involved child soldiers and, for most Westerners, were bizarre episodes that also seemed to them reassuringly foreign. Having been exposed to the sometimes sadistic bullying at his English boarding school, Hetherington was curious about why one child might end up as a victim of war and another the victimizer. At the same time, he saw an opportunity to replicate the soccer team's UK tour, this time with the blind children's choir, and he began enlisting sponsors and helping the school organize it. The August 27, 2003, *South Wales Echo* announced the choir's tour under the headline "War-Hit Children Sing for Us." The choir members had endured eleven years of a particularly brutal war, and many had known nothing else. Hetherington, who acted as the choir's spokesman, told the *South Wales Echo*, "7,000 people were murdered, thousands more abused, and half the city destroyed." The tour, Hetherington told the newspaper, was a way to begin "rebuilding their lives and healing the mental scars." For his part, he accompanied them on the tour, kept them entertained, and even washed and ironed their forty stage costumes before their concert at Westminster Abbey.

Corinne Dufka, who at the time worked for Human Rights Watch in Freetown, met Hetherington while traveling back and forth between Sierra Leone and Liberia, covering the conflicts and interviewing refugees. When she heard of his association with the Milton Margai School, she said, "I loved him for that. He wasn't one to go for the easy, obvious target." Most Western journalists were fixated on what she called Sierra Leone's "signature atrocity"—the rebels' penchant for hacking off their victims' arms or legs. The blind children had been largely overlooked and forgotten. Some of the choir members, she said, had had burning oil poured into their eyes because they could not stop crying after watching family members killed. In addition to organizing the tour, Hetherington introduced the blind choir to blind children in the UK through a pen pal program, and though he was understandably proud when he won a World Press Photo award for his portraits of the choir, his relationship with them—they called him Uncle Tim—"touched him on a far deeper level," Dufka said.

Hetherington's decision to move beyond the blind choir and the Millennium Stars to document the underlying conflicts was part of a natural progression, Brabazon said. It was "almost as if, by being there and interested in the people, he kind of got sucked into it," he said. Through the blind children's choir, Hetherington had seen the direct consequences of war. "He saw it physically, visually, graphically, literally on the faces of the children he was photographing," Brabazon said. "But what he didn't see was the mechanism of that violence. He didn't see how it was inflicted and by whom, and I think that what he went on to do in West Africa, when he came to Liberia with me, when he stepped into the middle of that war, was to see very clearly who was perpetrating these acts of violence and why. I think that the blind school was the beginning of the journey for Tim in some ways. It was the beginning of his journey in war and Liberia was the next logical step."

Because the Liberian president Charles Taylor had funded the rebels who committed the atrocities in Sierra Leone, "there was a very strong connection, both metaphorically and literally, between the war in Sierra Leone and the war in Liberia," Brabazon said. "And I think that Tim understood very, very quickly, you couldn't really understand what had happened in Sierra Leone, you couldn't understand what was happening in Ivory Coast, next door, you couldn't understand what was happening in Guinea unless you understood what was happening in Liberia. And I think that's what drew him back there, to understand what the center of this regional maelstrom was. Who was behind it and why were they doing this?"

The same year he had first visited Liberia and Sierra Leone, Hetherington traveled to Sudan and, in the years afterward, to the Democratic Republic of the Congo, the Ivory Coast, Namibia, Nigeria, Burkina Faso, and, again, India; he also covered the elections in England and photographed Afghan refugees following the U.S. invasion of Afghanistan in the wake of the events of September 11, 2001. He used freelance assignments and gigs for charities and NGOs to explore the lives of people who, for the most part, were struggling with seriously adverse circumstances. By 2002, the year James Brabazon's first documentary film about Liberia's LURD rebels was released, Hetherington was fully vested in Africa. The more he considered the harsh consequences of war, the more he wanted to understand its root causes.

During his time with Brabazon a theme began to emerge that would define much of Hetherington's work: the complex, persistent, and often baffling relationship between young men and war. War is undeniably grueling, so it was not surprising that young men played a key role. But what, Hetherington wondered, prompted them to fight, knowing they might die? Often, he found, it had nothing to do with the core reasons for the conflict. And why did so many of them relish combat? Liberia seemed a good place to find out, because he was familiar with the country and its second civil war was now under way. Though women too were drawn to battle, such as Black Diamond and her female fighters, and some of the rebels and government soldiers were mere children, it was the young men, Hetherington later said, who seemed hardwired to fight. Ultimately, he said, young men were used as tools in a violent political process as a direct result of their genetics and chemistry.

After seeing Brabazon's film, Hetherington cold-called him to say that he wanted to accompany him to Liberia when and if he returned. As Brabazon recalled, he was at first uninterested; he had received a phone call from a total stranger who basically said, "Hi, you don't know me. My name is Tim Hetherington, and I'd really like to come to Liberia with you and take photographs of the rebels." Brabazon initially said no, that it was his story and he was not interested in sharing it. But then Hetherington informed him that he already had a Liberian visa, "which was like gold," Brabazon said. "So I had the idea to divide the story, me with the rebels and Tim with the government troops." When he met with Hetherington to talk things over, Brabazon said he realized that "I actually really like this guy." He decided to hire Hetherington as a cameraman and associate producer, with the understanding that he could also take still photographs for his own use. Meanwhile, Brabazon got a call from the documentary filmmaker Jonathan Stack saying he wanted to go, as well, so Brabazon developed a plan for him and Hetherington to film from the rebels' side while Stack would film inside the city. Brabazon and Stack would coproduce the resulting documentary.

Brabazon and Hetherington spent a good bit of time hanging out together in the month following their meeting—triangulating, taking each other's measure before setting off for Conakry, Guinea, the final point of embarkation for what proved to be an intense, bizarre, and often terrifying journey. The Liberia trip was "kind of like our Rubicon," Brabazon recalled, when talking with Junger for the documentary film about Hetherington (which Brabazon coproduced). War, he said, is "like a pressure cooker, you know? It takes human relationships, puts them under a lot of strain, and accelerates them, and rather than you spending two or three months to discover that you don't particularly like someone you'll know like *that*." He snapped his fingers. "And rather than spend a year getting to know someone and become mates with someone it can happen overnight." Finding themselves alone together in a foreign jungle, during a war, and having surrendered their trust to a mercenary guide and a group of armed rebels who were intent on capturing a heavily armed city, there was "very little room for bullshit," Brabazon said.

Brabazon was encouraged that Hetherington had been to Liberia before, as well as to Sierra Leone, which meant that he knew how to get by in West Africa, though at the time he had never experienced armed combat. What mattered most was that Hetherington was game, even if he was a mannerly Oxford-educated type—Brabazon was also a Brit—prone to intellectual discussions and ruminating about truth and beauty and the aesthetics of his craft.

Hetherington loved what he knew about Liberia, but he knew there was no way to predict how he would react once the bullets started to fly. So as they hung out in Tubmanburg, and later as they advanced with the rebels toward Monrovia, he and Brabazon often talked about what would likely go down once the fighting started and the proper way to respond. Brabazon told him, "Stay close to me, do as I do. If you need to tell me something, physically grab me. If I don't respond shout at me. Worst case, lie flat on the floor." Hetherington listened to Brabazon's instructions in silence, processing the information. Afterward, Brabazon said, "He was very focused. He was never afraid to ask questions, never pretended to be more comfortable than he was—exactly what you want from someone in that situation. If he was afraid, he said he was afraid."

Unlike most photojournalists, Hetherington wasn't enthralled with using the latest technology. He owned a digital camera but decided not to take it with him to Liberia. He preferred to use his proven yet comparatively antiquated film cameras: a Mamiya Rangefinder and a Rolleiflex box camera, a type that had been in use since the 1930s, which required winding up and had a top-mounted viewfinder in which the image was reflected upside down. The images taken with such cameras were more textured and defined, Hetherington said, as opposed to highly pixilated, color-saturated digital images. Still, as Brabazon observed, the old-fashioned cameras tended to be difficult to use even on a tripod in a studio, much less during running combat or in the backseat of a car barreling through a firefight. Brabazon satisfied himself that at least Hetherington knew what to do with a video camera.

When Brabazon was deliberating about taking Hetherington with him to Liberia, he reviewed his work and found his photographs "disarmingly intimate," he said, "different from anything I'd seen shot in the region before." And once they were in the country, he saw a certain utility in the very slowness of the old-fashioned cameras, which put Hetherington on a slightly different plane during a firefight. "The fact that you had to slow down and look for the moment meant that he got these amazing pictures," he said. Among them was one taken before the assault on Monrovia of a woman tenderly bidding farewell to her rebel lover, a photo that a typical war photographer would not have taken and which later would attract attention to Hetherington's

Liberia work. In its stark, almost formal simplicity, the photo was a poignant reminder of the personal impact of war.

Unpredictable violence and formal photography may seem worlds apart but pairing the two made sense to Hetherington. There was a wide divide between a place like Liberia, where life was so challenging for everyone, and the comparatively cushy world of the West, and he was determined to find a connection that others would recognize. So began the career of an inquisitive artist, propelled forward to the front lines of war by demons he never described, to illuminate the darkest corners of the world.

Because Hetherington's career photographing wars began in Liberia that summer in 2003, Junger returned there in 2011 to interview people who had known him. At the start of his videotape Black Diamond sits in the dappled light of a beach cabana near Monrovia, apparently unaware that the camera is rolling. She pats her hair to make sure everything is in place, runs one hand across her face to smooth her makeup, and waits for the interview to start. She looks beautiful, framed by a backdrop of breaking waves, her large, expressive eyes and easy smile giving no hint of her infamous history as a war rebel. As soon as Junger begins his interview, Black Diamond tells him she does not want to talk about the past. She was now enrolled in school, and the whispers and stares that had followed her everywhere after the war had largely subsided. She lived in a house with small children who called her Aunt Diamond. But when Junger asks how she had met Hetherington, she is quickly transported seven summers back, to June 2003. It was near the climax of Liberia's second civil war, a period of violence climaxing more than a decade of intermittent fighting. By that point in the war Black Diamond stood out in the rebel crowd. In one of the photos Hetherington took of her she wears a long, stained T-shirt and jeans, indicating that she'd had little time to prepare as she ran out the door that morning. In others she is well dressed: she wears a long, animal-print coat, or a red tube top and matching beret and wristwatch, with gold earrings, necklaces, and bracelets. In every photo she carries an AK.

Her face in the photos looks very different from the way it does now. She is almost unrecognizable. Only later, in the last photo Hetherington took of her, after the war had ended, relaxing in Monrovia's Sharks Bar with a bottle of orange Fanta, does she resemble the relaxed woman Junger interviews in the film.

Black Diamond was exceptional among Liberian women and Hetherington liked photographing her, and she liked being photographed by him. She was so feared that during the war she was charged with enforcing discipline even among LURD's male fighters, and her personal story drew Hetherington in. He would later note in a book he published about his experiences in Liberia, *Long Story Bit by Bit: Liberia Retold*, that rape was a common denominator among the female fighters. The World Health Organization had released a report that found that among more than four hundred Liberian women surveyed in 2003, 77 percent had been raped and 64 percent of those had been gang-raped. Many such women were among Black Diamond's girls.

Black Diamond could barely remember life without war, and after having been abused at a young age, and having spent three years as a fighter, she was not easily impressed. But she admired the way Hetherington and Brabazon remained with the rebels during the worst of the fighting, despite being unarmed and not wearing bulletproof vests. Now, in the cabana in Junger's film, she speaks mostly of Hetherington, because he is the person Junger is most interested in. She says that in her observation he wasn't focused only on the fighting; he was interested in the lives of the people he met, perhaps because they were so different from those of people on the "outside," who "never experience the hard time." Some of the rebels, including Black Diamond, fought because they had been provoked; others fought because they were dissatisfied with the life imposed upon them by the government of President Charles Taylor, which offered almost no hope of advancement, education, jobs, or even a reliable supply of food. "I wasn't born with arms in my hands," Black Diamond says. "I was a good girl, and I think . . . I'm still a good girl . . . I stay who I am. I never change. I stay a good girl." She was also a perfect subject for Hetherington: a person with a compelling story, caught up in the intensity of war.

3
LIBERIA

Hetherington and Brabazon entered Liberia in the summer of 2003 from neighboring Sierra Leone, crossing the Mano River, which forms the border between the two countries, at night under a full moon. The river was wide and slow and shone silver in the moonlight as an old man in a pirogue ferried them across one at a time.

Brabazon, who was then thirty-one years old and had a flair for on-camera drama, was the first to cross, and he silently scanned the darkness of the far bank, unsure who or what awaited them. The border was closed because of the war and he'd been compelled to bribe a man on the Sierra Leone side to arrange the crossing under cover of night. Brabazon barely knew Hetherington, who was then thirty-two, but he knew his other traveling companion, Nick du Toit, only too well. Du Toit was the mercenary in the title of the memoir Brabazon later published, *My Friend the Mercenary*. Brabazon had hired Hetherington to help him film the rebels in the Liberian jungle. Du Toit was there to lessen the chances that they would get killed in the process. Though they did not know it yet, du Toit would soon abandon them.

When the bow of the pirogue nudged the bank on the Liberian side, Brabazon stepped out and the old man paddled away to retrieve Hetherington and du Toit. A group of LURD rebels with automatic weapons materialized from the darkness of the jungle, and Brabazon said hello and extended his hand. The nearest man grasped it, then others followed. There were smiles all around. In the documentary Brabazon had released the year before, *Behind LURD Lines: A Journey Without Maps*, his portrayal of the LURD rebels had been not altogether flattering—he had, essentially, broadcast documentary evidence of them committing war crimes. If the rebels had seen the film, apparently there were no hard feelings.

Because the rebels were preparing to attack Monrovia, Brabazon and his codirector on the new documentary, Jonathan Stack, had arranged to film simultaneously from opposite sides: Brabazon and Hetherington would approach Monrovia with the rebels, after which—assuming the rebels succeeded in their attack—they would meet up with Stack, who would film from inside the city. Now, as the men stood beside the Mano, a sudden tropical thunderstorm opened up, quickly drenching everyone to the skin. It was like standing under a waterfall, Brabazon remembered. When he and Hetherington had been packing for the trip at their hotel in Conakry, Hetherington had thought Brabazon was overdoing it by insisting that they put their photographic equipment and other essentials into plastic bags that were then placed inside other plastic bags. But now Hetherington understood. There was nothing to do but walk on in the rain, stumbling through the darkness of the jungle, drenched, by the light of headlamps and flashlights, for perhaps five or six hours until they arrived at a village where the rebels put them up for a night. There they slept with the aid of Valium that Brabazon had thoughtfully brought along. The next morning the rebels drove them to Tubmanburg.

Tubmanburg had been an iron ore and diamond mining center before the war, when the largest employer was the American-owned Liberia Mining Company, which had moved on once the iron ore was depleted. Now, the place was basically a garrison, largely abandoned but for the rebels. Hetherington and Brabazon stayed in the house of a rebel commander who called himself General Cobra, and it was there, as they sat on the balcony, that Black Diamond said she caught her first glimpse of Hetherington. Like Brabazon, he was tall and attractive, and he had a broad smile and a ready laugh. Brabazon said the question foremost on his mind during their time in Tubmanburg was "What happens now?" The answer, at least initially, was nothing. He and Hetherington spent their days sitting around General Cobra's house or roaming Tubmanburg, filming and interviewing rebels and foraging for food.

As they waited for the rebel attack on Monrovia, Hetherington had no idea what to expect, but the first harbinger came in the form of a gleefully crazed rebel in a green dress who danced provocatively close to him as he and Brabazon sat talking by a roadside. The Liberian civil wars were famously bizarre and remarkably brutal. During Brabazon's first trip, he had filmed prisoners being executed, shot and, in some cases, beheaded. Sometimes they were eviscerated and their corpses butchered and eaten. "It wasn't just that people were being killed in firefights," he later wrote. "There was murder, torture, even cannibalism. And that made the nature of the fighting very intense." Now, the rebels had made clear that if he or Hetherington were captured their safety would be far from guaranteed. "And depending on who captured us, we could expect to be tortured, murdered, possibly even eaten," Brabazon wrote. Many of the more outrageous rebel groups had since been killed off or absorbed into LURD, but during the first civil war, in the 1990s, one rebel force had been led by a man who called himself General Butt Naked, who, along with his men, paraded and fought naked. Other fighters dressed in strange attire, including orange life vests or women's wigs and wedding gowns, using theatrics as a weapon to instill fear in their enemies. The costumes and frequent dancing in the midst of battle also served to diminish the fighters' own fears. Some believed disguises would protect them like a talisman, that the bullets would not find them because they were not recognizable as themselves. Some also believed they gained the strength of their enemies by consuming their bodies.

Brabazon had seen rebels cut the hearts out of living men and cook them in stews, a ritual that had been practiced in West Africa for centuries. The mix of ancient ritual and superstition with modern weaponry had put the Liberian civil wars well over the top, "and Tim was thrown right into the middle of that—his first combat experience," Brabazon wrote in his memoir. "It wasn't just two armies facing each other off; it was two groups of young men who were absolutely enamored with theatrics of war—wearing dresses, eating each other, hacking off each other's limbs." As the crazed rebel in the green dress illustrated, there was still plenty of outlandish behavior to go around, though LURD sought to impose a semblance of military discipline, providing soldiers with a code of conduct toward civilians and advising them about the Geneva Conventions.

Brabazon's introduction to Liberia had come in the aftermath of the long civil war in neighboring Sierra Leone, during which he had met a group of South African mercenaries with a force called the Executive Outcomes Private Military Army. The mercenaries, who had settled in Freetown, told him stories about the Liberian fighting and said, as he recalled, "No one knows anything about it. No one's there, no one's covering it, and the Americans are quite involved in it, because they are very close to the rebels." The mercenaries claimed they had worked with U.S. intelligence in Liberia in the mid- to late 1990s. Intrigued, Brabazon had entered Liberia for what he expected to be about three weeks but turned out to be almost three months, during which the LURD rebels took him to their jungle bases. He accompanied them during a month of almost continuous, close combat.

On the eve of his second trip, as he and Hetherington had prepared to embark from Conakry, Brabazon paid close attention to the reactions of his new traveling companion and observed that while Hetherington spoke confidently, "I could see his eyes darting around, taking in the details of the scene . . . looking for whatever trouble might arise before it was too late." By then the Guinean army was helping arm the LURD rebels, who held more territory than ever before, and the United Nations had just unsealed an indictment of Charles Taylor for war crimes during the war in Sierra Leone, including murder, rape, sexual slavery, conscription of child soldiers, and the terrorizing of citizens. The indictment significantly upped the ante for Taylor's forces, and for LURD as well.

Remarkably, after more than a decade of deprivation and atrocities, one of the hallmarks of Liberian culture—its legendary graciousness and generosity—was still evident. Black Diamond was an alleged rape victim who'd witnessed her parents' murder, and who now had an AK and a license to kill, but she was generous and unfailingly polite. Liberia's cultural mix—ritual violence and high manners—was the product of one of Africa's most complex histories.

Liberia had been colonized by freed American slaves in the 1820s who, with the help of U.S. representatives, had persuaded the indigenous West African king at gunpoint to exchange land for various items, including gunpowder, iron, tobacco, silverware, clothes, canes, umbrellas, soap, and a barrel of rum. The tribes then had no concept of what they were agreeing to give up, and relations between them and the settlers quickly deteriorated. Liberia went on to become Africa's first independent nation, in 1847, and the Americo-Liberians, as the settlers called themselves, essentially reproduced the master-slave dynamic of the plantations many of them had escaped in the United States, replicating the architecture, manners, names, and, in some cases, institutions of the antebellum American South. They built columned mansions reminiscent of antebellum houses in Mississippi and Georgia, and, well into the 1980s, they dressed in top hats and hoopskirts on special occasions. In addition to indigenous villages and counties with names such as Nimba, Gbarpolu, and Grand Kru there were Americo towns and counties named New Georgia, Louisiana, Maryland, Mississippi, and Virginia, and their inhabitants' names could easily have been lifted from the roster of a country club in the American South. Meanwhile, the indigenous groups languished in poverty and were denied the right to vote. The Americos, occasionally backed by U.S. naval ships and armed with better weapons, prevailed in the frequent conflicts and ruled the country unilaterally for nearly a century and a half. Along the way, some of the Americos enslaved members of the indigenous groups, who had themselves been involved in the slave trade. As late as the 1930s the League of Nations had chastised Liberia for tolerating forced labor at the world's largest rubber plantation, which was operated by the Firestone Tire and Rubber Company.

The Americo president William Tolbert began instituting reforms in 1971, but they proved too little, too late. Simmering resentment resulted in a coup in 1980, in which Tolbert was disemboweled in his bed at the presidential palace, but the victor of the uprising, an army sergeant turned warlord named Samuel Doe, who was financially supported by the Reagan administration, was himself overthrown in 1990. His torture and murder were filmed by the perpetrators, who supported rival warlord Charles Taylor, a Liberian of mixed Americo and indigenous background who had been educated and briefly imprisoned in the United States and whose escape from prison there is still a mystery. Taylor had trained his invasionary force in Libya with the help of Muammar Gaddafi, who continued to arm Taylor's government in its fight against LURD until 2003.

Despite UN sanctions imposed five years earlier, Taylor was elected president in 1997 by a landslide, in what was generally considered a sham election, and began fomenting rebellions in neighboring countries. An oft-repeated mantra during Taylor's campaign was "You killed my ma, you killed my pa, I will vote for you." To make up for funds deprived him by the sanctions, Taylor tapped Liberia's ship registry program, the largest in the world, as well as the Sierra Leonean diamond industry, which extracted so-called blood diamonds using child and slave labor. LURD, which formed in 1999, was one of several Liberian rebel groups bent on overthrowing Taylor. By the summer of 2003, when Hetherington and Brabazon arrived, LURD was the preeminent rebel group, directly supported by Guinea.

Hetherington had done his homework on this complicated dynamic before traveling to Liberia during his previous trip in 1999. Though he had a good grasp of the history by the time he and Brabazon crossed the Mano River in June 2003, he wanted to see the fighters firsthand. Nearly half of Liberia's population of 2.5 million had been displaced by the fighting and widespread atrocities were still occurring.

In Tubmanburg, Hetherington and Brabazon slept in a storage room in General Cobra's house on a single dirty mattress on the floor. Soon after their arrival, du Toit, their guide and bodyguard, announced he was returning to South Africa, where he'd been called to do "another job." From that point on, Hetherington and Brabazon would be alone with a rebel army whose situation was growing more tense by the day. LURD had recently been embroiled in what the rebels came to call "World War I"—their first, disastrous attack on Monrovia, which started after a group of teenaged rebels encountered a number of government soldiers on the road, fired at them, and gave chase. The teenagers assumed the road into Monrovia would be heavily fortified, and when they found that it wasn't they continued pushing to the outskirts of the city. The teenagers in their enthusiasm had managed to fire something like 350,000 rounds of ammunition in just forty-eight hours, then returned to Tubmanburg, which meant they had spent nearly all of the rebels' ammunition, for nothing, over the course of a weekend. The result was the delay of the actual planned rebel attack, which left Brabazon and Hetherington stuck in Tubman-burg while the rebels awaited a delivery of ammunition. When the ammo finally arrived two weeks later LURD launched "World War II."

Brabazon and Hetherington spent the interim wandering around Tubmanburg, gathering mangoes and avacados from trees, discussing the war and what they'd rather be eating. During their conversations, Hetherington asked Brabazon if he would ever testify against du Toit, should he be called upon to do so, regarding his involvement in war crimes, indicating, in Brabazon's view, that Hetherington "was calcu-lating what compromises he'd already made or would have to make as we went further into this war." They also talked about the strange get-ups some of the rebels chose to wear, including the man in the green dress. If the idea was to instill fear, there was no arguing that a man running screaming toward you through the jungle with an AK and in a wedding dress would be unnerving.

Dante Paradiso, who worked as political director in the U.S. embassy in Monrovia at the time, later told Junger that both the reb-els and the government soldiers engaged in combat theatrics "to make themselves look like 1980s action heroes, because those were the mov-ies that they had seen, and in absence of any training that was basically what they would be imitating." Among the more notorious, he said, was Black Diamond.

It was common, Brabazon said, to see young fighters emulating those action figures as well as movie actors and American rap stars.

"That was a natural cultural reference for them," he said. "You know, they're strongly influenced by America."

Perhaps not surprisingly, there were very few Westerners in Liberia at the time, particularly outside Monrovia, where there were a few straggling NGOs as well as a skeleton crew at the American embassy, the last diplomatic mission still open. The LURD forces were supposedly in contact with U.S. intelligence but otherwise they were alone against one of the most feared regimes in West Africa.

Brabazon noticed that Black Diamond and the other female LURD soldiers—and at least one male, the one in the green dress—liked Hetherington, with his chiseled face, tall frame, polite manners, and easy laugh. In fact, they liked him "a lot," Brabazon said. The female fighters "were a strange bunch, really," he said. They were very young and "armed to the teeth. Some of them were very beautiful, and others not so much." One night, after Brabazon and Hetherington had been in Tubmanburg for a while, some of the younger fighters arrived at General Cobra's house with alcohol, cigarettes, and satellite phones for sale, which they had looted in Monrovia during World War I. Hetherington and Brabazon often received company on the balcony of Cobra's house, and that night, in addition to the young looters, Black Diamond stopped by. Brabazon had previously shared his supply of quinine with her when she was suffering from a bout of malaria, and as a token of her gratitude she brought a bottle of Drambuie liqueur, which she'd bought from the looters, and gave it to Hetherington and Brabazon. As a token of her esteem, Black Diamond also brought two young Liberian women to the house, whom she offered up for "jiggy-jiggy." Hetherington was embarrassed by the offer and immediately hurried inside without comment, leaving Brabazon to awkwardly decline. Black Diamond said she wondered if she'd been made the butt of a joke, though later when she recounted the episode for Junger she laughed it off.

All armies have their camp followers, and for a woman traveling with the LURD rebels "noncombatant" was a freighted term. If she was not a fighter, she was likely there to cook for those who were, or to sleep with them. Overall, the rebels were a lean, hungry fighting force, with far more access to ammunition than to food. Stories of rampant drug use among the rebels were typically exaggerated, though many used marijuana or ephedrine, Brabazon said. Likewise, the often horrific stories about the rebels' antics, though in some cases true, did not reflect the majority of the fighters and Liberian citizens Hetherington later described meeting, who were mostly average people living within a long-running war that had turned their world upside down. Because food was in short supply, Brabazon and Hetherington, like the rebels, subsisted on one bowl of rice per day, with some stewed cassava leaves and the fruit they picked from trees. They had packed staples including salt, sardines, tea, and sugar but were reluctant to dig into their stash. They knew they would miss a few meals once the fighting began.

One night, as he struggled to sleep under a mosquito net in the storage room, Hetherington heard gunshots in the distance and then what sounded like someone dying in the next room—low moans punctuated by occasional repetitive screams. It turned out to be a sixteen-year-old rebel who had been shot in the head, whom the rebels were feeding some kind of pills. Hetherington was surprised to find he was still alive the next day.

The night before the second assault on Monrovia they packed a light field bag for the journey, including videotapes, batteries, chargers, a flashlight, their satellite phone, a waterproof bag, and a medical trauma kit. They expected to be gone for a maximum of ten days. The next morning, one of the rebels appeared below the balcony of Cobra's house and said, "We're leaving," and told Hetherington and Brabazon they'd better hurry or they would miss the attack.

Before departing, the rebels participated in a cleansing ritual, splashing themselves with water and reciting Islamic and Christian prayers. The man in the green dress and bushy wig busied himself with dancing around Hetherington, alongside another rebel wearing red underpants who grunted loudly and danced with his Kalashnikov. Then the crowd began to move. Brabazon and Hetherington grabbed their bags and cameras and fell in line as the column of rebels walked out of Tubmanburg under a blazing sun occasionally interrupted by jungle downpours. They passed fire-gutted houses, farm fields, and swamps, walking nonstop for ten hours in a ragged column of several hundred men, women, and children. When Brabazon and Hetherington began suffering leg cramps they took Valium to ease the pain. They alternated running ahead to shoot panoramic footage of the entourage and walked into the night. At one point, as they stumbled blindly through the darkness, they heard strange voices and the alarming click of guns being cocked. Everyone in the column bolted to the side of the road and crouched in the underbrush. Then one brave or foolish rebel turned on his flashlight and discovered that the voices belonged to fellow rebels. With that, Hetherington turned on his own flashlight and told Brabazon it looked like things were okay. The rebels decided to camp there for the night, on the east bank of the Po River.

There was nothing to eat, and Brabazon and Hetherington slept uneasily on the concrete floor of a crowded sentry house. They awoke to an eerie, misty morning. "It was very atmospheric," Brabazon said. "You could see all these young rebel fighters standing by trees in the mist by the side of the road. You know what it's like in the morning when you've got that thick mist? All the sounds are muted, so you could hear the clicking of metal and stamping of feet and stuff, and people getting ready to go, but it was like you were sort of in a kind of big box, almost. You know, the enormity of the jungle had all kind of closed down, to what you could see in the mist." Hetherington shot a few photos and some video and they were soon under way again. He told Brabazon, "You know, man, if this really gets nuts, just tell me what to do, okay? No bullshit. Don't hold back."

Brabazon told him, as he had before, to stay low and, if necessary, to lie down, and also not to hesitate to say if he had different ideas about what they should do, including what to film. Brabazon said he has observed that people have a tendency to withdraw into themselves prior to combat, to search for inner strength and peace. "I've seen it happen a lot of times with soldiers, with other journalists, and I saw it then with Tim as well," he said. "It's very quiet. That kind of moment of self-reflection. It's very important." Hetherington was frightened, but he remained calm and focused. Being scared, Brabazon said, "that's a really good thing. Because if you're going into combat and you're not scared it means one of two things—either that you're an idiot or that you have not fully understood the nature of the situation you're in, and Tim was certainly not an idiot, and he very much understood that he was in a very difficult, challenging environment and had to treat it carefully and with respect, and that's exactly what he did."

The dirt track they had followed the day before had by now turned to pavement and took them thirty miles through more fields, swamps, and villages. As they walked, everyone was quiet, waiting for their first contact—"a horrible feeling" of anticipation, Hetherington later said. Then, on the outskirts of Monrovia, during a torrential downpour, the first ambush came. Everyone scattered. As Brabazon observed, it suddenly mattered that he and Hetherington were a foot taller than everyone else. Hetherington scrambled ahead of Brabazon on all fours, up a slippery red-clay bank, and crawled through a cassava field toward a house where a group of rebels were making a stand. A man who had offered to carry their rucksack followed. The wall of the house provided only the illusion of cover, because it could easily have been splintered by automatic weapons or RPGs, but it gave them some breathing room. The noise of machine-gun fire and rocket-propelled grenades was deafening. Peering around the corner of the house, Hetherington filmed rebels lying on their bellies firing AKs. Their raking fire soon routed the government soldiers, and the battle subsided as abruptly as it had begun. The government forces retreated. The rebels moved on.

A second ambush followed, then another. In each case the rebels managed to drive the government soldiers back, until they were inside the city, running through streets and across open fields, under fire. Many of the rebels were teenagers seeing a big city for the first time, and they were unnerved by it. In addition to fearing for his life, Hetherington initially found it extremely difficult to film on the run, but based on his footage he was getting the hang of it. Only later, during a moment of calm, did Hetherington and Brabazon notice that they were filthy, covered in mud, and drenched with rain and sweat. But the calm was short-lived. Soon they encountered yet another ambush, which turned out to be the worst. Brabazon shouted at Hetherington to get down and the two of them jumped into a ditch. A moment later, when they stood up, the rebel in front of them—who, they had observed, had been prone to running out ahead of the column—was immediately shot through the chest and collapsed on the ground. Hetherington bent over him, filming as the gaping wound in his chest gurgled blood. He continued filming as other rebels picked up the mortally injured man and carried him to a pickup truck. Brabazon watched with admiration. "I had spent so long working there alone, and suddenly I was there with someone who really had his shit together," he recalled, "who really knew what he was doing, who was filming great stuff, taking amazing pictures." By this point, he said, "Tim was just in it. There comes a point where that just is your reality. It stops becoming weird and different. It's just what you're living and breathing at that moment."

Such was not the case for some of the younger rebels, who were only children and started to cry, which prompted their commander to shout at them, "What's the matter? Have you never seen a man die before?" Then they were on the move again, with General Cobra angrily whipping the reluctant boy soldiers into battle with a length of electrical cable.

As the rebels neared a bridge leading to the center of the city they were attacked from both sides. Bullets tore through the trees, and bits of bark rained down upon them. The man carrying Hetherington's rucksack was shot in the head. Hetherington was trying to take it all in, his head pivoting in one direction and then another. Brabazon passed the video camera to him and motioned for him to follow, and they ran toward the cover of a school building, Hetherington filming all the way. In hindsight, Brabazon observed, "There was definitely someone aiming at us when we were running, definitely. You can tell the difference." As they ran, he heard Hetherington hit the ground behind him very hard and thought he'd been shot. To his later regret, Brabazon kept going. When he reached the cover of the building, where a group of commanders' wives cowered, he saw Hetherington running behind him.

Once there, Hetherington told Brabazon, with considerable distress, that he had dropped the wind cover of the video camera's microphone. As machine-gun fire continued to rake the field, they hurried back to the spot where Hetherington had fallen to search for the cover. A small group of rebels joined them in the search, asking, "What does it look like?" It was, Brabazon said, "absolutely insane." When Hetherington found the cover they rushed back to the comparative safety of the school, where the commanders' wives watched incredulously from behind the wall. Hetherington later laughed at the absurdity of the episode. There was still incoming and outgoing machine-gun fire, growing louder by the minute. With the video camera, Hetherington slowly panned the group hunkered down behind the wall, lingering on Brabazon. Then he put the video camera down, shot a few still photos, reloaded the video camera with a new tape, and filmed as the rebels unleashed a massive truck-mounted machine gun that finally succeeded in driving the government troops away. In the calm that followed, Hetherington walked into the field to photograph dead bodies in the grass. He noticed that some of them were men who had died days before.

As they emerged back onto the road they came upon another column of rebels that had preceded them and been cut off by Taylor's army. There was jubilation over the reuniting of the two rebel forces, and Hetherington and Brabazon accepted an invitation to climb aboard a looted four-wheel-drive. As they sped toward the center of town, Hetherington photographed more dead bodies along the roadside, including many with their hands tied behind their backs who had obviously been executed. Some appeared to be civilians, though it was hard to say. As he later wrote, Hetherington had not considered the consequences to civilians as the LURD forces fired their mortars indiscriminately into the city, without accurate coordinates or triangulation. In fact, their mortars resulted in widespread civilian deaths, including in a part of the U.S. embassy compound in Monrovia, where Sebastian Junger was now covering the onslaught from the other side. Junger reported seeing people rushing the injured to a field clinic in wheelbarrows or carried over their shoulders or dragged by their arms and legs. Another photojournalist covering the conflict from inside Monrovia, whose path would intersect with Hetherington's in Libya eight years later, was Chris Hondros, who managed to take what would become an iconic photo of the second Liberian war: an exultant, manic-looking government soldier, shirtless and dreadlocked, carrying an RPG launcher and jumping into the air as he runs across a newly won bridge.

When Hetherington and Brabazon reached the rebels' temporary headquarters in the city, which was located in a beer factory, they
found more than a thousand refugees gathered there without food or
water. "It was just a disaster," according to Brabazon. The rebels had
set up an emergency clinic in the beer factory, and among the injured
and dead bodies Hetherington was surprised to find their bag carrier,
still alive though brain-damaged. Seeing that the medical workers
were having trouble administering pain pills, Hetherington tried to
force-feed the man a watery rice soup to help him keep the medicine
down. From the beer factory Hetherington and Brabazon ventured
out to the Freeport area, which Taylor claimed he controlled—now,
obviously, a lie because, as Hetherington observed, "We were there."

In one of his self-portraits, Hetherington smiles broadly, his hair
soaked with rain, looking as if he is enjoying being there. In reality,
the atmosphere was tense, not only because they were behind enemy
lines but because many of the rebels were suspicious of the locals
among them. Even the presence of a civilian doctor, or medic—the
only trained medical worker—sparked controversy. Outside the beer
factory, Hetherington felt compelled to intervene when the medic
was surrounded by rebels, who were shouting at him, slapping him,
and hitting him with the butt of a gun, accusing him of having treated
government soldiers. As Hetherington and Brabazon filmed, a rebel
known as Iron Jacket, wearing a bright yellow T-shirt, pointed a hand-
gun at the doctor's head, and in Hetherington's footage we see mortal
fear in the doctor's eyes. It seems he is about to be executed.

Brabazon, who had filmed executions before, was preparing to
document another, but Hetherington was unwilling to stand idly
by. In Brabazon's video we hear him protest, "He's a medic!" Then,
while Brabazon films, he walks into the shot, still filming with his own
Handycam, and with his free hand he grabs Iron Jacket's gun hand and
starts negotiating for the medic's life. "This is the only doctor you've

got," he protests. Brabazon watched in amazement. Hetherington, he said, "had this ability to just do very surprising things. He did the right thing. It was this very humanitarian act, which put him partially in a very great deal of risk, and he just intervened, and they led the guy off."

In the footage of the encounter, which made its way into Brabazon and Stack's documentary about Liberia, *An Uncivil War,* the conflict is left unresolved but, Brabazon said, "They didn't shoot him. And very shortly, he was back, treating wounded at the hospital again. So Tim probably saved his life." It was a defining moment for Hetherington, who, although he did not know it yet, was embarking on a decade-long career in which he would push the boundaries of journalistic detachment and become closely involved in the lives of people he photographed in war zones.

Hetherington spent the rest of the afternoon filming and photographing refugees who congregated at the beer factory as well as soldiers and civilians being treated for their injuries. He and Brabazon ended up staying that night in the radio room at the beer factory, unaware that the next day a fight would unfold with the aim of capturing or killing them. For now, they had an endless supply of warm beer to drink as they sat on the street. By then, Brabazon said, they were "completely high," as a result of physical exhaustion and the Valium they'd taken for their leg cramps and to calm their nerves. As Hetherington later told Dante Paradiso of the American embassy, they were so spent, and so deep into the moment, they were almost oblivious to the awful hyperreality of the scene around them. "There's that thing about war—it's pretty shameful, really," he said. "Your sense of everything is distorted, it's warped." At the end of the tumultuous day, he said, "I remember sitting down that night on the side of the road and drinking a Club beer, and then saying to James, 'What's that smell?' and we're like, 'ahhh' . . . We turned around and nearby was a couple of bodies. And I remember he said, 'Should we move?' and I said, 'I'm too tired.' I was exhausted, and I said I'm too tired to move. And we sort of sat there." In hindsight, he said, "the weird thing about being a reporter is you're caught up in these two things. On the one side, you have an adrenaline side that makes it all quite exciting, and on the other side you're seeing that it's pretty appalling. The range of emotions that washes over you, I suppose now in some ways you sort of feel ashamed. Ashamed—that's not the right word, but . . . something."

Later that evening Brabazon was interviewed on CNN and the BBC via his satellite phone and reported that Freeport was actually in rebel hands, which infuriated Taylor when he heard about it. After the interview, which people on the streets of Monrovia listened to on transistor radios, Brabazon and Hetherington turned in for the night. Junger, who also listened to their interviews, was astonished. "I'm like, damn, these white guys are with LURD," he says in his documentary about Hetherington. "As scary as the government guys were, the LURD guys seemed worse."

In his book *Long Story Bit by Bit,* Hetherington included several photos of Black Diamond, including one of her interrogating a young girl during the fighting in the Monrovia suburb of Duala. In his caption, he notes that Black Diamond's real name was Mayama Sesay. She later expressed similar amazement with Hetherington being there, telling Junger she was as curious about him as he was of her. She wondered, "How can this man leave his family, everybody, just to sacrifice and come, just to do a piece of job? He may not be doing this on his own, but maybe he doing it for a cause. I don't know the cause."

Whatever it was, she says, "He was all in there, on the front line."

4
ESCAPE

The shooting resumed at dawn. Though the fighting was distant, it would soon make its way to the beer factory, where Brabazon received a piece of disturbing news: Charles Taylor had put a bounty on his and Hetherington's heads and had dispatched two units of soldiers to find and kill them.

Taylor had heard enough of their radio interviews. In his view, the two were working for the rebels, and he wanted them removed from the public relations equation. They were, indeed, closely aligned with LURD. Brabazon and Hetherington had discussed the journalist's need for objectivity, which Brabazon felt was an empty concept during a war. "The idea that you can be objective in war is just ridiculous," he said. "The idea of the journalist as an impartial, neutral, objective observer is just a lie. It's a very pernicious lie, as well. If you work in war, you know—not just as a journalist but in whatever capacity, but particularly as a journalist—there will come a point at which you inevitably have to exercise your natural, inalienable right of self-defense, and the point at which you do that means you're no longer an observer. You are necessarily a participant. And to what degree you participate

41

is kind of irrelevant. The fact is, you are participating, and I think Tim understood that very carefully."

During his later interview with Paradiso, Hetherington essentially confirmed this, saying, at one point, "We ran out of ammunition," then correcting himself to say that the rebels had run out of ammunition.

As Junger observed in his book *War*, "Journalistic convention holds that you can't write objectively about people you're close to, but you can't write objectively about people that are shooting at you either."

Hetherington saw very little distinction between being a journalist, a humanitarian, an observer, a witness, or a participant. "He was just Tim at war in the same way that he would be Tim having a drink with you at a pub, or Tim talking to you about why he favored one kind of aesthetic over another in his images," Brabazon said. He was also very aware that some things were worth fighting for, and not only ideology. During their first visit to Tubmanburg, Brabazon had returned to their little storage room to find him with "this rebel soldier up against the wall by his throat, pinned to the wall. I walked in, looked at the two of them, walked over to my bags, and said, 'Everything all right?'"

"No, not really," Hetherington said.

"I'm like, 'Okay. What's going on here, then?'" Brabazon recalled saying. "And he's literally got this guy off the ground, I mean, pinned against the wall." Someone had been stealing Hetherington and Brabazon's precious supply of sardines, the only protein they had, taking one tin at a time over a period of weeks, and Hetherington had come back to the storeroom and caught the guy red-handed. Eventually, Brabazon said, he let the guy down, "and this kid was saying, 'Please, please don't tell the commanders. Please, please don't tell anyone. They'll shoot me.'" Because they realized this was probably true, they told no one.

Hetherington had a strong will and a forthright disposition but Brabazon wasn't sure how he would take the news that Taylor had issued an order for them to be killed. Taylor had been spreading false propaganda, how he'd reoccupied Freeport and was winning the war, and only two people seemed to be getting in his way—Brabazon and Hetherington. U.S. intelligence agents whom Brabazon spoke with over his satellite phone had delivered the information. By that point the rebels were running low on ammunition and trying to decide whether to regroup and resume their assault. "It became very clear that they just weren't in a position to do that," Brabazon recalled. "They were going to have to withdraw." So he asked the American agent whether he could send a helicopter to evacuate the two if the rebels were cut off, and "he said, 'Absolutely not,' which was great news," Brabazon drily observed. "And he said, 'Look, you need to know that Taylor is very unhappy with you. There is an execution order out on you, and he has dispatched two death squads to find and kill you, and there is a ten-thousand-dollar bounty on each of your heads, in case they can't do it and someone else wants to pick up on the prize money.'" Brabazon thought: close combat was one thing, an execution order was another.

It was actually in the interests of U.S. and UK intelligence for Brabazon and Hetherington to stay in Liberia, he said, "because there was no other information coming out of northern Liberia, north of the rebel lines, nothing other than the work that Tim and I were doing." Still, the intel guy was adamant that they should leave. "So I said, 'Well, that's very easy for you to say, but I'm surrounded by government troops in central Liberia. How exactly do we do this?'" The agent said if they could manage to get back to Tubmanburg, U.S. officials would arrange for the closed bridge across the Mano River to be opened for them.

Neither Hetherington nor Brabazon had slept or eaten much for three days, and the chemistry of their brains was seriously out of whack, Brabazon said. Now they had to think, to focus. As Brabazon considered the ramifications of this latest bit of news, a rebel commander miraculously appeared with a plate of chicken. Seizing the moment, Brabazon sat down on a ledge with the commander and the two had a little apocalyptic picnic, while Hetherington went back to filming the refugees. "There was a pretty good firefight going off down the street about eight hundred yards away," Brabazon said, "and the rebel commander looked at me, and he looked at Tim, and he could see Tim kind of working . . . and he said, 'James,' and he looked at Tim, 'shouldn't you be filming this too?' I said, 'No, I'm really hungry.' So we ate the chicken and what we didn't eat got put in a bag and sealed, which later Tim got so hungry that he ate the chicken and it floored him with the most spectacular diarrhea."

By then the rebels had decided to retreat from Monrovia, and when Brabazon and Hetherington found a ride they got mired in a traffic jam of stolen vehicles. The government troops were soon upon them, and their driver "freaked out," Brabazon said, and started shooting wildly. He ended up putting an AK round through the engine block of his own car, which killed it. As Brabazon and Hetherington deliberated what to do, the rebel in the green dress, who had been harassing Hetherington in Tubmanburg, ran up, grabbed his arm, and shouted, "I'm going to fuck you up the ass."

"So," Brabazon said, "Tim's like, 'Wow,' you know, so I at this point, slightly becoming numb with fear and apprehension, I really, actually, didn't know what to do." Hetherington got out of the disabled car and found a guy who went by the name of Bushmaster, who had possession of an old, looted red Range Rover. The driver of the Range Rover, known as Joe T., said, "Yeah, come and get in with us," Brabazon said. "And he was smoking a spliff the size of a carrot. I was like, okay."

Slowly, the traffic began moving, but soon the car behind them was hit by an RPG. High-velocity rifle rounds tore into the vehicles on either side of them, yet Hetherington continued carefully taking photographs through the window, one frame at a time. He later said as he braced for getting shot the whole time that "It was almost like a certainty that I was going to be hit." Then, after one of the windows of the Range Rover was shattered by bullets, he and Brabazon jumped out and leaped over a nearby wall to take cover. To Brabazon's astonishment, Hetherington then went back over the wall and ran back to the Range Rover to retrieve his rucksack, which contained their film, satellite phone, videotapes, and medical kit. When he was safely behind the wall again, Brabazon said, "Right, that was fucking bonkers. 'Don't do that again.' He was like, 'Yeah, actually, that was a bit insane.' But I was really glad he had the bag. I mean, we were just off our tits on adrenaline at this point." They ran to a line of buildings for cover, where one of the units that Taylor had sent out to kill them had intercepted the rebels, and encountered Black Diamond again.

As Brabazon recalled, "Tim and I were pinned up against the wall and I just said to myself, Right, that's it. You know, you've got to go forwards. You can't just stand here. You've got to film this. So I ran forward to start filming. Bushmaster had opened up a .50-cal, trying to punch through the roadblock. And this guy out of nowhere just came up and threw his arms around me and said he was a civilian and he was terrified and would I save him—a young man—and I didn't know who he was, what was going on, so I slapped him really hard and told him to get a grip and get himself together. One of the rebels saw it, and Tim was there, and the rebel just stuck his AK into the guy's guts and said, 'Do you want me to shoot him?' And Tim is standing there with me, and, 'No, I don't want you to shoot anyone. Just get him away from me.' And it was this very paranoid feeling, They're after you. It's no longer just chancing your luck at the front. It's . . . it's . . . this is something else. You're being hunted."

Just then, the rebel traffic jam was freed up. The fighters up ahead had cleared the roadblock with machine-gun fire, so Hetherington and Brabazon ran back to the Range Rover, got in, and Joe T. cranked the engine and hit the gas. In Hetherington's footage, we hear him shouting from the backseat, "Faster, faster, go fast!" As they crossed an intersection with government troops firing upon them, he shouted, "Jesus Christ!" Then, "Fuck! I can see them!" He handed Brabazon a roll of exposed film while loading a fresh roll into his camera.

As they drove, Brabazon recalled, "Tim and I were trying to constantly work out how many rivers we crossed, how many bridges we'd gone over, so that if we had to get out of vehicles, would we be able to walk north, or would we have to go to the coast and try and get a fishing boat? We were really like, okay, this is it. I mean, we are going to have to walk out of this. And somehow, you know, the rebels opened up a hole big enough and long enough to get out, and then something really, really difficult happened." They came upon a stolen World Food Program truck—a fifteen-ton flatbed, Brabazon said—that had slid on the rain-slicked road and overturned in a ditch. Perhaps thirty refugees were pinned beneath, many of them dead. Because they were then out of range of the fighting, Joe T. stopped. Everyone got out of the Range Rover, and, "Tim and I sort of walked up to it," Brabazon said, "and they just had no means of turning the truck back over, because the biggest truck they had was the one that was upside down. They had no means of doing anything, you know, and there were government troops coming up the road after them, so . . . and you could hear people in the truck screaming, and Tim and I sort of looked at each other, and one of the rebels said, you know, 'Don't you want to film it?' and Tim said, 'No. No, I don't want to film this.'" So after helping the rebels offload food from the truck and retrieve as many of the injured as they could, they headed back to Tubmanburg.

As they drove, Liberian reggae music blared on the stereo and young rebels hung off the side of the vehicle, passing a joint back and forth. In addition to their guns, some of them had grenades in their hands, and they were arguing. Hetherington warned them to be careful, an odd but logical admonition under the circumstances. He then placed the video camera on the dash and filmed the scene as they drove. While listening to the rebels argue about who had looted what, "I thought, Is this what it's all about? It just seemed so absurd." But most of all, he said, he felt relieved to be alive.

Before reaching Tubmanburg, the Range Rover broke down, and as the rebels worked on it Hetherington noticed a speedboat on a trailer by the side of the road. A group of rebels had been towing the boat and had run the wheels off of it and abandoned it after dragging it for some distance on the metal rims. When they finally got the Range Rover up and running, Hetherington glanced into the boat in passing and noticed a dead body inside.

Back in Tubmanburg it continued to rain, and the mood was gloomy. The rebels had very nearly been defeated and they'd run out of ammunition. Brabazon, who had not yet told Hetherington about Taylor's order, saw him sitting by the side of the road, "white as a sheet, smoking a cigarette, very still. I mean, he was really in shock.

"We'd been forty-eight hours of almost nonstop combat, right up to the point of that truckload of civilians being killed, and I just looked at him and thought, This is a man at the edge of what he can take. And we had an option. We either stayed in Liberia . . . to wait and go back in with the next attack, knowing everything we did about what Taylor wanted to do with us, or [we'd leave]. And I felt a very strong sense of responsibility toward Tim."

As Hetherington later told Paradiso, Brabazon "looked really straight-faced, and he said, 'You want the bad news or the really bad news?'" He chose to hear the least bad news first, which was that the rebels were almost out of ammunition, after which Brabazon told him, "They say there are death squads coming to get us" and that they had seventy-two hours to get out of the country. In typical understatement,

Hetherington later told Paradiso he had a "daunting feeling." He finished the scotch he was drinking and asked Brabazon if he might have another. After that, he said, their abiding concern was, "We've got to get out, we've got to get out," though they were cautious about who they told.

As they packed their bags they were surprised to find that the young man who had awakened them during their first night in Tubmanburg with his moans and cries—who had been shot in the head—was still alive, and he was feeding himself. Tim photographed him and noted that he was sixteen and went by the name Rocket.

They were unable to depart right away but the rebels eventually got a convoy together and drove them to the Mano River bridge, where they were handed over to the Sierra Leone army. In one of the last images Hetherington recalled of the LURD rebels, he saw an exhausted commander on the bridge wearing a T-shirt emblazoned with the words, "This is not the life I ordered."

Hetherington and Brabazon would not be there for the subsequent, brief rebel invasion of Monrovia known as World War III, nor for the departure of Taylor, which marked the end of the second Liberian civil war. They would be watching from afar, and Hetherington would return only after Taylor had fled into exile. But he would never disengage from Liberia after his experience with the LURD rebels. In Brabazon's recollection, Hetherington had, by then, gone "from someone very eager to go to war, who'd never been to war, sitting in a café in London with me, pitching me for coming along on the trip, through to someone who'd gone to the absolute extremity of what you can do as a human being without snapping, in four weeks." When he looked at Hetherington now, Brabazon thought, "There was a man who'd found another part of himself."

5

MONROVIA

The sun was setting as James Marparyan sat in his battered old taxi in the queue at Liberia's international airport Roberts Field, watching the last passengers on the final flight that day from Brussels make their way to awaiting cars. Months had passed since the end of the second Liberian civil war, but the country was still reeling—basic infrastructure was largely destroyed, the majority of the population was unemployed, and money was extremely tight. Marparyan didn't relish the thought of making the one-hour drive back to Monrovia without a passenger, so when he spotted a tall white man coming out of the terminal, looking slightly out of sorts, he got out of his cab and asked if he needed a lift. The man was Tim Hetherington, who asked how much the ride would cost, and when Marparyan gave him a price he said it was too high and began to walk on.

Marparyan thought Hetherington looked irritated, that perhaps he'd been expecting someone to meet him at the airport and they hadn't shown up. Whatever the reason, Hetherington stopped when Marparyan called to him and they negotiated a fare. Marparyan loaded his bags in the trunk and they set off for Monrovia.

The road from Roberts Field wended its way through remnants of jungles, past thatched huts in palmy clearings, many of which had small, perennial campfires in the yard, and at the time of day that Hetherington and Marparyan were traveling oil lamps could be seen glimmering in the windows in the fading light. The road was well maintained, unlike most in Liberia, which were often dirt or mud tracks or bomb-cratered tarmac, and remained largely empty of traffic for long periods. The route became congested only before and after the rare departure and arrival of planes, when the phalanx of taxis descended on the airport—mostly old yellow Nissans with shattered windshields and hand-painted, often ungrammatical slogans on the side, such as "God is in control" and "A watched pot never boil."

On the way to Monrovia the taxi was overtaken by gleaming new Land Rovers with darkly tinted windows, transporting UN and NGO personnel. Now and then a luxury SUV passed, carrying men whose business was unknown, and whom Marparyan, a wiry, dark-skinned Liberian with an even temper, had learned long ago not to ask about. During the war, such people had likely been arms dealers, illicit diamond or timber merchants, mercenaries, or spies. Now, however, who knew? Some were missionaries. More outsiders were trickling into Monrovia now that the war was over, and the city's population, which had been fluctuating for years depending on the flow of refugees, hovered at around one million. It was still rare to see a white person on the street, an event that was usually interpreted as a sign that things were looking up. When security deteriorated, or was about to, the white people vanished.

After fifteen years of intermittent fighting Monrovia was in shambles. Many buildings had been blasted by rebel mortars, and the streets were riddled with gaping holes. Families squatted in abandoned Americo mansions along the beach and in high-rises with no glass in the windows, nor electricity or running water, cooking on hibachis or makeshift grills. In a derelict mansion next to the Mamba Point Hotel, squatters could sometimes be heard singing in the evening, their songs something like a mix of tribal chants and American gospel music. Despite pervasive poverty there were few beggars. Monrovians were more likely to offer services in hopes of getting tipped; unemployed women swept the streets with homemade brooms on the chance that a better-situated passerby would give them a few coins.

Liberia's second civil war—the one that Hetherington and Brabazon had covered in the early summer of 2003—had ended the preceding August, when Charles Taylor, faced with increasing international pressure and another in a series of attacks by LURD rebels, saw the writing on the wall and agreed to voluntary exile in Nigeria, under the presumption that he would not be extradited for his war crimes. Also facilitating Taylor's departure was the menacing presence of U.S. naval ships off the coast, a phenomenon with powerful meaning in Liberia in that the arrival of such ships had historically tipped the balance during conflicts between the Americos and the indigenous groups. The ships, waiting just beyond the horizon, indicated that Taylor would no longer be left alone, or rather that he was now very much alone, against a world that had lost patience with him.

After escaping with the LURD rebels, Hetherington and Brabazon had caught a ride in a truck from the Mano River to Freetown, Sierra Leone, where they spent the night with a friend of Brabazon and were debriefed by U.S. and UK intelligence agents. They had then flown to Conakry, and from there to London, but on the way back Hetherington realized he hadn't had enough, and almost as soon as he got to London he booked a flight to Conakry, from which he hoped to find a way back into Liberia. That proved impossible; the U.S. Navy was threatening to fire upon any vessel off the Liberian coast, which was the only route back in. So he abandoned that idea and returned to London, where he experienced the inevitable letdown of a war journalist reentering the mundane world back home. Returning to his apartment in the leafy South Kensington neighborhood seemed more like an interruption than a respite. One minute he'd been sipping coffee in London, trying to insinuate himself into James Brabazon's African domain, and the next he had watched, with a mix of excitement and terror, as the world unraveled around him, to the point that an enraged despot had called for his head. Safely ensconced in South Kensington, he thought of nothing but going back to Liberia. He wasn't sure precisely what he wanted to do, but he had the feeling that the story was unfinished. So after Taylor fled and it became easier to book a flight into Monrovia—at a time when most Western journalists had lost interest and departed—Hetherington returned, rented an apartment near the Ducor Hotel, and settled in.

Hetherington's experience was typical of many new war journalists, who find themselves straddling two very different worlds—one where people grapple with mortal threats, which has the odd effect of making them feel more alive and more aware of what matters, and another, back home, which is comfortable and routine. They seesaw between periods of high drama, when they're driven beyond their own perceived limits of endurance and nerve, and the inevitable reduction of life-altering events, as if recounting for family and friends a dream or a summer vacation gone bad. When they attempt to bridge the gap by sharing their experiences, their stories elicit the same series of responses—acute interest at first, then a kind of awe that slowly turns to worry and bewilderment, at which point there is nothing to do but nudge the conversation back to safer ground. Running for your life in a place no one else has heard of is one thing, but there is still the matter of picking out the new sofa.

As war reporters and photographers experience further combat, the feeling that they inhabit a parallel universe typically becomes more pronounced, and as Hetherington spent more time in Liberia and in subsequent conflict zones he found himself struggling to reconcile the two. In an effort to explore both the contrasts and the connections, and to understand his own attraction to both, he would later make a short film, *Diary,* juxtaposing snippets of his war footage with more prosaic scenes in hotel rooms, coffee shops, and cabs, highlighting the obvious contrasts but also unexpected, repetitive patterns. In *Diary's* title sequence, Hetherington explains that he made the film as "an attempt to locate myself" after years of war reporting, and that his aim was to "link our Western reality to the seemingly distant worlds we see in the media." The intellectual tone was typical of his writing style, but the images and film footage are provocative and, at times, lyrical.

Diary opens with a scene filmed from the vantage point of a person lying in bed while a ceiling fan, partially shrouded by folds of softly rippling mosquito netting, slowly turns overhead. The effect is mesmerizing—like lying in bed, staring at nothing, between waking and sleep. But soon the whirring of the fan is transformed into the sound of a helicopter rotor gaining momentum, while in the background a slightly garbled woman's voice, from a message on an answering machine, says how much she misses him. From that point on, the familiar and the extraordinary mix. A shot through a round peephole in a doorway to an apartment where an argument is taking place becomes the full moon over a pair of American soldiers, whose bonfire sends cinders flickering upward into the night sky, where they hang like constellations until slowly transformed into the twinkling lights of windows in New York City skyscrapers. The smoke from an exploding bomb fades into the smoke from a soldier's cigarette, which dissolves into clouds viewed from an airplane window. A yellow car fleeing a firefight in Monrovia becomes a yellow cab in Times Square, above which can be seen a newsreel about the Liberian war—Hetherington's own footage, in which Brabazon appears, projected onto a large outdoor screen. Toward the end, soft-focus scenes of autumnal English countryside at sunset segue to shaky footage shot from the Range Rover during the firefight in Monrovia. In a strange and disquieting way, the juxtapositions make sense. It's all about trying to reconcile seemingly irreconcilable worlds.

After Taylor's departure, Hetherington returned to Monrovia several times and eventually settled in. Postwar Monrovia provided a natural halfway point, a home base that was comparatively stable yet agreeably challenging, in a war zone that was no longer at war. Once there, he encountered people who were straddling their own opposing worlds, between the violence of war and the subdued chaos of its aftermath, in which they struggled to find normalcy again. He felt at home.

Jenkins Vangehn, a Liberian who worked at the American embassy in Monrovia, met Hetherington during his first return trip, in August 2003, after Taylor had gone into exile and a tentative peace had returned. They were at the Mamba Point Hotel, whose bar was a favorite networking site in Monrovia, and which, during the war, had been the preferred place for journalists to stay because it was protected by armed guards and was, as Hetherington's friend and roommate Zubin Cooper noted, "a three-minute sprint from the U.S. embassy." Vangehn noted that Hetherington knew a lot of the diplomats, and as they conversed, "Our friendship just clicked, like *that*," he said. When Vangehn eventually saw *An Uncivil War,* the film Hetherington, Brabazon, and Stack made about the war, he was grateful that they had shown the world the situation in Liberia and said the film had the unexpected effect of revealing what was going on behind the rebel lines to other Liberians, many of whom knew nothing other than hearsay and Taylor's propaganda.

By late August 2003 the UN mission in Liberia and the African peacekeeping organization ECOWAS were more or less in charge, but it was still risky to be there. Half of Liberia's three million people were living in squalid refugee camps, and the capital was without electricity, sewage treatment, garbage collection, and pretty much every other basic infrastructure. Paradiso, who became friends with Hetherington during the time, described Monrovia as "the shell of a city, with people living in that shell." He had also met Hetherington at the bar of the Mamba Point, which felt like one of the safer places in Monrovia, perhaps because so much danger was corralled there. During the war, men who sold arms to warlords, diplomats who were undercover intelligence agents, international drug dealers, clueless missionaries, and hungry journalists all found a spot in the lounge, or on the terrace overlooking the crashing surf of the Atlantic, framed by palms. The Mamba Point was "the place that as a journalist covering Africa you always imagined you would find," Paradiso said. Summoning a description by his friend Karl Vick, a correspondent for the *Washington Post,* he observed, "You had the washer women gossiping in the hallways, and you had the little government guy lurking around . . . spying on people, and you had some hard-bitten journalists over in one corner, and the Lebanese arms dealer in the other corner, and that's the type of environment that the Mamba Point has been in these times of crisis." There was an odd mix of allies and enemies, with a caged parrot and pink geckos sunning themselves on the terrace rail and, occasionally, haunting singing from the ruined mansion next door. Notably, there was no African food on the menu.

Starting with occasional photographic assignments for human rights organizations and Western newspapers and magazines, Hetherington carved out a life for himself in Monrovia, coming and going between the Liberian capital and the UK, the United States, and other countries in Africa. Eventually, he was appointed to the UN's panel of experts on Liberia to help document disarmament and sanctions compliance programs and to report on the activities of militia groups and their own and Charles Taylor's erstwhile war crimes. When Paradiso met him, Hetherington rarely talked about this work in great detail. He preferred to discuss the Liberians he photographed—adults and children bringing unexploded ordnance and weapons to UN collections sites, and others he met on the streets and in outlying villages. Corinne Dufka said all she knew about Hetherington's UN work was that "He certainly did a lot of deep intel interviews." Among other things, Hetherington concluded that because rebuilding efforts were focused on Monrovia, at the expense of other regions, a power vacuum had developed that local militias were only too happy to fill.

He spent a lot of time drinking tea in cafés and getting to know the people of Monrovia, taking photos and shooting video and producing segments for the U.S. news program *Nightline*. By the time Marparyan met him he was very much at home in Monrovia, sharing an apartment with Zubin Cooper and dating a woman who worked at the U.S. embassy. On the evening they met, Marparyan and Hetherington chatted amiably, and when Marparyan dropped him off at his apartment Hetherington asked for his phone number, telling him he had a driver in Monrovia but that the man frequently arrived late, which was an inconvenience when he had appointments to make, and that perhaps he would call when he needed a lift. A week later, as Marparyan was preparing to drive his children to school, Hetherington phoned and made arrangements to be picked up for an appointment. From that point on they became friends.

In his photography book *Long Story Bit by Bit*, Hetherington described the neighborhood where he lived and alluded to some of its hidden postwar dramas.

Above a clock in the dry cleaners on Benson Street hangs a small framed picture of President Tubman. Upstairs there used to be a place called the Lighthouse. That's where I met Jacqueline. As is the case with conversations in Liberia, we meandered, searching to get the measure of each other. I told her that I'd been coming and going to Liberia for several years and pointed through the window to my apartment. She asked me if I had been here during the 2003 war, to which I replied—somewhat cautiously—that I'd been on the "other" side with the rebels. "We were trying to kill your ass!" she said with a smile.

She looked up and checked my face, "You really don't know who I am, do you?"

I looked at her blankly. I hadn't a clue.

"I'm Jacqueline Toe. General Jacqueline Toe. I was Taylor's aide-de-camp from 1997 to 2002. I was in the NPFL [National Patriotic Front of Liberia] from the start."

Toe, Hetherington wrote, had told him that she had two young children when the war broke out and had no way to defend them from warlords who committed all sorts of atrocities, including drugging and conscripting child soldiers. During Liberia's first civil war, she had joined the National Patriotic Front of Liberia, a rebel group, and drove to the front line each day with her children in the backseat. As she discussed her experiences, as Hetherington put it, "She became excited by the memory like a person who has been through combat or seen strange things and had their moral compass turned so much so that the springs inside have become a little unhinged."

After talking with her, Hetherington offered to give her a ride home. Marparyan was waiting in his car outside. In his book, Hetherington describes Marparyan as a quiet, polite man who went to church on Sundays and who "was one of the only people I trusted in the entire country. I could give him a hundred dollars to keep safe and then ask him for it back a year later and he'd hand me the same exact bill. Untouched." As Marparyan silently drove them to Toe's home in the Congo Town neighborhood, she and Hetherington chatted in the backseat, and at one point she told him that Charles Taylor was "a great man." After dropping her off, Hetherington noticed that Marparyan seemed uncharacteristically "tense and serious. I could tell that there was something inside him that he was barely keeping control of. His hands tightened on the steering wheel and then he started shaking his head." When Hetherington asked what was bothering him, Marparyan went off, lambasting Jacqueline Toe, Charles Taylor, and the NPFL. "You know, the N-N-N-NPFL," he said, "they came to our house, and we gave them everything. They asked us for food, and we gave them everything we had, everything. And then they beat my father to death, they beat him to death. They beat him so bad he died. For nothing. Nothing!"

"After Marparyan finished," Hetherington wrote, "he took a deep breath and composed himself. We climbed the straight incline in silence and passed the large grey walls of the White Flower compound on our left," where Taylor had lived. "Its small dark windows seemed like peepholes into the past. Dangling above it, inoperable now, were fairy lights spelling out the words 'Season Greetings.'"

The episode stuck with Hetherington, who had always shown interest in the lives of the people he met. Once, when he and Marparyan visited an orphanage, they met an old blind woman who worked there, and as they were about to leave Hetherington gave Marparyan money to give to her and asked that he not say where it had come from. His genuine interest made him lots of friends, Marparyan said, adding that he could remember only one case where Hetherington tangled with anyone during the time he knew him in Monrovia. In that case, he said, a man on Centre Street became angry after Hetherington took his photo, "jumped him," and tried to take his camera. A crowd of the man's friends gathered around and Marparyan was compelled to run and find a policeman. After the officer intervened, he and Hetherington hurried away.

Hetherington was well known around Monrovia, and he became something of a local celebrity, particularly after he bought a motorcycle. As if it weren't enough that he was one of the few Westerners on the streets of a city of a million people, he was now the tall white guy on a motorcycle in a sea of pedestrians dodging battered, honking cars. He also soon became the go-to guy for Western journalists who visited Monrovia, though those were rare except during the country's historic postwar elections, held in 2005. He was the one who could tell you who was trustworthy and who could give you directions to the Americo Baptist church on Broad Street or to the diamond merchants' shops that had recently sprung up in the area "where the burnt out cinema used to be," or to "Raja—the big Lebanese guy in Diana's," who made the best chicken shwarma in town.

In *Long Story Bit by Bit,* Hetherington reveals his intimate knowledge of the city, down to the hustlers who hung out on the corner of Carey Street, the petty traders who sold secondhand baseball caps and creased trousers nearby, and, farther along, A.B.'s phone recharge stall and finally the steps leading to the apartment where he and Zubin Cooper lived "in the damp and the mold." Cooper, an affable guy with a close-cropped beard who described himself as a media producer, was a Monrovia native whose family had fled to the United States during the first civil war and had been introduced to Hetherington while the two were working with Brabazon and Stack on *An Uncivil War.* "We knew *of* each other," Cooper later said, since they had communicated only by phone and e-mail before Hetherington moved to Monrovia. When Hetherington and Brabazon were doing a follow-up story about the national elections for the UK's Channel 4, he and Cooper met and ended up renting an apartment together.

Soon after the 2005 elections, Hetherington and Cooper were covering a protest march to the U.S. embassy when, as Cooper recalled, "Tim raced up to the front, and then it degenerated." The crowd began throwing rocks and one struck Hetherington hard in the back. He initially thought he was all right, but after he and Cooper went to a bar for a beer, "He was like, 'Oh, my back's aching where the rock hit me, you know, but it's not too bad.'" When it continued to hurt, Hetherington decided to go to the hospital, "and he has three cracked ribs, it almost punctured his lung, or something," Cooper said, "and he had to leave a week later to go to the UK for serious treatment, but that was just the kind of person he was. He didn't even notice it at the time. He shrugged it off and kept on taking pictures."

Like many others, Cooper had first met Hetherington at the Mamba Point, when the two, along with Brabazon, were working on the TV documentary *A Violent Coast*. In the days after, he noticed that Hetherington was meticulous in his work but, as he later told Junger, he was alarmed by his behavior during a confrontation with former fighters at a checkpoint outside the city. "I just thought, 'This guy is fucking crazy,'" Cooper said. Many of the former fighters were drunk or high on amphetamines, and armed with automatic weapons, and they were not happy when Hetherington began photographing them with his old Hasselblad camera. Cooper watched in alarm as a few of them began firing their guns into the air, while Hetherington continued taking photos, even moving in for close-ups. One of the former fighters pointed his AK in Hetherington's face, with his finger on the trigger and the safety off, and Cooper said, "I'm like, 'Tim, Tim.' And he's so concentrated, he's not even hearing what I'm saying, and then I told James, 'Can you talk to him or something?'" Brabazon's response, he said, was, 'We all know the risk, man.' And so he's just taking these pictures, and this guy is high. He can pull the trigger at any time. And he's just standing there. He's not really even paying attention to Tim. Tim is circling him and the other guy, just taking pictures," Cooper recalled. Cooper then said, 'You're insane,' and he was, 'What?' I'm like, 'Forget it.'"

All that mattered to Hetherington, Cooper said, was, "'This is the picture I want to get,' because it would tell the story of where this young person, who this man is, this fighter is, at this time, so he's just focused on that to the exclusion of everything else, including his own safety."

It was all about telling a story, and Hetherington had learned that the story was delivered in bold relief during moments of high tension. As he later told his friend Stephen Mayes, the "software" of war was young men, and in Liberia, "It dawned on me when I was with the fighters that if there would be a choice between sitting in a refugee camp or being on the front lines and fighting I would be fighting . . . My interest is in the zone of conflict, with that software, where you can see the code more clearly." Yet the aftermath mattered, too, because he felt a responsibility to follow the story to its conclusion.

Around the time that he began working for the UN, Hetherington gave up the apartment with Cooper and moved in with his girlfriend. Cooper was himself working for the UN, and Hetherington sometimes asked him for background information, he said. Though Hetherington had access to a UN vehicle, it wasn't always the best way to arrive at interviews, so he often rode his motorcycle or, in cases where he wanted to travel incognito, had Marparyan drive him. He enjoyed being in Monrovia so much that at one point he and Cooper talked about opening a pub together.

"He wanted some justice for the Liberian folks," Cooper said, "so he kept on doing it in his own way, which was taking pictures, whatever information could be gleaned, and putting it out there." Hetherington was also considered one of Monrovia's most eligible bachelors, Cooper said. "I remember we went out once . . . there was a bar we used to like to go play pool, right up the road from our apartment. We went out, and this girl was throwing herself at him all night, and then afterwards, we went to another hotel where they had a pool table and a bar, and this girl followed . . . We just walked to this other bar and this girl just stalked us all night, until around three o'clock in the morning, and he's like, 'Zub, how can I get rid of her?'" Cooper told him, "Either you sleep with her or just tell her you don't want to be bothered." Because he already had a girlfriend, Hetherington said that "number one" was not an option, and "number two" he'd already tried. "I said, 'Okay, then three, we can run away.' We took option number three," Cooper said.

Beyond being chased after by women, "Tim was universally loved," Cooper said. "I've never really met anybody who said they didn't like Tim. . . . Tim knew the name of almost every photographer on Broad Street. He knew the boys, the ex-combatants . . . Everybody would know Tim because he'd go and sit down, he'd go and see a guy with a camera and he's like, 'Oh, that's nice. Can I see your pictures?' They'd talk. He'd show the guy a camera. They'd take pictures of each other. You know what I'm saying? . . . He was very engaging in how he would talk to people."

"I would run him from place to place, place to place, he photograph all day long," Marparyan said. "Most every day, except when he was going, the road so bad my car could not go there. Then he would take the four-by-four Jeep. Or if it is in a rural area, he took a helicopter." Marparyan said that when his daughter, Mercy, was accepted to nursing school and Marparyan couldn't afford the tuition, Hetherington paid half.

During the time that Hetherington was in Monrovia, *An Uncivil War* premiered at the Human Rights Watch Film Festival, and he was beginning work on his book *Long Story Bit by Bit,* which was published in 2009. The book includes long captions that accompany telling and sometimes stunningly beautiful photographs—portraits of young fighters wearing T-shirts emblazoned with the words "Too Tough to Die"; the woman bidding farewell to her rebel lover; a lush jungle landscape framed by a bombed-out hospital window; a haunting scene at the site of a massacre in a sacred forest; the shiny shoes of Jacques Klein, the special coordinator of UN operations in Liberia. His captions and side notes are rich in detail, such as his account of what Charles Taylor had in his possession when he was arrested on the Nigeria–Cameroon border: two cartons of sliced Korean ginseng; a videocassette titled *A Goofy Movie Cartoon;* a Liberian flag; five pairs of shoes; five walkie-talkies; eleven bottles of mouthwash; two bottles of perfume; one bottle of Nivea lotion; two books (*Effective Thinking Skills* and *The Laws of Team Morale*); seven submachine guns; one Luger; one bulletproof jacket; a safari suit jacket; twenty-one vests; a green raincoat; and a walking stick. As Marparyan later joked with Hetherington, he seemed to know more about Liberia and its history than he did about his native country England.

His friend and fellow photographer Benjamin Spatz, who also worked in Liberia, said Hetherington told him he liked that the country challenged him. "Nothing was ever easy," Spatz said. "Everyone was always testing you, and he loved that challenge, and he loved their openness, but he also loved how they were testing him, and the challenge to get the real story underneath." Spatz said the fact that Hetherington remained for the war's aftermath, which presented new complications, was "a testament to his ability to rise to that challenge."

Ultimately, it came down to the subjects of his photographs. In the acknowledgments to *Long Story Bit by Bit,* Hetherington wrote that he hoped the book's value would lie "in demonstrating how history is not the product of random chaos but is defined through the actions of individuals—hence the emphasis I have placed on naming people. With witnessing comes responsibility."

Magali Charrier, who edited Hetherington's *Diary,* observed, "There's this character in *Sans Soleil* who makes a list of all the things that quicken the heart, and it seems to me that Tim was addicted to the things that quicken the heart, maybe . . ." Hetherington was interested in "showing the beauty even in the darkest images," Charrier said.

It wasn't just about the excitement of war, said Caroline Irby, a photographer and friend who had also accompanied the Milton Margai blind choir on its UK tour. Irby noticed that Hetherington was "curious about everything and everyone—not just people in the context of war." Still, she added, "You find everything and everyone in their most extreme version when you're at war."

6
ACROSS AFRICA
AND SOUTH ASIA

In December 2004, while Hetherington was living in Monrovia, the South Asian nation Sri Lanka, which was embroiled in its own decades-long civil war, was hit by a devastating tsunami. The tidal wave killed an estimated 35,000 people, and soon after a rebel group known as the Tamil Tigers began recruiting children in refugee camps who had been orphaned and had no place to go. Child soldiers had been used in the civil wars in Liberia and Sierra Leone, and the Tamil Tigers had previously recruited and armed thousands of them, using threats and even abduction, and sent some on suicide missions. Now, after having lost hundreds of fighters to the tsunami, including nearly four hundred women and girls washed away from a rebel training camp, the Tamil Tigers were looking for ways to replenish their ranks.

At the time, Hetherington was working a variety of assignments across the African continent, most of which focused on the hardships of people in conflict and post-conflict zones. As he watched news accounts of the tsunami, he had no idea of going there. He was focused on his work for the UN and on documenting other stories in

Africa and didn't feel a particular connection to South Asia. Then he got a call from Panos Pictures, his photographic agency, offering him an assignment to make a short film about the tsunami for Britain's Channel 4. So he packed his bags and went to Sri Lanka to document the aftermath.

Hetherington's photos and footage from Sri Lanka and the similarly devastated nation of Sumatra showed a different kind of turmoil, the result of a natural disaster rather than a human conflict zone, though it reminded him of images he had seen of wartime destruction in Dresden and Hiroshima. As he had done in Liberia, Hetherington remained in South Asia after "the news-bandwagon moved relentlessly onward in search of the next thing," as he put it, and felt "dumbfounded by the sheer surreal nature of what had happened." Always intent on making connections across the void, he looked for images that people elsewhere in the world—people who were comfortable in their homes, as the residents of Sri Lanka had been when the tsunami hit—could relate to, such as a sodden photo album or a favorite chair lodged in debris amid a seemingly endless landscape of devastation.

He returned to Asia in 2005 to document the one-year anniversary of the disaster, spending most of his time in Banda Aceh, Sumatra, where he wandered the ruins and, as he later put it, "developed an isolated routine and got into a fairly surreal state of mind, which I think is reflected in the images I produced during that time." He observed that people whose lives revolved around the sea were grappling with mixed feelings about the ostensible calm of the post-tsunami world, that even seasoned fishermen felt intimidated by the thought of returning to their boats. Among his photos is one that has the quality of an impressionist painting, of several dozen schoolgirls shrouded in white veils and matching lavender garments known as *salwar kameez*, enjoying themselves at the edge of the surf, illustrating that people were growing comfortable with the sea again. It revealed an aspect of

Hetherington's work that would sometimes be overlooked amid the more dramatic war photos and footage: his search for beauty amid scenes otherwise characterized by sadness, terror, or despair. He chose the image as the end point of a later photo exhibition.

Hetherington's coverage of the tsunami was a geographic departure, but like his previous work it focused on people in distress, and the Sri Lankan civil war was part of the backdrop. There, as elsewhere, he found himself blurring the lines between journalism, art, and humanitarianism; as always, he wanted to explain the world to the world, through vivid and telling imagery, but he also wanted to prompt action. Between his initial foray into Liberia and Sierra Leone in 1999 and the second war he covered, in Afghanistan, in 2007 and 2008, Hetherington crisscrossed a series of troubled countries, often working on projects with a humanitarian focus. During that time, he staged a performance by children from the choir of the Milton Margai School for the Blind, at Cardiff's St. Donats Arts Centre; published *Healing Sport,* about soccer in post-conflict countries in West Africa; photographed street kids in Kinshasa in the Democratic Republic of the Congo; and in Nigeria participated in a project called Crossing Borders, hosted by the London-based British Council, in which he mentored young photographers to help them "record their own history," as he explained it, to find a voice beyond documenting their experiences in cell phone pics. Anyone could snap a cell phone photo and post it online, after which it might be endlessly forwarded, but he believed there was still a need for sharp, resonant, artfully composed images that told a deeper story and had staying power—in any case, that was his great hope. On more than one occasion he had pronounced photography a dying art, and in his own work he was moving steadily toward film and multimedia projects.

Hetherington also traveled to Nigeria to photograph an insurgency in the oil-producing Niger Delta, the scene of terrorist attacks on the facilities and pipelines of multinational companies that were reaping huge profits while devastating the sensitive marine environment. Far more oil had contaminated that environment than in the much-publicized BP spill in the Gulf of Mexico, fouling water supplies, ruining farms, and slowly killing the local fishing industry. In protest, rebels, insurgents, terrorists—the chosen term was a reflection of one's perspective—roamed the labyrinth of jungle waterways, mangrove swamps, and open bays in boats, often dressed in T-shirts, head rags, and underpants, their faces hidden by masks, sabotaging oil industry facilities with explosives and AKs and occasionally kidnapping oil field workers. As in Liberia, Hetherington wanted to get beyond the more provocative images to illustrate the personal stories behind them.

The journalist Dino Mahtani later recalled that when he traveled to the Niger Delta in 2006 for Hetherington's first trip, Mahtani took the lead, and when Hetherington arrived there the second time, "he called me regularly for advice and contacts. But before long the tables had turned. I was no longer his guide down there. Rather, he was mine, ensconced in the new underworld he had found." The result was Channel 4's *Unreported World—Nigeria: Fire in the Delta,* which Hetherington filmed, produced, and directed.

When he returned to Sri Lanka in 2007, Hetherington accompanied Olivier Bercault, a researcher for the Human Rights Watch emergencies program whom he had met while working in the Darfur region of Sudan, covering the unfolding genocide there. As Bercault pointed out, they traveled through some very dark places in Darfur, having come upon partially decomposed bodies of people hacked to death with machetes, half buried in leaves, and dark stains in the dirt left when other bodies had been removed. They traveled through Darfur with the Human Rights Watch researcher David Buchbinder, visiting abandoned villages and refugee camps—exhausting work that required long, rough rides in four-wheel-drives over bumpy desert roads, during which Hetherington somehow managed to edit his photos on his laptop while being constantly jostled. At one point, Bercault said, the three of them were so giddy with exhaustion that they got into a sort of photographic tousling match, taking pictures of one another as they drove. One of the photos, of Hetherington laughing, later ran in *Vanity Fair*.

Despite the gravity of their work—evidenced in the title of the short film Hetherington made about Darfur, *Echoes of Horror*—the three of them spent a lot of time laughing, Bercault said. Some of it was laughing-to-keep-from-crying but their shared sense of humor helped ensure that the friendship would last.

In Darfur, Hetherington, Bercault, and Buchbinder inhabited a different kind of front line, one that was little known in the outside world and which gave Hetherington's tandem interests in photography and humanitarianism a critical focal point. Their focus was the genocide of African villagers by Sudanese government forces and their murderous surrogates, known as the Janjaweed. Hetherington, Bercault, and Buchbinder were the first to document a horrific massacre of civilians by the Janjaweed, and during their extended drives through Sudan, as well as neighboring Chad, they had long conversations about the role of photography in humanitarian efforts. Before Hetherington went to work for Human Rights Watch in Darfur, the group's work was "a bit dry," according to Bercault. Hiring a war photographer and cinematographer had been a new approach, and Hetherington's assignment was basically a trial run. Because it worked so well, and drew worldwide attention to what was going on in Darfur, Human Rights Watch began hiring other war photographers and has since become an organization known for quality reporting from conflict zones, in addition to being an important source of freelance assignments for photographers.

At issue in Sudan was the government-supported genocide in Darfur, which was then spilling into Chad. Darfur is part of a largely unmapped area known as the Sahel—a swath of arid plains and stark escarpments between the Sahara Desert and the jungles of Africa, where the cultures of Arabs and black Africans, and nomads and farmers, overlap and frequently collide. In Darfur, the Janjaweed were engaged in genocide and the looting of traditional African villages, and hundreds of thousands had died and millions were displaced. When the Janjaweed began expanding the genocide into Chad, refugees streamed back into Darfur. Buchbinder and Bercault had recognized that atrocities were occurring in the town of Djawara after making the rounds of local hospitals in March 2006, when they encountered numerous people with machete injuries. They then traveled to Djawara to find out what had happened and discovered the aftermath of the massacre.

The Janjaweed were murderous, thieving gangs, and when they began rustling cattle in Djawara, the local militia gave chase. Because the Janjaweed had automatic weapons, vehicles, and backup from Sudanese gunships, the local militia—armed only with bows and arrows, clubs, spears, and boomerangs—was annihilated. In retaliation for the militia's show of self-defense, the Janjaweed massacred the entire village. Buchbinder and Bercault found three mass graves and many unburied bodies; the total killed, by their reckoning, was 118 in four villages, including Djawara.

Bercault had contributed to a 2005 Human Rights Watch report, "Smallest Witnesses," about children caught up in the genocide. In the course of Bercault's interviews with refugees, he and his colleagues had supplied crayons and paper to children, largely to distract them so the researchers could talk with their parents. The children had proceeded to draw revealing pictures of what had happened. As Hetherington had found back at Cardiff, the best way into the story proved to be an approach from an unfamiliar angle, in this case, through the eyes of children who might otherwise have been seen merely as a source of distraction.

Bercault conducted interviews in nine of eleven refugee camps and observed the same results in each one. He and his colleagues amassed hundreds of children's drawings, evidence of war crimes so detailed it was possible to identify which types of guns the Janjaweed had carried. The drawings corroborated accounts that the attacks began with the arrival of gunships (which proved the Sudanese government in Khartoum was involved), after which the Janjaweed arrived on horses and camels, in jeeps and on foot, to finish off the villages. At the time, there were no photos or videos of the crimes, so the children's drawings filled the gap. Human Rights Watch recognized the need—and opportunity—to further document what was going on, and the footage Hetherington shot eventually made its way into two films: *Darfur Bleeds,* which he directed, and *The Devil Came on Horseback,* a feature documentary about a former U.S. soldier who photographed the genocide.

Darfur Bleeds has some of the pacing and arrangement of *Diary,* which also incorporates some of Hetherington's Darfur footage (as well as Bercault's voice), though the narrative is more straightforward. The scenes, most of which were shot in the aftermath of the Djawara massacre, are nonetheless haunting. Hetherington narrates against a background of eerily monotonal music and the voice of a man reading the victims' names in Arabic. He interviews survivors of the attack as they roam the now abandoned village, and one recalls that there would be "five, eight, ten people" rushing at injured victims with machetes to finish them off, shouting, "Kill the Nuba!" The villages were primitive and had been occupied since ancient times, their thatched huts arranged in geometric grids on the seemingly endless plain. Life had always been hard there, and the balance was easily tipped by armed marauders backed by gunships.

Buchbinder and Bercault had arrived in the capital city N'Djamena in April 2005, a few days before Hetherington flew in from Monrovia. A week had passed since Chadian rebels had invaded Darfur, and around N'Djamena they observed the tracks of tanks that had flattened houses and visited a prison where two or three hundred Chadian rebels were being held. During their investigations, which would continue until May 2006, they visited refugee camps on the Darfur–Chad border, where there were a great many forced conscripts, including numerous children. Hetherington shot particularly stunning video footage of the kids after the official interviews were over, in which they stare silently into the camera for two or three minutes—a long time to maintain an unwavering gaze and a long time for a viewer to watch. Buchbinder found the silent footage "very poetic" and said at that moment he realized Hetherington wasn't a typical war photographer.

The second phase of the mission took the crew into eastern Chad, where they documented the massacre at Djawara. "It was very dangerous at the time," Buchbinder said. "Snipers were picking people off in that area." The resulting footage empowered an international effort to intervene to stop the genocide.

Toward the end of the mission, Buchbinder and Hetherington talked a lot about the role of photographers and the blurring of the line between journalism and humanitarianism. Hetherington felt it wasn't enough merely to show what had happened, that photography could convey a deeper narrative and influence the direction that narrative would afterward take. Prompting action had likewise been the aim of the former U.S. marine Brian Steidle, who had photographed his journey through Darfur in 2004 while serving as a paid military observer for the African Union, monitoring a cease-fire between the predominately Muslim north and the animist-Christian south. Steidle's journey, chronicled in *The Devil Came on Horseback*—Janjaweed translates as "the devil on horseback"—incorporates footage by six photographers, including Hetherington. At the time of the film's release, in 2007, an estimated 400,000 people had died in the genocide, which the film places at the feet of the Sudanese president Omar al-Bashir, while implicating Chinese oil companies that enjoyed cozy deals with the Sudanese government. At the time Steidle was taking his covert photos, the UN could not even agree to pronounce the killings as genocidal, though entire villages had been murdered, their residents shot, hacked to death, or burned alive.

Darfur Bleeds and *The Devil Came on Horseback* generated worldwide interest, albeit briefly. Despite rallies and intense media attention the world was slow to take meaningful action. Steidle, who went so far as to travel to Rwanda to see how that nation had ended its genocidal war between the Tutsis and the Hutus, was frustrated, and he broke down in tears during one interview. His only tools, he said, had been his monitoring reports, which went nowhere, and his camera.

Echoes of Horror was "very graphic," Bercault said, and despite the film's limited response, "I knew we had an impact. It triggered something. Nobody had heard about Darfur before we went there." And though its subject matter was tragic, Hetherington's *Darfur Bleeds* "was a beautiful piece," Bercault said, "an artistic approach to a massacre."

When he returned to Sri Lanka with Bercault, in 2007, it was to work on a project that was indirectly related to the Sri Lankan civil war, about the human rights activist Sunila Abeysekera. Because the government was embarrassed by the focus of their work, Human Rights Watch became concerned for their safety and canceled a planned trip to the east of the island, telling Hetherington and Bercault to leave the country or, if that wasn't possible, to "at least keep quiet in Colombo." Hetherington and Bercault were unable to change their flights, so they stayed for a few days in a touristy hotel by the beach south of Colombo.

While stranded at the resort, Hetherington and Bercault spent a good bit of time editing footage in their hotel rooms, and Bercault said it eventually occurred to them that the hotel staff thought they were a couple. They occasionally went shopping together and visited art galleries in downtown Colombo, all of which reinforced suspicions, Bercault said, that the two were on a romantic holiday. Though they had separate rooms the staff seemed to consider that a cover for their romance, and it didn't help that each evening they enjoyed a candlelit dinner on the beach. "Tim often told this story when talking about doing undercover work," Bercault said, laughing at the memory. "He joked that the best way to work undercover was to pose as a gay couple." Few people questioned their reasons for being there and, if they did, the questions were typically veiled attempts to determine their romantic status.

Bercault said he enjoyed traveling with Hetherington under any circumstances, not only because he was committed, and talented, but because he was "a very funny guy, and such a joyful companion, very witty, even in the worst situations."

7

AFGHANISTAN

When Staff Sergeant Kevin Rice saw the Taliban fighter taking aim at him with an RPG, he was on his hands and knees on a remote mountainside in Afghanistan, bleeding from his stomach and shoulder onto the ground. At that moment, Rice thought, "Wow, this is the last thing I'm going to see."

Rice was a farm boy from Wisconsin and had never been outside the United States before deploying with the U.S. Army in Afghanistan. Now he was about to be blown away on a mountain ridge known as Abas Ghar, or so it seemed. A few seconds later, after the grenade had gone off, Rice was surprised to find that he was still a Wisconsin farm boy fighting in the Afghan war, but with new wounds. "Okay," he said to himself, "I'm still here. I'm still alive." The explosion riddled his body with shapnel, and he was now bleeding from multiple places rather than the original two wounds. But what really mattered was that he could hear Taliban fighters talking nearby, so rather than wait for them to come and finish him off he rolled himself down a ravine, into the bushes, and lay there until the voices went away. Then he pulled himself to his feet and went looking for his guys.

On another part of the ridge Hetherington, who was filming with a machine-gun crew, ran to where the scouts attached to the army platoon were under attack. The Americans' position had been overrun. Hetherington was embedded with a conventional army for the first time—technically, this was only his second war, and that day, and that war, proved a turning point for him, as it did for many of the soldiers around him. In his footage we hear someone yell, "Abdul, get the fuck over here!" Someone else shouts, "I don't know where they're at!" It's clear the enemy is close but they're always outside the frame. Then Hetherington comes upon the body of Sergeant Larry Rougle, a scout commander whom everyone loved, who had been shot through the head and had died instantly. Sergeant Mitchell Raeon sees Hetherington filming the scene, quickly covers Rougle's face, and shouts, "Get the fuck out of here!" Hetherington switches off his camera.

When a group of Afghan soldiers who had accompanied the Americans began dragging Rougle's dead body away by the feet, Raeon yelled at them to stop, saying it was no way to treat him, that they should show some respect. Hetherington helped hoist Rougle's body onto Raeon's back so they could transport it to a landing spot to be helicoptered out. Not far away, Private Misha Pemble-Belkin, a boyish-looking Oregon man whose hippie parents had forbidden him to play with toy guns, heard Miguel Cortez calling for a medic and bounded to the spot where Specialist Carl Vandenberge lay, shot in the arm and neck. Vandenberge was rocking from side to side, bleeding out, saying, "Help me," over and over. Cortez and Pemble-Belkin began wrapping his arm and neck with gauze, and Pemble-Belkin pushed Kerlix bandages into the worst wound until his fingers were knuckle-deep inside, applying pressure to the artery. Vandenberge's eyes looked ghostly. "You could see it in his face that he [was] slowly dying," Pemble-Belkin later said. Vandenberge told them the Taliban had been only twenty feet away. No one knew where they were now.

Cortez then went to check on Rice. A bullet had entered Rice's shoulder and exited through his stomach, and he had multiple shrapnel wounds, but Rice didn't want any help as he staggered through the woods, so Cortez ran back to Vandenberge and helped Pemble-Belkin carry him to the top of the ridge. Once there, Cortez saw Rougle's body. He felt like crying but held it together. When Rice stumbled up, he also saw Rougle's body, but it didn't fully register. Then he saw Vandenberge, bleeding profusely from his shoulder, and Rice lost it. Hetherington, hovering nearby, filmed the scene. The Taliban had broken through the position Rice had been trying to hold, and all he could do was tell Vandenberge how sorry he was. In Hetherington's footage, as soldiers fire into the valley below, we hear someone shout, "Shut up!" then someone else saying, "Calm down, there are still guys out here. Okay? Just stay with me, all right?"

Everyone was in a state of shock, including Hetherington. Afghanistan was the first time he was working among fighters who looked like him, and it felt different. When people back home asked how he continued photographing and filming during a firefight, he always said he had a way of shutting off a part of his brain—the part that instinctively compels a person to fight or flee—so he could keep doing his job. But here he was shaken. As he zoomed in on the soldiers' faces, we see that they're all young, American, of different ethnic backgrounds. They look alternately angry, confused, scared, determined, distressed. When soldiers began helping Rice and Vandenberge off the mountainside, to a distant landing zone for evacuation, Hetherington thought perhaps he should go with them, that maybe they could use his help. But he was riveted by the scene unfolding around Rougle's body. In his footage, a scout named Clinard sees Rougle's body, cries out "Rou—" and begins to sob. Another soldier embraces him and says softly, "Don't look at him. It was quick."

Hetherington pans the ridgetop, and everyone we see, including those who are not injured, is bloodstained. Hetherington glanced at his own hands and saw that they were too. Raeon, who had taken position with his gun, is scanning the valley through his scope, looking for the retreating Taliban attackers, his fatigues and bulletproof vest drenched with Rougle's blood. Hetherington moves in for a close-up of Raeon's blood-crusted fingers gripping the trigger as he unleashes a fusillade of bullets into the forest below. Confusion and blood: these are the dominant themes of Hetherington's footage.

Elsewhere, Captain Daniel Kearney is on his radio, speaking breathlessly between gulps from a bottle of water, his face taut and grimy with greasepaint and dirt. He calls in helicopter gunships, telling them to follow the trail of blood from the last Taliban fighter his guys had hit, which he says will lead them to the rest. We see the gunships firing into the evergreen forests below, clipping the leaves off trees. Then, as abruptly as it began, the firing subsides. The Taliban guerrillas have disappeared.

In the quiet that followed, Hetherington felt chastened, not only because Raeon had shouted at him to stop filming but because he knew Raeon was right. But why was that? He had photographed and filmed countless bodies in war zones and was unsure why it was different now. Was it because Rougle wasn't a nameless African? Hetherington had come to Afghanistan to film the Second Platoon of the 173rd Airborne Brigade's Battle Company for a documentary he was working on with Sebastian Junger, who had been covering Afghanistan for more than a decade. The idea was to live with the platoon at their small, remote bunker in the Korengal Valley, which was known as Outpost Restrepo, to show what life was like for American soldiers there. The Korengal was the most dangerous place in Afghanistan, where the majority of U.S. ordnance was being dropped during the platoon's fifteen-month deployment. Over the course of a year, Hetherington and Junger would spend a month or so at a time with the soldiers, sometimes traveling there together, sometimes separately. This time Hetherington was alone.

On his own, Hetherington would probably have been drawn to photograph the world of the Afghans, but now—with the film in mind, and with tandem assignments for *Vanity Fair* and ABC News— he found a way to show that war is hellish for everyone, including the soldiers of a highly trained and well-equipped invading force.

Abas Ghar was the focus of a weeklong operation known as Rock Avalanche, which involved about seven hundred soldiers spread out across the ridge. Going in, everyone knew it was going to be bad, but no one knew just how bad, that it would mean the end of Rougle, a veteran of six combat tours since he had enlisted following the September 11 attacks, who was twenty-five and had a three-year-old back home in Utah. Yet there he had been, lying dead on the ground, waiting for a body bag. And the fight was far from over.

In the film that Hetherington and Junger made, which they called *Restrepo* after the name of the remote outpost and the soldier it had been named for, the battle scenes are prefaced with earlier, grainy footage of the soldiers on a train, traveling across Italy on their way to Afghanistan. The platoon medic, Juan Restrepo, films with a Flip cam. When he turns the camera on himself, we see a handsome guy, wearing shades, with a broad smile and perfect teeth. He looks cool. Another soldier, Brendan O'Byrne, jokes with him, talking nonsense, beer bottle in hand—one in a long series, by the look of things. We're going to party in Italy, O'Byrne says.

Restrepo, a native of Colombia who grew up in Florida, says, "Tune in next time, we're going to be still loving life. We're getting ready to go to war. We're going to war." A month later PFC Restrepo was dead.

Like Kevin Rice, most of the soldiers in Second Platoon had never been out of the United States before and had never lived anywhere other than with their parents. On their first day in the Korengal they were involved in seven firefights. Their first casualty was a nineteen-year-old private named Timothy Vimoto, the son of the brigade's command sergeant major, who was shot through the head during the first volley from a Taliban machine gun positioned about half a mile away. As Junger later wrote in his book *War,* "One minute he was in the first firefight of his life, the next moment he was dead." Rice had carried Vimoto's body away on his shoulder. "Doc" Restrepo was killed a few weeks later, when the Taliban ambushed a patrol in Aliabad, mortally wounding him, then attacked a convoy of Humvees that tore out of the Korengal outpost to try to save him. Restrepo was still alive when he was loaded on a medevac helicopter but died en route to the hospital.

Battle Company's First Platoon had traveled alongside the Second Platoon to Abas Ghar, the Taliban stronghold at the far end of the six-mile-long Korengal Valley. The soldiers had been helicoptered in to a remote landing zone during the night and walked into the village of Yaka China just before dawn. Everyone was nervous, because everyone else—the villagers, the Taliban—had obviously heard the choppers and knew they were there. Soon, the soldiers began hearing mortars exploding and gunfire in the distance, as American gunships fired rounds and planes dropped bombs on suspected Taliban locations. As Hetherington filmed, they came upon a home that had been hit. In his footage, the family is terrified; at least one child is dead, her body covered with dirt and rubble. An old man stares at the soldiers with hatred in his eyes.

The next day the soldiers searched another house and found ammo, a pistol, an AK, and a stash of RPGs. When they interrogated the owner, who claimed he was only a sheep herder, he said that if he told them anything about the Taliban he would be killed. His wife looked on, holding a baby. When night fell and the temperature began to drop, the soldiers bedded down in the forest in sleeping bags. By morning they had identified four Taliban positions, and in Hetherington's footage everyone speaks quietly now. At one point, Kearney says over the radio, "What the fuck was that? Did you hear that? Am I just jumpy?" Soon their voices are reduced to whispers. They walk with guns at the ready, peering through their scopes.

When the attack finally came they were atop the Abas Ghar ridge. It was worse than expected, and in fact was the worst fight of their fifteen-month tour. Not only was Rougle killed, the Taliban had managed to overrun all their positions, steal weapons and ammunition, and get away. Considering that thousands of people sometimes die in a single combat episode, the loss of one man on a lonely ridge in Afghanistan was an example of war on a very small, intimate scale, but it hadn't felt in any way small to those who were there, including Hetherington. An intimate perspective was what he and Junger were looking for. The point was to show war from the inside for an American soldier in the twenty-first century. If Hetherington shied away from being described as a "war photographer," which he felt reduced what he was trying to do to something facile, it was going to be a difficult distinction to make now. His footage and photos in the Korengal would be the most famous of his career and among the best produced by any photographer in any war.

After the fighting subsided, Hetherington and the Second Platoon spent an uncomfortable night camped on Abas Ghar. The soldiers "slept on their arms," in military parlance, with grenades and guns within reach. In fact, few of them got much sleep; circumstances required that two soldiers stand guard while one rested, and considering where they were it was all but impossible for anyone to let their guard down for long. All night, Apache helicopters monitored

Taliban fighters who were walking in their direction, and Kearney eventually called in a bomb drop that missed its target but dispersed the fighters, many of whom were then killed by fire from the gunships. The next morning everyone was tense and exhausted. They were picking up radio chatter that indicated the enemy was closing in again, and when Taliban fighters were seen moving along a nearby ridge the entire American line opened up on them with mortars, gunfire, and RPGs. By late afternoon, once it became clear that the Taliban fighters were not going to attack again, the men of Second Platoon finally got some rest. They were told to move out around midnight.

First Platoon had left the night before and made its way back to the Korengal Outpost but had been dispatched that day with a portion of Third Platoon to reconnoiter the valley for Taliban fighters who, according to the army's intel, might be planning an attack on Outpost Restrepo, and also another remote base, Phoenix, each of which at the moment had only a skeleton crew of ten men. After nightfall, when the soldiers of First Platoon were walking single file along the crest of a ridge, ten or fifteen yards apart, they were ambushed by three Taliban fighters waiting ahead of them with AK-47s, and ten more to their side with belt-fed machine guns and RPGs. Sergeant Josh Brennan was walking point, followed by Staff Sergeant Erick Gallardo and Specialist Salvatore Giunta. "Within seconds," Junger wrote, "every man in the lead squad takes a bullet. Brennan goes down immediately, wounded in eight places." The enemy was perhaps twenty feet away. As the men fought back while trying to rescue their wounded comrades, Giunta threw his last grenade and sprinted to where Brennan had fallen, and in the moonlight he saw two Taliban dragging him away. He emptied his M4 magazine at them and began running toward Brennan, Junger wrote. As Giunta later told Junger, "I didn't run through fire to do anything heroic or brave. I did what I believe *anyone* would have done."

One of the Taliban fighters who was dragging Brennan fell to the ground, dead, and the other let go of him and escaped. Giunta dragged Brennan behind cover, cut the ammo rack from his chest, and pulled the ripcord on his bulletproof vest to free him and search for wounds. Brennan had been shot multiple times in the legs and had a large shrapnel wound in his side; he had also been shot in the lower part of his face but he was still conscious. When a medic arrived, he gave Brennan a tracheotomy and, with the Taliban now gone, a medevac chopper landed and evacuated him and the other casualties. Brennan later died, as did another soldier, Specialist Hugo Mendoza, who had also tried to rescue him. Whether Giunta saw his actions as brave or not, he was later awarded the Congressional Medal of Honor for his efforts to save Brennan, the first time it had been awarded to a living soldier since the Vietnam War.

By the time Second Platoon moved out from Abas Ghar at midnight everyone was in an exhausted daze, weighed down with their body armor, weapons, and heavy packs. "We waited for First Platoon for hours," team leader Sergeant Aron Hijar told Junger, "and once we linked up with them it was still two and a half hours' walk back to the KOP," as the soldiers called the Korengal Outpost. By then they had heard about the ambush and, "You could just tell on the guys' faces, it wasn't the right time to ask," Hijar said. "You already knew what the answer was going to be. Some of them were walking around with bullet holes in their helmets." As they stumbled quietly through the darkness, Hetherington had time to consider what had happened on Abas Ghar. He wondered about Raeon's verbal assault, for which Raeon later apologized, and about why he saw these soldiers differently. He had gotten blood on his hands. He had entered a different kind of war zone, inside and out.

Most of the soldiers wore night-vision goggles but Hetherington didn't have any, which put him at a disadvantage as they hiked through the rugged terrain in the darkness. At one point he caught his foot between two rocks, fell to the side, and felt something snap. Intense pain shot up his leg. When the medic approached, Hetherington tried to downplay his injury. There wasn't much anyone could have done to help anyway. No one was going to carry him, and there was no way to call in a medevac chopper. He had learned during his time at Restrepo that one of the worst things anyone could do was become a burden on the other soldiers, which would increase the risk for everyone. So he took some Advil or whatever it was that the medic gave him, found a stick to use as a kind of crutch, and walked on, for the rest of the night, on what turned out to be a broken leg.

Hetherington had felt a need to prove himself to the soldiers from early on. He was a journalist, a British guy, approaching middle age, among a group of rowdy, young, tattooed soldiers from California, Florida, New Jersey, and Wisconsin. He had a tendency to view war intellectually, with an artist's eye, and in some ways he stood out as much as he had when he was the white guy on the motorcycle in Monrovia. It was much the same for Junger, but at least he was an American.

Over time, Hetherington managed to prove himself. The men of Second Platoon had accepted him, joked with him, and sometimes shared their innermost feelings with him. And once they found out what he had been going through as he hopped and limped—and occasionally slid and tumbled—down the mountain trail that night after Abas Ghar, their admiration for him increased. But for now it wasn't clear that anyone would make it back to Restrepo alive, and Hetherington was undoubtedly the most vulnerable. As they walked through the darkness, the platoon picked up radio chatter from the Taliban indicating that they were aware of their movements. According to the Afghan translator, the Taliban fighters were basically saying, "We've got these guys." There was no way out for the soldiers other than the

84

mountain trail, and due to his lack of mobility Hetherington felt especially frightened, and he tried to mentally prepare himself for whatever might lie ahead. At one point he turned his camera on himself and recorded a short message for ABC News, the essence of which was: I'm in a bad situation.

The anticipated attack never came. Perhaps the Taliban had only been trying to scare them. When they finally reached the landing zone at Landigal, Hetherington could afford to say how bad his injury was. The medic already knew but hadn't mentioned it for fear that knowing his leg was broken would have made it harder for Hetherington to endure the pain. He was evacuated to the hospital at Bagram Air Base, where he underwent surgery for a broken fibula. The rest of the soldiers returned to Yaka China, and from there to Outpost Restrepo.

Junger, who relieved Hetherington for the next stint of filming at Restrepo, said that when they met up in New York City it was apparent that Hetherington didn't feel anything like pride over having soldiered on with his broken leg, that he was, in fact, "traumatized and ashamed." His misgiving about filming Rougle's death scene, the fear he'd felt over being partially immobilized, the blood on his hands—all of it stuck with him. "I don't think he ever got over it," Junger said. Operation Rock Avalanche had been what the military called, prosaically, a "tactical walk-through" aimed at locating and engaging the Taliban fighters who'd been attacking American military outposts— including Restrepo—in the Korengal Valley. For Hetherington, it proved to be a rite of passage into a new and, in many ways, darker kind of war zone. His physical, emotional, and psychological immersion may have been useful for a journalist who needed to empathize with his subjects, to better portray their experience, but it was damaging for him, just as it was for them. The point of Hetherington and Junger's project was to get inside the soldiers' world, but it was equally important that they be able to get back out. It was obvious the latter was going to be difficult for Hetherington.

The idea for the documentary had come to Junger after he had published an article in *Vanity Fair* about an episode in which a group of Taliban fighters had cornered a four-man Navy SEAL team that had previously been dropped onto the same Abas Ghar ridge. The Taliban had killed three of the Americans, and shot down a Chinook rescue helicopter, killing all sixteen commandos on board.

Junger, who had been covering the war in Afghanistan from the outset, saw the trauma inflicted upon the soldiers and decided to embed himself with a platoon to get a clearer view of their world. He decided to return to Afghanistan with a *Vanity Fair* assignment and ABC News credentials to collect enough material for both a book and a feature-length documentary on one platoon. "I realized I needed to work with a photographer who was really comfortable shooting video as well. I needed someone who was in shape, who could carry a lot of gear, and who could alternate between a still camera and video, and who had been in a lot of combat. Basically, I needed someone like Tim. And then I met Tim."

Introduced to Hetherington by editors at *Vanity Fair,* for which Hetherington was a contributing photographer, Junger found him to be the perfect companion. He knew Hetherington had been with the LURD rebels while working on *An Uncivil War,* which meant he'd been in combat and could handle himself. During a subsequent telephone interview, after Junger's first trip to the Korengal Valley, Junger recalled telling Hetherington that he would have to be in good shape to cope with the conditions and the workload in Afghanistan. Hetherington had laughed and replied, "When you meet me you'll realize I'm rather lean."

The two met for the first time at London's Heathrow Airport, en route to Afghanistan. Junger was reading a newspaper in the gate area when he had the sense that everyone around him had suddenly looked at something simultaneously. It turned out to be Hetherington, who was approaching in full stride. "He had a kind of electricity," Junger said. "They were all looking at him. He had this huge stride, I mean, after he broke his leg, on crutches, I would literally have to run to keep up with him as he walked down the sidewalk. He was just this sort of giant of a man, and he was striding through the airport, through the gate, towards me, and everyone was looking at him, because he was just that kind of person. And here was this tall, good-looking, and incredibly energetic person, and I thought, 'Oh, my God. This is the guy I'm going to be working with for the next year?' His head is swiveling around, scanning for me, while he's got a backpack on, and in each hand he's got some kind of communication device, and he's multitasking [with] both of them."

The two subsequently missed their connecting flight in Delhi and were stuck in the terminal for twenty-four hours, during which they got to know each other, and slept for a while on benches, Junger said. They discussed the relative merits of being embedded with a military organization, which some journalists felt compromised their objectivity. Junger had refused to cover the Iraq war because he vehemently opposed it, which would have gotten in the way, because the point of what he wanted to do in Afghanistan was to tell a story from the perspective of the soldiers themselves, separate from the politics. Toward that aim, he had lined up the assignments with *Vanity Fair* and ABC News, the latter of which provided him with a video camera, so they could use his footage in their broadcasts. After Hetherington came on board, the two traveled together to Restrepo three times for month-long stays, and otherwise alternated trips. Junger also planned to write a book, what would become *War*. Though he had shot some video during his earlier coverage of the Afghan war, he had no idea how to make a film. He decided he would figure it out later.

During their first trip together, Hetherington shot mostly still photographs. The plan was to remain at the Restrepo outpost for a month at a time, each of them shooting video, with Hetherington continuing to shoot stills as well. After Junger tore his Achilles tendon during their first trip while carrying a heavy load up a steep hill, he was forced to spend some time recuperating at home, so Hetherington returned to Restrepo alone. It was during that trip that the soldiers were dispatched on Operation Rock Avalanche; because Hetherington had broken his leg, Junger had to take up the slack the next time around. They returned together the following April, after which they went back to alternating their stays, arriving at the main Korengal Outpost by helicopter and walking the two hours from there to Restrepo, which was notoriously primitive by the standards of the American military, where most bases are equipped with Wi-Fi and gyms. At Restrepo there was no running water, Internet or phone communication, nor, in the beginning, electricity. Until small hooches were built, "You slept out in the open," Hetherington recalled. "Filming conditions were pretty tough. You couldn't take a tripod and every so often you'd go down to the Korengal Outpost on the valley floor to recharge your batteries." In *War*, Junger describes Outpost Restrepo as "a dusty scrap of steep ground surrounded by timber walls and sandbags, one of the smallest, most fragile capillaries in a vascular system that pumps America's influence around the world." By then, Hetherington had given up his apartment in Monrovia, having finished his work for the UN, and was intrigued with the idea of covering a different kind of war, in a different part of the world.

The soldiers of the 173rd Airborne would later hold the distinction of being deployed more times since the September 11 attacks than anyone other than the Tenth Mountain Division, which handed the Korengal over to Battle Company in June 2007. At that time,

Battle Company effectively became the tip of the U.S. spear, as the entire southern half of the Korengal Valley, which included Abas Ghar, was controlled by the Taliban. American patrols that pushed even a few hundred yards into the area were immediately attacked. Lots of rocks and dust and pyrotechnics arose each time a mortar was fired from Restrepo, or a bomb dropped by a plane or a missile fired from a helicopter gunship, but with the Taliban fighters scattered over steep, forested mountainsides it was hard to know how effective the counterattacks were.

Second Platoon had a reputation as a tough crew, guys who tended to act up and sometimes got in trouble back at the base, but who were unparalleled soldiers during combat. They were, Junger wrote, a cross section from "mainland America and from wherever the American experiment has touched the rest of the world: the Philippines and Guam and Puerto Rico and South Korea." At Restrepo they came under daily fire, sometimes three or four times a day, from distances as close as fifty yards, inside a small fortification delineated by Hesco containers and sandbags that the soldiers filled with rocks that they'd laboriously broken with pickaxes in 100-degree heat. Seventy percent of U.S. munitions in Afghanistan were being dropped in and around the six-mile-long Korengal Valley, and though Outpost Restrepo wasn't far from the main American staging area in the valley, the KOP, the men of Second Platoon were extremely exposed there, always under threat of being overrun by the Taliban. All it would take for the outpost to be taken would be for the Taliban to pin them down with machine-gun fire from above while fighters flanked them and overran the Hesco barriers and concertina wire.

The Korengal was a remote, starkly beautiful valley in eastern Afghanistan that marked the demarcation line between the American forces and the Taliban's last, best stronghold. It was a place where life had changed little for centuries, where people unaccustomed to outsiders lived in stone houses perched precipitously on the mountainsides of the Hindu Kush. Korengal culture was essentially feudal, and it was staunchly tribal. Though the Taliban had been driven out of the valley during the Soviet invasion of the 1980s, the locals now tolerated their presence as the lesser of two evils. Everyone either supported the Taliban or feared opposing them because it would likely get them killed. During the Soviet invasion, the Korengal had been a safe haven for the local mujahideen, who had used it to launch strikes against the occupying forces. After the September 11 attacks and the subsequent NATO invasion, the Taliban had been driven from political power, and U.S. Special Forces arrived to track down militants believed to be linked to al-Qaeda. Hetherington, who later wrote about his experiences in Afghanistan in the narrative for his book of photography *Infidel,* noted that in 2005 a series of deadly attacks on U.S. forces in the valley had led the Americans to conclude that the Korengal was once again becoming a militant stronghold, and the decision was made to establish outposts there and, meanwhile, to build a road that might more firmly connect the region to the central government.

The people of the Korengal were notoriously suspicious of outsiders, even from elsewhere in Afghanistan. They spoke a version of Pashai that was unintelligible even to speakers of other dialects of the obscure language, and they practiced their own strict version of Islam. To soldiers from Wisconsin and New Jersey, the village elders may as well have come from another planet, with their traditional hats and robes, mascara-rimmed eyes, and long beards died with henna to a strangely bright pink or orange hue. The people of the Korengal likewise saw the Americans as strange, with their high-tech weapons, rambunctious behavior, and inscrutable tattoos (many of which boldly proclaimed "infidel"). The villagers were likewise incensed that U.S. military presence had halted the valley's important timber trade, which was being used to support the Taliban, and had better enabled the government in distant Kabul to enforce its policies. Due to their antipathy, and the valley's rugged terrain, the Korengal attracted both Taliban militants and foreign jihadists from Pakistan and Saudi Arabia; as a result, everyone, including journalists, knew they'd see combat when they arrived.

According to the American rules of engagement, anyone other than U.S. military personnel who carried a weapon or a radio handset was a viable target for American troops. Yet, as Hetherington noted, "the difficulty of distinguishing an insurgent from a farmer became quickly apparent to the U.S. soldiers. Local men could earn $5 by agreeing to fire a weapon against U.S. forces, and by the time the Americans had become fully deployed, there was a noticeable absence of young men of fighting age in the villages." Most had either joined the insurgents or fled to Pakistan to sit out the war. "Other villagers were caught in the middle of the fight," Hetherington wrote. "Insurgents threatened anyone who collaborated with the Americans, so the locals refused to supply workers. One father and son, lured out of the main American outpost to buy a goat, were seized and beheaded." Further complicating matters, insurgents often fired on American soldiers from inside homes, then herded women and children to the rooftops as human shields. Many of the people who were used in this way died in the resulting strikes by Apache helicopters.

By any measure the Korengal was unusually dangerous terrain. During one day in July 2007, Cpt. Kearney counted thirteen firefights, illustrating precisely why Restrepo was built where it was. When Hetherington and Junger arrived at Restrepo that summer most of the world was focused on the war in Iraq, and Hetherington recalled being "gobsmacked" by the intensity of the fighting in the Korengal. American troops in the Korengal had a 25 percent casualty rate, and because of the frequency and intensity of combat Hetherington reverted to what he described as classic war photography, though his footage, as well as the photos he later published in *Infidel*, are anything but conventional. The reason, he said, was that he became bored with shooting stock fighting scenes. Dangerous as Restrepo was, the fighting soon became routine.

In an interview with NPR during one of his trips back home, Hetherington said he had not anticipated how intense his time at Restrepo would be. "I imagined that we'd be walking around, kind of in the valleys there, and meeting village elders, and kind of sitting down for meetings and cups of tea and occasionally being shot at. And I didn't expect to have the kind of intense combat experience that actually happened there, the intensity of the fighting—fighting, basically, or being attacked, or attacking, every day."

Being embedded with a fighting force, whether Liberian rebels or American soldiers, carried risks beyond coming under fire. A journalist whose life depends on a group of armed men cannot afford to alienate them, which is easy to do if the coverage is truly objective. But Hetherington and Junger said no one placed limits on what they could do, beyond the logical ones that applied to the soldiers as well, which involved physical endurance and strategic risk. No one asked to see their footage before *Restrepo* aired. Outpost Restrepo was far from "the machinations of the U.S. military bureaucracy," Hetherington said. "We were in some ways forgotten about." What the military brass did see, in *Vanity Fair* and on ABC's *Nightline,* apparently did not offend them, and Junger and Hetherington studiously avoided editorializing about the reasons the men were there. Their work focused on the soldiers themselves. The soldiers, though initially skeptical, warmed up over time. As Hetherington told *PBS NewsHour,* "They realized that we were going to go to the furthest extents that they would go to. We went on every patrol, into every combat situation. And that made a bond between us and allowed me to document their lives in this very full way."

The men of Restrepo were far from the archetypal soldiers of old war movies. Kevin Rice, the farm boy from Wisconsin, had a tattoo of dancing bears on his left arm and the names of fellow soldiers who had been killed in battle in Zabul on the other. As Junger wrote of Rice, "He keeps an expression of slight bemusement on his face except during firefights, when he simply looks annoyed. Rice is known for his weird calm under fire. He's also known for fighting with the kind of slow, vengeful precision that most men can barely maintain on the pool table. I ask what he thinks about an all-out attack on Restrepo, and he just chuckles. 'I'm kind of looking forward to it,' he says. 'It would be very entertaining. It would be up close and personal.'" Pvt. Pemble-Belkin, twenty-two, had not been allowed to eat any sugar until he was ten, nor play violent video games or watch violent movies, and his parents had taken away his turtle-shaped water gun because it resembled a weapon. On his left forearm Pemble-Belkin had a tattoo of the *Endurance,* Sir Ernest Shackleton's ship, which became entrapped by sea ice in Antarctica in 1915. "It's the greatest adventure story ever," he told Junger, who watched as he cut a pocket from his shirt and sewed it over a rip in the crotch of his pants while he was still wearing them.

"The men spend their days clambering around shale hillsides dotted with holly trees, and most of their uniforms are in shreds," Junger noted. "Pemble-Belkin uses his free time back at the KOP painting and playing guitar, and says that his father was a labor organizer who supports the troops absolutely, but has protested every war the United States has ever been in. His mother sends him letters written on paper she makes by hand."

Contrary to the prevailing image of American soldiers, the men assembled each morning with their pants untucked from their boots and their faces streaked with dirt and stubble, Junger observed. "They wear flea collars around their waists and combat knives in the webbing of their body armor. Some have holes in their boots. Several have furrows in their uniforms from rounds that barely missed. They carry family photographs behind the bulletproof steel plates on their chests, and a few carry photographs of women in their helmets, or letters. Some have never had a girlfriend. Every single man seems to have a tattoo." Aron Hijar, a short, brawny young man, told Junger he enlisted because he felt that if people like him didn't sign up everyone his age would be subject to a draft. When he told his family about his decision he was urged not to go, though no one could say why. At the time, Hijar was a fitness trainer in California, bored with his life. His grandfather had fought in World War II, so he went to the army recruiting office and enlisted. He decided to keep a journal while at Restrepo so others could understand what it was like. "When my children, if I have any, decide to go into the military, I'll say, 'You can do whatever you want, but you got to read this first,'" he said. "It has everything, the good times, the bad times, everything that ever meant anything to me."

Specialist Brian Underwood was a bodybuilder and probably the strongest man in the platoon other than Vandenberge, who was six-five and weighed 250 pounds. While Junger interviewed Underwood, he dropped to the ground and began doing push-ups in full body armor. Vandenberge, who had turned down a basketball scholarship to join the army, was more reticent and was reportedly something of a computer genius back home. Perhaps the most telling comment any of the soldiers gave Hetherington and Junger came from Specialist Kyle Steiner, who said, of getting shot at, "You can't get a better high. It's like crack, you know. Once you been shot at, you really can't come down. You can't top that." When Junger asked how he would manage life in the civilized world after having experienced that, Steiner said he had no idea.

During his stints at Restrepo, Junger said only one soldier told him he joined the army because of September 11. The rest were there because they were curious or bored, because their fathers or grandfathers had been in the army, or because the courts had given them the choice of combat or jail. Frightening as combat was, the soldiers in many ways thrived on it, as soldiers do in every war. The quiet times were alternately unnerving and boring; they sat for hours doing nothing, with little to occupy them other than each other, their iPods, and magazines about surfing, cars, or naked women. They spent time sunbathing, playing guitar, lifting weights, driving golf balls into the abyss, tussling and roughing each other up—especially the "cherry bitches," the new arrivals. They mock-molested each other, which occasionally got out of hand. But they also had fun in ways that might have been unacceptable back home. In *Restrepo,* one of the soldiers says of another, "He's a beautiful man, I'd fuck him back in the States," and everyone bursts out laughing. As Junger later wrote, "Ultimately, it made me think that if you deprive men of the company of women for too long, and then turn off the steady adrenaline drip of heavy combat, it may not turn sexual, but it's certainly going to turn weird." The result was a mashup of pantomimed rape, struggles for dominance, and what Junger described as "grotesque, smoochy come-ons that could only make sense in a place where every other form of amusement had long since been used up." At one point the soldiers held a dance party inside a hooch, bumping and grinding to a song where a female vocalist moans about feeling another person's body close to hers.

The odd interaction had a lot to do with trying to get outside the war for a moment, using whatever means available, Hetherington said. The soldiers had a lot of pent-up energy, they had music, they had each other. "And, you know, many of these young men were going through some of the most traumatic experiences of their life. They were dealing with big existential questions, the most that anybody'd deal with as we get older." The idea of killing or being killed, or having a friend die in their arms, affected them deeply, he said.

On one incredibly hot day, with flies buzzing all around, when there hadn't been any combat to speak of for a week or two, everyone was "bored out of their minds," remembered Junger. "There was a lieutenant [who] walked by—you know, shirtless, sweating in the middle of the day, muttering, 'Oh please, someone attack us today.' I mean, that's how boring it was out there. They were actually praying to be attacked, right? And I'm sort of lying there in this . . . heat daze, and everyone's asleep, except the guys on guard duty. Everyone's asleep. And I see Tim scuttling around with his camera and he's photographing the soldiers who are asleep, in their bunks. . . . It looks like the outpost has been overwhelmed by some kind of poison gas attack and everybody's dead."

Meanwhile, he said, "Tim's scuttling around, and he's photographing them, and I'm like, 'Tim, man, what are you doing?' I mean, this is the ultimate situation where nothing's going on, and there's nothing to report on, and you can just switch your brain off because there's no work to do as a journalist, and until someone starts shooting at us, just turn yourself off."

Hetherington, he recalled, said, "Don't you get it? You never get to see soldiers like this." Junger explained, "You always see them in their gear with their weapons and they're indomitable, and whatever. Look at them now. They're—they're like little boys. They're asleep. They're totally vulnerable. And he said, 'This is how their mothers see them.' This is the other side of them, and this what their mothers see, and this is what the American public never gets to see because America, any nation, is self-selecting in the images it presents, and we want to see our soldiers as strong, and they *are* strong. We don't want to know that they're also these vulnerable boys, and we just don't want to know that, because then it would be too painful, as a nation, to send them off to war where they're going to get killed." The photos Hetherington took would later become part of an exhibition titled *Sleeping Soldiers,* which mixed still photos of the men in their bunks with battlefield footage evoking the nightmares within.

Through *Restrepo, Infidel, War,* and *Sleeping Soldiers*—no one could accuse them of not fully mining the terrain—Hetherington and Junger wanted to show a side of soldiers that noncombatants could relate to, as well as to foster a sense of responsibility for helping reintegrate them into American life afterward. Most of all, they wanted to find out what mattered most, and every man at Restrepo knew the answer. As Junger wrote in *War,* "The willingness to die for another person is a form of love that even religions fail to inspire, and the experience of it changes a person profoundly."

Along the way, Restrepo revealed a truth about war that, on the surface, was disturbing: that it could be fun. As Hetherington, Bercault, and Buchbinder had experienced firsthand during that gleeful photo frenzy on their way to a massacre site, the men of Restrepo could endure only so much excitement, terror, and sadness before their psyches changed the channel. And despite his serious approach to his craft and his tendency to intellectualize, Hetherington and Junger were happy to join in the fun. Hetherington, in particular, was known for cracking jokes in the middle of firefights, and more than once he had run up a hill and pretended to plant a small British flag, claiming it for the British empire. "He was a complete freak in some ways," Junger said of Hetherington, with a laugh, "and he thought being British was kind of inherently funny. And he had no problem rolling with that and entertaining people with that, and in a place like Restrepo entertainment was, you know, in some ways as precious as ammo or food. It was something that, psychologically, people desperately needed, and he came in and provided that. He was amazing."

The soldiers responded in kind, occasionally harassing him, and each other, to wild laughter. They took relief where they could find it, such as when they shot and butchered a local farmer's cow—against regulations, with no apparent empathy for the poor, elderly man who owned it, and consumed it during an impromptu barbeque. "The cow incident," as it came to be known, led to a minor controversy after a group of village elders arrived at the outpost demanding payment. The soldiers told them the cow had gotten caught in the concertina wire surrounding the outpost and that they'd shot it to put it out of its misery. The elders wanted $400 or $500 but in the end were reimbursed with the cow's estimated weight in rice, beans, and sugar. The cow incident was a reminder that although the men were focused on their own small world, which the cow had wandered into, their actions were certainly not contained. They were firing weapons into a valley where people lived, some of whom were innocent, and others not so much. Sometimes the air strikes they called in tragically killed people who weren't trying to kill them. On more than one occasion, the gunship attacks hit the wrong target, as had happened at Yaka China. Remorse was not a useful emotion in a time of war, but it was inevitable in such situations. Kearney recognized it, too, when he counseled the soldiers about the deaths of nine men in a sister company, Chosen Company. His advice: feel bad about it, and move on. Change the channel.

The idea of looking beyond the obvious to see what was really going on had characterized all of Hetherington's work, but Restrepo opened a new window into the subject that had long fascinated him: how young men are attracted to and exploited by war. As Junger noted, it was a story that was "universal and timeless. His search for images that tell the soldiers' true stories is why the guys in the platoon loved him just as the rebels and the blinded children did. He wanted to know what they know."

Being British meant that Hetherington was slightly removed from the American soldiers, which actually helped him get closer to the story, as he later told *Cineaste* magazine. "I was a bit of an anomaly for them . . . They'd repeat and laugh at things I'd say. If anything, it helped break the ice. I also don't know all the American societal codes. If you're born into the codes, you don't recognize them, but you're much more governed by them. As an outsider to America, I've known East Coast and West Coast America, but I hadn't really known Middle America. Getting to know the soldiers was my first really coherent experience with Middle America, and that was fantastic. In reporting, you have to be able to know something well enough to be able to understand it, but you also need to be enough of an outsider to have fresh eyes."

Brendan O'Byrne said that, when Hetherington showed up at Restrepo, he saw him as most people did: "A good-looking British guy was here and I didn't really understand why he was there." But what struck O'Byrne as he watched Hetherington work was his determination, which impressed him because it was a quality the soldiers possessed too. "He never stopped filming, he never stopped trying to get the right shot, no matter how bad it got," O'Byrne said. "I can compare him to the Tasmanian Devil, you'd just see a whirlwind of Tim passing by . . . All you hear is the snapping of shutters and he was gone, you know? Filming the next person, and that was Tim. That was the blur of Tim."

Among the photographs Hetherington shot at Restrepo was one that won him a World Press Award. Considering how hard he tried to find and record atypical moments, the photo—dark and slightly blurred—was surprisingly conventional; aside from a few small details it could easily have been taken in Vietnam. An exhausted soldier slumps with his hand to his head after a firefight. At the time, Hetherington was exhausted too—everyone had been up since around 4 a.m., as they were on most days, and there had been two intense fights that day, which brought the inevitable floods of adrenaline and, afterward, the withdrawal. Hetherington said during an NPR interview that even when he was hopelessly tired he remained focused on photographing the soldiers, whether during battles or in the relative quiet of the outpost, because if he stopped for one moment he wouldn't know what to do with himself. Particularly in the heat of battle, he said, "the fear would paralyze me, I think. And it's very interesting when you watch the soldiers as well, how they operate in this situation. They're used to, in combat, really getting on with their jobs and being extremely focused. I mean, focused to a point that sometimes, you know, you think that the level of danger for them or the risks are almost like a—quite an abstract idea. You know, that the actual bullets become abstract."

Though he wasn't protecting anyone, it was much the same for him, he said. He had to remain focused on what he needed to do, whether that meant putting himself at risk to photograph others who were doing so or recognizing, in his own exhausted state, the exhaustion of a solder, and recording that. Fear, he said, never went away, but like exhaustion it could be suppressed until later. He recalled one incident at Restrepo when a soldier was firing a grenade launcher from his knees, and Hetherington was filming about a foot away. The soldier later asked him if he'd noticed the tracer bullets passing between their heads. Hetherington hadn't, but once he heard about it he was terrified. He later went back to the spot to see where the nearby trees had been shattered by the bullets he had never seen.

Such delayed reactions were useful during combat but had to be dealt with afterward, which wasn't always easy for Hetherington. Back in New York City, his friends and colleagues noticed that he was having a difficult time assimilating his experiences in Afghanistan. Olivier Bercault, who had worked so closely with him in Darfur, had lunch with him in New York City after his release from the hospital at Bagram and later said he could tell that Hetherington was deeply affected by his experience during Rock Avalanche. "He definitely was not himself," Bercault said. "He was extremely nervous, agitated, kept talking and talking, his eyes staring at nothing. After having lunch he had it in mind to buy a new bag, and started to walk so fast with his crutches on Eighth Avenue that I almost had to run to keep up with him. At some point I put him in a cab and sent him home to rest . . . I had the strong impression that day that death had grazed him."

Junger recalled being "profoundly scared" twice during his time at Restrepo. The first was during a firefight at the outpost, "and bullets were hitting everywhere and I just froze, and Tim jumped across this gap—I could see the bullets hitting the ground, and I couldn't make that ten feet, and Tim did it and threw our stuff back—the camera, my vest. He also threw ammo to soldiers. As soon as I had my camera on I was fine." The second time was when he and Hetherington were descending a hillside with a squad of scouts and the snapping of bullets suddenly filled the air. "Tim and I threw ourselves to the ground, but the enemy gunner was firing down on us—*plunging fire*—and it was extremely hard to take cover from," he said. "I remember leaves getting clipped by bullets and floating down on Tim. I remember looking back and seeing bullets raise evil little puffs in the dirt around my feet. We lay there until the American mortar tubes got going, and then we jumped up and ran. I noticed a soldier who had watched all this from the safety of a bunker laughing hysterically. There's almost nothing you can't learn to laugh at, I guess."

Oddly, Junger wasn't frightened during one of the most dangerous scenes in *Restrepo*. At the time, Hetherington was recuperating from his broken leg and Junger was riding with soldiers in a Humvee that got hit by an improvised explosive device in the road. The explosion went off under the Humvee's engine block, which prevented those inside from being killed. Junger was in the backseat filming at the moment of the explosion, and his footage became the opening sequence for the film. He remembered feeling no fear, which made him wonder if he was injured and in shock. "I patted my way down to my feet to see if both of my legs are okay," he said. He found that he wasn't injured, he was just numb. But, he said, "I had horrific nightmares that night. I was really depressed afterward, saddened and bummed out." After the explosion, the Humvee's cabin had filled with smoke and, once a soldier gave the order, everyone jumped out the doors and ran. Though he was initially stoic, Junger found himself increasingly unnerved by the experience, and he wanted to take a couple of weeks off afterward, so it was Hetherington's turn to take up the slack and he returned to Restrepo on his own.

O'Byrne said he had often wondered what attracted guys like Junger and Hetherington to war. "Same thing with a lot of my buddies [who] were drawn to this," he said. What O'Byrne couldn't quite fathom was that, as he put it, "nowhere in my life did I feel more sure of what my purpose was. I knew I was to lead men in combat. I knew that I was to . . . For example, I was supposed to do this patrol and lead the men to this and I knew exactly what my job was that day. I think Tim found a lot of purpose in what he was doing. I think that it fulfilled him in a lot of ways to tell that story because he was looking for the answers also."

Hetherington said he saw many of the same patterns of behavior among both Liberian rebels and American soldiers, despite the outward differences. He also saw the same patterns of behavior in himself. They were all looking for a sense of purpose, which the extremes of war gave them, and which created a bond between those who shared it. The group bond was "incredibly strong," he told *DAV* [Disabled American Veterans] *Magazine*. "As one soldier said, 'There are guys in the platoon that outright hate each other, but they would all die for each other.' So he's talking about a brotherhood rather than a friendship that is particularly profound, and which adds a lot of significance and meaning to their lives. It's no wonder they come home and actually miss being 'out there,' a fact that most civilians can't get their heads around."

Hetherington and Junger also felt it. Benjamin Spatz, the photographer who came to know Hetherington in Liberia, said he had an experience similar to Bercault's while talking with Hetherington about Rock Avalanche. Rougle's death, he said, "was much more intense than anyone else in the past . . . He often used the words, 'That almost broke me.'" Spatz recalled having dinner with Hetherington after one of his tours in Afghanistan, "and he was just so antsy. He could hardly sit still. He was fidgeting constantly, you know, with almost just no pause. He could hardly breathe. He was just constantly either asking questions about what I was doing, I think as a way to maybe separate himself from what he was thinking about, or he was just nonstop opening himself up to what he was working on and how he thought about it. It was a really intense experience for him."

As Junger explained, Larry Rougle was killed "about eighty yards away from where Tim was, and at one point, he had this choice. Go to where Rougle died or follow Vandenberge and Rice down the hill, wounded, because they're going to the medevac, and he went towards Larry, and he shot incredibly painful video of the soldier, of Larry's dead body, and the soldiers braced for another attack, crying, trying to process having lost their squad leader, just convulsed with grief, and Tim came back from that, and he said to me, he said, 'You know, I'm so—' He's like, 'I'm sorry. You know, I should have followed Rice and Vandenberge. They were the guys in our platoon, they were wounded. I should have followed them, but I got sucked into the death.' He said we all did. And we were all up there with Larry. And he said it made him feel bad that he had shot video of a dead soldier, and the reaction of his brothers. That's a private moment. And I think he had a sense that there was a somewhat vulture-like aspect to journalism. It's unavoidable. God forbid these stories not get covered. There's no good alternative to journalism, but it does leave you feeling slightly impure."

In defense of journalistic voyeurism, Hetherington said on NPR that the soldiers allowed him to get close because they wanted their stories told; "they said listen, just let people at home know what this is really like. What we're going through. That was the only thing that they really asked me to do." Aside from the incident with Raeon and Rougle's body, "they never controlled what I could or couldn't photograph," he said. "They just asked me that. And therefore I had a responsibility to live as closely as possible to them and what happened to them."

"War is very confusing to soldiers," Junger said, "and the main thing that's confusing about it is that it's so terrible when it's happening, and then you miss it so terribly when it's over." Regardless of your age, if a person finds himself in a group like that, "it's incredibly reassuring, and everything else feels—everything else back home in society feels inadequate and like a pale version of reality, and so you miss it. You want to go back, not to the killing, but to the connection.

"The lure of a place like Restrepo inhabits a much more profound place in young men than, 'Oh, I need some adrenaline,'" he said. "Tim called it the Man Eden. It was, for the young male psyche, this just sort of easy place to be, like you don't have to wash. There's no e-mail. There's no fights with your girlfriend. There's no hassles." Starting out, the soldiers of Restrepo were laden with gear—with body armor and heavily loaded packs. Later, they're engaged in firefights in their boxer shorts and flip-flops, along with their bulletproof vests and helmets.

Some of the footage Hetherington shot at Restrepo made its way into *Diary*. Junger recalled that when Hetherington first told him about the short film he was then working on, he described it as a trip through his brain. He wanted to explore the relationship between what was going on inside his mind and what he observed during war. When Junger saw the finished version of *Diary*, he felt Hetherington was trying to process the transitions that he was compelled to make, "that we all have to go through, between the experience of war and the experience of normalcy and peace back home. You know, of course the danger is that war becomes normalcy, and back home actually becomes the battleground you have to fight on, psychologically, as a journalist or as a soldier. That's the danger of doing this work, and Tim, I think, struggled very hard with that problem."

Hetherington acknowledged that his emotions were sometimes intense. As Junger put it, "Whatever it was he was experiencing, he went quite far with it, until he got a grip on it and then he would lock it away. Sometimes he would start crying. He just wasn't working in any interior way on the things that made him feel bad and they would kind of ambush him." *Diary*, Junger said, was Hetherington's effort to open the compartments. But, he asked, "How do you turn pain into art? If you can run the engine on pain, it's a very seductive idea . . . but I don't know if anyone's ever written a really cathartic novel and felt better later. I don't know how many times I told Tim, in the wake of an emotional storm, when he was being ambushed in the middle of nowhere, 'You need to talk to a shrink.' He was on the go constantly, it got in the way of romantic relationships, even our friendship." Hetherington, he said, "never did see a shrink. I have a feeling he thought he would work that out by making a film about it, which was what *Diary* was."

Sometimes Hetherington's determination to understand and explain the nuances of war—which was, after all, an exercise in sheer brutality—got the best of him, Junger said. After Hetherington won the World Press Award, Junger was playing chess alone while Hetherington drafted his acceptance speech, and "I'd look up once in a while, and you can feel this machine at work while he's crunching this topic, just demolishing it, right? I just remember thinking, Oh boy. This is going to be something. And so he finally finishes, and he reads it to me, and it is so complex, it's so analytical, it's so theoretical, it's so filled with words that I literally had no idea what he was talking about. I knew it was brilliant. It had to be brilliant, but I couldn't—I couldn't even understand it.

"And I said, 'Tim, man, that's probably great, but what you really want to do is talk about how this all makes you feel. How does it feel to win this award, but more importantly how does it feel to be out here? We're at Camp Blessing. We're about to go into the Korengal. We're spending a year off and on with these guys. What does that do to you? How is that affecting you?' And he was like, 'Okay, all right. I think I got it. I'm going to go back to work. I'm going to redo it.'

"So I went back to my chess game. He went back to his laptop. A couple of hours later, 'Hey, Sebastian. I—I think I—I think I got it.' 'Ah, great, man. Read it to me.' So he started reading. And he got about three sentences in and he went silent, and I looked up, and his shoulders were shaking, and he was just sobbing, and he—what he had gone into in his essay was the pain of all this, and how much it moved him and affected him to be accepted into a group that was struggling so hard to deal with physical survival and emotional survival, and both were going on out there, and Tim and I were brought into that world, and we helped, and we were a part of it, and that may have been . . . You know, Tim wasn't married and he didn't have kids, and I think that experience of being brought into that platoon in those circumstances may well have been emotionally the most profound experience of his life."

"As anyone who has experienced it will know, war is many contradictory things," Hetherington wrote, in typically measured language, in *Infidel*. "There is brutality and heroism, comedy and tragedy, friendship, hate, love and boredom. War is absurd yet fundamental, despicable yet beguiling, unfair yet with its own strange logic. Rarely are people 'back home' exposed to these contradictions—society tends only to highlight those qualities it needs, to construct its own particular narrative. Rather than attempt to describe the war in Afghanistan, I have sought to convey some of these contradictions."

8

HOLLYWOOD

The red carpet at the Academy Awards ceremony was about as far as Hetherington could imagine being from that day in Monrovia when he'd sat with James Brabazon, surrounded by corpses, drinking warm beer, or the night he'd hobbled on his broken ankle after Rock Avalanche. Yet there he was, looking debonair in his black tuxedo, with his lovely girlfriend Idil Ibrahim beside him. Junger was also there, with his wife, Daniela Petrova, and all of them looked stunning as they strolled past the flashing cameras.

Hetherington told a correspondent for *The Hollywood Reporter* that the Oscars, with its crush of stars and voracious media coverage, scared him more than Charles Taylor had. He was joking but the point was clear: this was not his natural habitat.

The success of Hetherington and Junger's documentary film *Restrepo*, which had won the Grand Jury Prize at the Sundance Film Festival a year before, was a huge affirmation for Hetherington. *Restrepo* was an unvarnished look at a harsh reality, not normally a recipe for popular success. Yet the reviews had been uniformly positive, audiences had approved, and *Restrepo* was now up for an Academy

Award for the best documentary film of 2010. "It's incredibly strange," Hetherington told a National Public Radio reporter in an interview he gave while in Hollywood for the event. "Our foremost thought when we started this project wasn't winning an Academy Award, it was not getting killed making this movie. And we succeeded in doing that, barely, I think. But it's absolutely thrilling to be with other such great filmmakers. And it's a really once-in-a-lifetime experience."

Among the many photos of their time in Hollywood is one that shows Hetherington posing, with a slightly bemused look, beside the statue of an oversized, gilded Oscar—a requisite photo op that was as predictable and contrived as *Restrepo* was original and unwaveringly authentic. Here I am in Hollywood, the photo proclaims. Junger observed that their being there, in the pantheon of superficiality, made Hetherington a little uncomfortable, that he had seemed more at ease in the Korengal Valley, where he had been, for the most part, very relaxed: "I had the sense that he felt like he was the most him out there . . . Here he was faking it."

War zones made a kind of emotional sense to Hetherington, despite the recurring trauma, which had, in a bit of irony, landed them at the Oscars. Being there, Junger said, "was very intoxicating to Tim and kind of alarming. You can't go to the Oscars and not be alarmed." The Oscar nomination, Junger said, "was a huge affirmation but it was from a world we didn't feel much in common with. I think it would be a little like having a cheerleader like you in high school—it's tremendously flattering but you didn't have much in common with this person. Hollywood is this very plush, gorgeous, and flaky world. We both decided it would mostly be just fun, and it was fun. It was pretty clear that in the food chain we were basically plankton . . . documentaries are down there with animation and sound design. All the cameras and attention are focused on the stars. It's really about the stars. But even at that level of attention . . . it was thrilling, and our movie was about something of urgent importance to America, even in Hollywood."

Despite Junger's disclaimer about the Hollywood hierarchy, Hetherington attracted his share of attention. He was that tall, handsome Brit, an attractive subject for the photographers and TV crews. It didn't hurt that he and Junger were also accompanied by Aron Hijar and Misha Pemble-Belkin. "I don't know if soldiers had ever walked the red carpet, and people loved it," Junger said. In his interviews, Hetherington appeared charming and relaxed, but the conversation he was having with Junger behind the scenes was typically about the ongoing Arab Spring, the series of uprisings that was turning the Arab world upside down. Both of them felt the Academy Awards represented a hiatus from their work, not the culmination of it. "Did you ever think about being here when making *Restrepo*?" one interviewer asked. "No," was the answer.

Hetherington and Junger looked more at home posing with the two Second Platoon soldiers who accompanied them, both fresh from Afghanistan. Hijar wore a tuxedo, but Pemble-Belkin wore his dress uniform. The soldiers' presence, Hetherington said, made the event feel more authentic. He and Junger had authenticated the soldiers' experiences and now the soldiers were authenticating theirs.

Hijar had been discharged from the army the day before the main Oscar event, Pemble-Belkin was about to deploy to Afghanistan for another year, "and we're walking the red carpet, and they're in their dress blues, very handsome and, you know, how many soldiers in uniform have walked the red carpet? Maybe none," Junger said. "And some famous person comes up to Pemble, recognizes him from *Restrepo*, and says, 'Hey man, I saw *Restrepo*, just incredible. I love your work.' And Pemble came up to me after that, and he was like, 'Love my work? What's he mean? Does he realize *Restrepo* is a documentary?'

"We made a movie that's real, that, because we're in Hollywood, people think isn't real," Junger said. "And then you have people out there in America who are watching Hollywood movies thinking they're real. That stuff drove [Tim] crazy. I mean, he loved it. He loved it."

Beyond the obvious risks of filming the action, making *Restrepo* had not been easy. The glamorous life of a journalist covering war often means paying your own way, and despite their magazine and TV assignments Hetherington's and Junger's expenses had quickly added up, even before they started editing the film—a long, arduous process during which they could work on nothing else. In addition to their travel expenses, there was equipment to buy for their newly created entity Outpost Films. "After that, we put all our spare cash into the edit, several hundred thousand dollars over the course of the next year," Junger said. He and Hetherington hired an editor, Michael Levine, and his assistant, Maya Mumma, to assemble a "one-hour sizzle reel—the best stuff," he said. "We showed that to Nat Geo [the National Geographic channel]; they weren't interested. We went to HBO, A&E—no one was interested. Five thousand dollars a week was coming out of our pockets." But they continued to work and by October 2009 had put together a rough cut of the film, which National Geographic bought. They then submitted it to the Sundance Film Festival and won the Grand Jury Prize for documentaries. Junger's book *War* came out a month after the film aired on TV, and a few months after that *Restrepo* was released in theaters. Then it was nominated for the Academy Award.

Before going to the Academy Awards, Petrova said she had to force Junger to buy new black shoes, because his old ones looked terrible. Hetherington, on the other hand, went on a shopping spree and bought a new black tux and a suit to wear to parties. If he looked awkward posing in front of the giant Oscar, and felt the artificial world of Hollywood wasn't what it was all about, he knew that being nominated for an Academy Award was important. "Most of all," he said, "it feels like the film is really connecting with people."

The Hollywood Reporter observed that at the nominees' luncheon Hetherington was seated across from the actor James Franco, and that the two appeared to have bonded. "I'm new to all this, the dynamic of Oscars," Hetherington told the reporter. "So I just mentioned I knew his work and we sparked on the conversation." Like Franco, the article noted, "Hetherington disregarded art boundaries: His Afghanistan work spawned the film, the brilliant art book *Infidel* and an art installation, *Sleeping Soldiers*." Lapsing into his favored intellectual mode, Hetherington told *The Hollywood Reporter,* "News and entertainment are the two primary ways we accrue images into our visual library. Things are getting more and more open, and boundaries are breaking down between media. You're image makers, you kind of mine your craft in different kind of ways." In other words, they did something new here and it paid off.

During the pre-voting buzz, *Restrepo* was often compared with the highly successful movie *The Hurt Locker,* a wholly unrealistic—yet *seemingly* realistic—fantasy about an American bomb squad in Iraq. In an interview with Anne Thompson, of Indiewire, Hetherington said he felt *Restrepo* better captured the truth of war. "There's only been two IED scenes from inside a Humvee, where you've been blown up," as Junger and the soldiers' vehicle had been, he said. "And I've never known of a situation where somebody's filmed people crying over their friends, the body of their dead friends. So I think there's a lot of stuff in the film that is completely unique to documentary."

Junger was a veteran of many interviews, owing to the success of his books, particularly *The Perfect Storm,* which was made into a blockbuster movie, and to his war reporting. Hetherington had been around the block a few times, too, though he received far more attention than he was accustomed to at the Academy Awards. He rose to the occasion, Junger said. "He'd take someone who—an interviewer— who should kind of make you nervous in some way, because you don't know how they'll react, and he'll just go in and be very, very familiar and joking, and somehow it works, and everyone loved him. Literally, every single person who met Tim loved him. And I watched it with taxi drivers and waitresses and old guys on the street and soldiers and officers [and], you know, nice old ladies out in LA at the Oscars. Whatever. Everybody. And it was almost like he understood that the thing that he did well, the thing that he had as a person on this planet, was that he could engage any kind of person and get them to open up, and he knew it, and he went out of his way to do it, and that was one of the things that gave him emotional access as a journalist, as a photographer to his subjects."

It also made him an irresistibly attractive subject at the Oscars. As Junger described it, "Here we are in this superglamorous, beautiful environment, all these beautiful women, all these beautiful cars, all this beautiful food. Everything is gorgeous. And so weird, and so unreal. And Tim, he was able to roll with it. He just—in some ways, he treated it like Restrepo, like, 'Wow, this is a trip, you know? Let's experience this for a while.'"

Hetherington and Junger had cared deeply how the soldiers would react to the film; they were the audience that mattered most. Regardless of how the film fared commercially, and even before its Oscar nomination, Restrepo had accomplished a remarkable feat, Hetherington told a Cineaste reporter. After the film was released in theaters he described how one of the soldiers, Santana Rueda, reacted. "Rudy was really speechless because he said, 'You won't believe it, but I'm on the street, and I'm looking at the cinema, and in big letters outside the cinema is the name of my dead friend. I never would have believed I would be standing here looking at his name written so large.'" Cinema, Hetherington said, "has this kind of effect on people and yourself that you can't calculate at the time. It has its own life force after you've finished it."

Brendan O'Byrne said the film validated his personal story, that it was no longer just a story he told; it was now "the truth," because it had been documented on film. Its Oscar nomination was a further affirmation. Pemble-Belkin, who attended promotional screenings with Hetherington and Junger, later told the military newspaper *Stars & Stripes* that sharing his experiences with audiences was cathartic. As the newspaper noted, "Memories of friends claimed by the Korengal had trailed him home, triggering sporadic 'night terrors' that jarred him awake. On other occasions, his wife, Amanda DeVos, found him sleeping under a makeshift fighting position he built from furniture and blankets in the middle of the night." Pemble-Belkin added, "Seeing the movie and talking about it actually helped me. It kind of gave me a chance to work through things."

Though Pemble-Belkin was rarely recognized on the street as a result of his appearance in *Restrepo,* it raised his visibility within the military. The Academy Awards was a different animal. At *Vanity Fair*'s Oscar afterparty, *Stars & Stripes* noted, "the likes of Justin Timberlake, Josh Brolin and Kevin Spacey sought out Pemble-Belkin to discuss the film. Tom Hanks knifed through a crowd to reach him. 'I know who you are,' Hanks said. 'I just want to say thank you.' The two talked for several minutes when the actor remarked on the soldier's composure. 'You don't seem nervous at all,' Hanks said. 'Why would I be?' Pemble-Belkin replied. 'You're just a person like me. I'm about to deploy to Afghanistan two months from now. I'm a little more nervous about that.'" In *Restrepo,* Pemble-Belkin says that when he hears the name "Restrepo," he doesn't think of the outpost; "I still think of the person."

In Hetherington's book *Infidel,* Kyle Steiner says, "One of the things that makes me happiest is knowing that people who make millions of dollars standing in front of a camera, smiling and acting— they're pretending to do what I do. I don't go out and pretend to be an actor. I don't go out and pretend to do their job, but they pretend to do mine. They pretend to be able to react the way I do in a fire-fight. They pretend to know how to do medical training the way I know it and my boys in Second Platoon know it. They make $10 million pretending to be me. That feels pretty good. I make $30,000 for being me. And they make 10 million to pretend to be me. Shit's fucked up!"

Before the main event at the Oscars, while Petrova and Ibrahim were in their rooms getting dressed, making sure their makeup was right and fussing over their hair, Junger and Hetherington lounged by the hotel pool, savoring the moment. To the main event at the Kodak Theater, Petrova wore a shimmering midnight blue dress with a plung-ing neckline; Ibrahim wore a green, form-fitting crepe gown. Both looked beautiful. In the limo, Hetherington was still getting dressed. Ibrahim held a small mirror for him as he tied his bow tie, and Petrova noticed that, in contrast to his black tuxedo, he wore pink socks. She laughed and looked at Ibrahim, who shrugged and said it wasn't her idea. Hetherington laughed, too, but offered no explanation.

It was undeniably exciting to be seated among the glitterati at the Kodak Theater, though they had been warned that *Restrepo* was not favored for the award. "The Oscars is very political and *Inside Job* was well positioned to win," Junger said, "and Sony Pictures, I think, car-ried it, financially. They put a huge amount of money into promot-ing it. We were pretty much prepared not to win." Oprah Winfrey announced the winner of best documentary: *Inside Job*, about the financial crisis. The *Restrepo* group gave polite response, though it felt a little weird to be applauding the announcement that they had lost. "You don't know where the cameras are, you don't want to look bitter," Junger said. In fact, they were very disappointed. "It's kind of a weird empty feeling, but all the glamour and pomp and dazzling beauty of all this gets you to care about something you don't really care about,"

Junger said. "It gets you to kind of invest in it, so you're way more disappointed than you would have been or should have been. You do care, and I was disappointed, and you realize pretty quickly it's ridiculous."

They had a good time at the afterparty, the soldiers in particular. "They're young and surrounded by the media gods of their generation," Junger said. "They couldn't believe who they were talking to . . . They were kind of in awe. The place was crawling with celebrities, people they'd only seen on TV. I don't know these people's names but they did. No one took it very seriously and that allowed us to have a good time. Tim went up to Ben Affleck and started talking to him and enlisting him in some project. They traded e-mails." The next day, Petrova said, Hetherington was back beside the pool, networking with people on his two cell phones.

Once they got back to New York, Hetherington e-mailed Junger to say, "While we didn't get to take home the little gold man, going down the red carpet with those soldiers from the film was one of the highlights of my life so far and a real finale to an incredible journey. Although this particular journey may be over, the film lives on." By then, Hetherington was making plans to travel to Libya, where the Arab Spring had spawned yet another uprising, aimed at taking down the country's longtime despot Muammar Gaddafi.

He and Junger had discussed traveling to Tunisia, Egypt, Libya, and Bahrain, to look at the backstory of the uprisings, but "I'd already made a decision to not cover outright combat," Junger said. He had told Hetherington he was more interested in the politics of the uprising, that "the fighting is a symptom of a more important process, not the process itself. It's dangerous and I just want to move to the next level as a journalist. All that combat in *Restrepo*—I remember saying to Daniela, 'I basically want to do this and then I'll stop doing this.' To be totally honest I was saying those things but I wasn't sure myself." Combat, he said, is actually easier to cover than in-depth war reporting.

"It took Tim a while to get to that," Junger said. "I was saying I'm not going to do an assignment that involves getting shot at, and he was a little resistant to that. He flew into Cairo on his way to Libya, started establishing contacts, then I couldn't go, and he was already in Benghazi." *Vanity Fair* editors had declined to assign Hetherington a story, not because it was too dangerous but because there was no writer attached. Due to a combination of personal issues Junger was unable to go, so after his first foray into Libya on assignment for Human Rights Watch, Hetherington stayed back in New York City for only three days before returning to Benghazi on his own. As had happened in Liberia when he was with the LURD rebels, as soon as he left he wanted to go back. He saw Libya as the logical next step in his long-running project about the relationship between young men and war. A big part of that was how young men see themselves at war—the performance, the feedback loop, how they emulate images they've seen in movies and on TV. He had observed that soldiers often styled their behavior and appearance after actors playing soldiers, and that the mass media reinforced that behavior.

For thousands of years, Junger noted, "young men have been sucked into the death, sucked into the violence, and Tim wanted to understand that, and the first stage of his understanding, I think, was trying to understand how the media informs and affects these young men and sends them into conflict, and that creates more images of young men in conflict that then get processed, digested by the next generation of young men, and it keeps feeding itself." The relationship intrigued and sometimes disturbed Hetherington, but there was no question that—despite its obvious contrivances—it was an authentic part of the equation of modern war. And to explore it, he didn't need to go to the front line, and he assured his friends he wouldn't.

After his last trip to Afghanistan, Hetherington had said that he was ready to move on from photographing war, but in the end, Junger said, "he couldn't really do it." He saw himself as an artist searching for the truth about human nature in conflict zones, and he was happy, for a moment, to play the role of a dashing journalist at the Academy Awards. His willingness to accept such contrivances informed the way he approached the war in Libya, as a raw source of artistic material.

The photo that won Hetherington the World Press Award for 2007, of the exhausted U.S. soldier in Afghanistan, appeared conventional in many respects, yet in an era of highly pixilated, sharply focused digital photography, it was oddly dark, moody, even a little blurred, which magnified its impact. The photo was, in fact, about the loss of focus—the soldier's, the photographer's, and, as Hetherington said, the nation's as a whole regarding the war in Afghanistan. In Libya, Hetherington planned to restrict himself to a more artistic approach, using equipment that was unsuitable for conventional combat photography, as he had during his first combat experience in Liberia. He would take cameras designed for careful, nuanced photography in controlled environments, along with a small video camera. He planned to take war portraits, not action shots, although, as he had done in *Diary* and in his *Sleeping Soldiers* exhibit, he wanted to have the option of mixing media later.

Sleeping Soldiers was the bridge between Hetherington's desire to create art and his fascination with the intensity of war. When it opened at the New York Photo Festival, it had been accompanied by an exhibition of related photos from Afghanistan. After passing through the exhibit hall, visitors walked into a small theater where a five-minute montage of still photos and videos was projected on three screens. Amid the sounds of soldiers talking and the thumping of helicopter rotors, war footage and still photos faded in and out on the screens. "*Sleeping Soldiers* is probably the closest I've come to expressing what it's like to be in a chaotic war situation," Hetherington said. "I like this idea that the project challenges what we think we know war is about. I'm interested to reveal parts of conflict outside of the mass media dialogue."

The nexus of *Sleeping Soldiers* had occurred during that lull in the fighting when Junger observed Hetherington creeping around, photographing the men in their bunks. "The truth was that Tim saw things very differently from the way I did," Junger wrote in his introduction to Hetherington's book *Infidel*. Hetherington, he wrote, "wasn't looking for dynamism so much as for beauty or strangeness or even ugliness. There were a lot of pin-up girls in the hooches, for example, and there were also a lot of fly-strips and a lot of ammunition. Sometimes those three things converged on a bedpost in ways that were easy to overlook until you noticed Tim staring at them intently while adjusting the aperture on his camera. I'd watch this and realize that what he was capturing on film was utterly essential to the experience out there." Hetherington, he wrote, "somehow navigated this world of boredom and killing in a way that extracted the maximum meaning out of both. 'I got an amazing picture of the latrine,' he told me one day. 'I'm just worried the guys will think it's weird that I was taking photos of it.'" If he had thought about it, Hetherington might have worried the guys would think it weird that he was taking photos of them while they slept, many of which do evoke sleeping children, but others of which are undeniably sexy. He conceded, to one interviewer, "They look almost like nudes. They're very soft and intimate pictures." As it turned out, the soldiers were cool with it. Anyone could see the photos' power and beauty and, besides, they were flattering.

The contrast beween innocence and horror that characterized *Sleeping Soldiers* was also a product of Hetherington's psyche, Junger said. "He was never psychically, physically, emotionally in the same place for more than three seconds," he said. As he and Hetherington became close friends, Junger began to suspect that all the forward momentum was being driven by some kind of torment, that "those demons kept him moving, and they kept him in pain, but because of that he was also extraordinarily aware of the pain of others, and you cannot be a good journalist, not to mention a good human being, if you're not aware of the pain of others."

Whatever inspirations Hetherington drew from, *Sleeping Soldiers* was original. As Hetherington's friend and fellow photographer Mike Kamber, who also covered the war in Afghanistan, said in an NPR interview, "I went over there to take pictures of guys doing raids and firing guns, but Tim was interested in their interior lives. He was interested in what was going on in their heads. And so he did this amazing series of portraits of these soldiers asleep in their bunks, and then he came back and created this whole multimedia piece based on their dream states, sort of tying in, you know, their interior worlds and the exterior violence that they faced every day. And I don't think there's any other photojournalist in the world that could have done a piece like that or who has done a piece like that."

In Hetherington's view, war was the catalyst and the backdrop, not the subject itself. His last book, *Infidel,* includes only a handful of battlefield scenes yet page after page of portraits, still lifes, landscapes, and those sleeping soldiers. So as he prepared to depart for Libya he assured his friends that he wouldn't take unnecessary risks, that he was going to focus on the faces of individuals during a time of war, and for that there was no reason to go to the front line.

9

LIBYA AND THE ARAB SPRING

At first glance, Katie Orlinsky might have been mistaken for a coed. Pretty, animated, twenty-eight but looking younger, she did not fit the mold of a gritty photojournalist, and in fact had never experienced combat before arriving in Libya nor, for that matter, had she studied photography in school.

A native of New York City, she had studied political science and Latin American studies at Colorado College before landing her first newspaper job in Oaxaca, Mexico, where she was drawn to photographing the city's drug wars. In Oaxaca, she proved to have good news sense, a remarkable eye for composition, and more than a little nerve. The drug wars were notoriously dangerous, particularly for journalists, who were often targets for assassination. Orlinsky threw herself into it.

Libya presented a different kind of danger. Orlinksy first arrived in Benghazi in early February 2011, near the start of the uprising, without an assignment, though she received some funding from her photographic agency. She wanted to cover the uprising, she later said, because she was fascinated by Gaddafi and by Libya in general and was under the impression that the government would quickly fall, which would provide "an incredible moment in history to witness and document as a journalist." At the time, she was disheartened over the deteriorating situation in Mexico and looking for a change.

In Benghazi, Orlinsky managed to pick up a few assignments, but when a close friend with whom she was sharing expenses decided to leave she found herself on her own at a time when the uprising was escalating into a full-scale war. She didn't have her own BGAN—a portable satellite Internet device—nor a satellite phone, flak jacket, or helmet, all of which she considered essential for working in a combat zone. She had meanwhile run out of cash and there were no ATMs or Western Union offices in operation, so she decided to accompany a friend to Cairo, and after a few days there she returned to New York City to get what she needed.

There were plenty of unprepared journalists in Benghazi at the time, young people caught up in the allure of war reporting, many unaffiliated with any news organization, whose photographic equipment consisted primarily of an iPhone and whose work largely appeared in blogs, tweets, or Facebook posts. They were looking to get their foot in the door and hoped the zeitgeist of the Arab Spring would provide a breakthrough, that they'd capture a powerful image that would jumpstart their career. Their presence was sometimes a distraction to more seasoned, professional photographers, not only because they represented a competitive shift in the dynamics of war reporting but because their inexperience posed risks for everyone. Novices were sometimes oblivious to the dangers both to themselves and to the groups in which they traveled. Some had a good grasp of what Hetherington called the basic grammar of storytelling yet knew little about what and whom to fear.

Orlinsky was more circumspect. She had learned important lessons while covering the Mexican drug wars, including the importance of finding people she could trust, being mindful of danger even as it is an inevitable consequence of the job, and preparing as best she could for whatever might arise. When she returned to Benghazi in early April she linked up with fellow American photographer Chris Hondros and, through him, Hetherington. She had known Hondros through mutual friends in the comparatively small photojournalist community in New York, and both had covered the earthquake in Haiti. She'd met Hetherington once, at a party. Seeing him in Benghazi, she thought, "Wow, this is a big story. Tim Hetherington's here." She was charmed by Hetherington's smile, graceful manners, and confident yet humble air. She was also a big fan of his work and happy to find that he had a great sense of humor.

For the first few days the three roamed Benghazi, visiting hospitals, morgues, and public gathering places and traveling by hired car to the front lines west of the city, or as near to them as they could get. A few days in, they spent a comparatively quiet day near the front in the town of Ajdabiya, where they encountered isolated shelling and a few injured rebels who had accidentally shot themselves. The Libyan fighters were as unversed in war as many of the young photographers, and it showed. On that day Orlinsky said the war was "kind of boring," so in midafternoon she, Hondros, and Hetherington decided to take a taxi back to their hotel and freshen up for dinner.

War reporting does not lend itself to dressing for dinner—journalists invariably travel light and often wear the same clothes for weeks at a time, particularly during the height of conflict. In Liberia, his first war assignment, Hetherington had packed two T-shirts, two pair of pants, and two pair of socks—one for the day and one for when he felt the need to clean up at night. That evening in Benghazi, everyone looked forward to rinsing off the sand and changing into fresh clothes. Hondros was an exception among typically grungy war photographers in that he was something of a clotheshorse, apt to show up at the front in a tweed jacket and cords, with a smart scarf

Liberia. Monrovia. September 2004. Ex-Liberians United for Reconciliation and Democracy (LURD) rebel fighter 'Black Diamond' at Sharks Bar.

Liberia. Virginia. June 2003. Journalist James Brabazon takes cover from incoming fire while filming with the rebel group Liberians United for Reconciliation and Democracy (LURD) during the height of the civil war.

Liberia. Monrovia. June 20, 2003. Photographer Tim Hetherington at the LURD front-line headquarters during the Liberian civil war. (Photo by James Brabazon)

© Tim Hetherington/Magnum Photos

Liberia. Monrovia. June 25, 2003. A member of the AA (Anti-Aircraft) brigade exchanges a brief tender word with his girlfriend during heavy fighting in Monrovia.

© Tim Hetherington/Magnum Photos

Afghanistan. Korengal Valley. 2007. A soldier from 2nd platoon rests at the end of a day of heavy fighting at the "Restrepo" outpost. This photograph was named the World Press Photo of the Year.

Afghanistan. Korengal Valley, Kunar Province. July 2008. Sergeant Elliot Alcantara sleeping, a photograph from Hetherington's "Sleeping Soldiers" series.

Afghanistan. Korengal Valley. 2007. Writer Sebastian Junger during an assignment for *Vanity Fair* magazine at the Restrepo outpost.

Afghanistan. Korengal Valley. 2007. Hetherington at the Restrepo outpost during an assignment for *Vanity Fair*.

Afghanistan. Korengal Valley, Kunar Province. June 2008. Men of 2nd Platoon have an inter-squad brawl at the Restrepo outpost. Boredom is a constant companion as men wait for the fighting to resume.

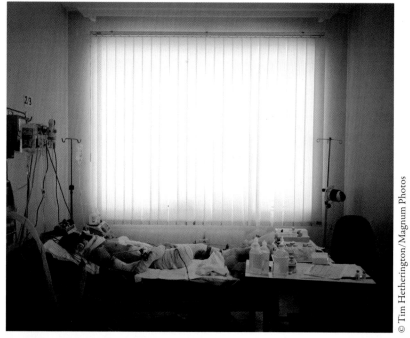

Libya. Hospital. April 18, 2011.

© Tim Hetherington/Magnum Photos

Libya. Misrata. April 20, 2011.

© Tim Hetherington/Magnum Photos

Libya. Misrata. April 20, 2011. Rebel fighters take a break from the morning battle to push through and secure the strategically important Tripoli Street.

Libya. Tim Hetherington, self-portrait. April 2011.

Libya. Misrata. April 20, 2011. A small group of photographers that were present at the scene concluded that the helmet had been shot through by rebel forces at close range. Hetherington's last photograph.

draped around his neck. By now, Orlinsky expected that from him, but she was surprised at how dashing Hetherington looked when they met for dinner. It was a common reaction among women, and, for that matter, among men. He always looked good, but when he gave it a little effort everyone noticed him entering a room.

Hetherington had been to Libya once before, having traveled to Benghazi in March on the heels of his experience at the Oscars, when he was yearning for the honest reality of a war zone. During his first trip he had been dismayed to find that many of the rebels in Benghazi, Ajdabiya, and Brega seemed more interested in posing for photographers than in actually fighting. More than most fighters, they appeared to be channeling characters they had seen on television and in war movies, using the media's tools to frame their own self-image—flashing the V for victory sign for the cameras while wearing rakish head scarves, army helmets, or baseball caps and belts adorned with carefully polished bullets. The posturing was nothing new, as photos and daguerreotypes from conflicts going back to the American Civil War attest, and Hetherington was intrigued by the idea, dating to his time with the LURD rebels in Liberia. But in Libya it was amplified, and seemed disproportionate, perhaps because the Arab Spring was one of the most visually documented conflicts in history.

The series of uprisings that constituted the Arab Spring had drawn much of its power from the technology of instant communication and documentation. Cell phones and social networking sites were used to galvanize public discontent and to frame and publicize the results. Having seen the influence of media imagery in Egypt, the Libyan rebels were mindful of its power and, like people everywhere, enjoyed seeing themselves portrayed in larger-than-life roles. Dramatic images of fighters, forwarded countless times on the Internet, were both self-affirming and useful for attracting outside support. For Hetherington there was something staged, even fake, about it, as if the war were an elaborate photo op, and the proliferation of cell phone cameras meant that the presentation of war had become congested. The line between news and propaganda was becoming unsatisfactorily blurred.

Hetherington had long fretted over the relationship between war and the media, wondering if his very presence sometimes influenced the action. The issue was largely moot—he was going to be there, but in Benghazi that first time around the dynamic seemed unacceptably skewed, and his inclination had been to disengage. It hadn't helped that he was uncomfortable with the attention focused upon him as a result of the Academy Awards. To most Libyans, he was just another Western journalist but to his peers he was Tim Hetherington, Academy Award nominee. Some of his fellow photographers were envious of his success; others were attracted to it. The Oscar nomination had elevated his professional status and, he hoped, increased his chances of gaining representation by the vaunted Magnum photo agency, but he was uncomfortable with artificial roles, including the one that was currently being assigned to him. As it turned out, being relatively famous had not helped that much when it came to getting an assignment. After working for the nonprofit Human Rights Watch the first time around, he had returned to Libya on his own.

Before his first trip, Hetherington had discussed going to Libya with the photographer Chris Anderson, with whom he shared a studio at the Brooklyn Navy Yard. As Anderson recalled, "He'd been making this film for a year, *Restrepo,* editing it, sitting in an editing booth, dealing with contract lawyers, conference meetings, whatever, and then another year promoting the film . . . walking on the red carpet of the Oscars, doing all that needed to be done, and itching to get back to work, and not sure exactly what his next thing was going to be, what his next great story was going to be." The two had discussed an offer Hetherington had for an assignment in Libya, but Anderson convinced him it wasn't the right story and Hetherington had turned it down. He eventually picked up the Human Rights Watch gig, pho-tographing the Libyan archives, to ensure the images weren't totally lost if the originals were destroyed by the war. Peter Bouckaert, who worked as emergencies director at Human Rights Watch, had noted Hetherington's discomfort with his newfound fame while working with him in Benghazi that first time around. Hetherington, Bouck-aert knew, was accustomed to working in relative anonymity and did not like traveling in a pack of photographers, shooting the same story as everyone else, particularly when it involved heroic portraits of fighters who weren't doing much actual fighting. After encountering small hordes of photojournalists in Benghazi, struggling to document the war without intruding into one another's frames, Hetherington thought of the simultaneous war in the Ivory Coast, in West Africa, which no one seemed to care much about, and considered forgoing Libya for that. In the end, he had decided to return to Brooklyn to regroup.

Back in New York, over dinner one night at his Brooklyn apart-ment with Mike Kamber, Hetherington said his first experience in Libya had made him wary of becoming a tool of war propaganda. "The media has become such a part of the war machine now that we all have to be conscious of it more than ever before," he said. He felt no compunction about being embedded with Liberian rebels or with U.S. soldiers; the difference was that those guys were actually waging war. He had been disappointed with the photos he'd taken during his first foray in Libya, which he asked Anderson to look over with him and which were, in Anderson's view, "pretty banal war images," albeit technically correct.

At some point Hetherington had latched on to the idea that the fighters were "acting out these characters" within a literal and met-aphorical theater of war, as Anderson put it. The seeming fakery of inexperienced rebels posing with guns they barely knew how to use struck Hetherington, in retrospect, as an authentic response to having been thrust unexpectedly into war. It also said something about the relationship of today's young men and war, the recurring theme of his work. It occurred to him that if he wanted to explore that idea further he needed to come up with "another visual language," as Anderson described it. "It couldn't look like news photography. It couldn't look like the pictures that we were seeing every day. He needed to find another way to, sort of, make that visual imagery separate from journalism, in that sense."

On the day that Hetherington departed for Libya the second time, he and Anderson talked about fear, a subject they had discussed many times before. "Working the numbers," Anderson said, it was inevitable that at some point a war photographer would have survived more than his share of dangerous episodes; the law of averages dictated that he wasn't going to survive many more, at which point it would be logical for him to get out of the business, to move on to something else. "It was just the natural mature realization that . . . I am going to have to go do something that's very dangerous, and the likely outcomes of that are not good, and having already kind of pushed my luck enough times, is this the time that it's . . . that my number's up?" Anderson said. Libya was particularly dangerous because there was so much ordnance falling and the photographers were so frequently exposed, running around with fighters who didn't know what they were doing. But he assured Anderson that, because his approach to photographing the war would be different the second time around, he would not have to put himself right up on the front line. Anderson warned him not to get sucked in, "and he was, like, yeah, you know, you're right, and don't worry, I'm going to stay back on this one." Hetherington, Anderson said, was "genuinely scared to go back, not because he had any premonition but because he was experienced enough to know that he was going to do something that was really dangerous, and the outcomes were potentially not good at all."

Still, Hetherington seemed to have a strange fascination with his own fear, Anderson said, "and maybe we all do, in that sense. Maybe, as photographers who cover those situations, we do have a little bit of a screw loose in that sense of being like moths to a flame, being drawn to experiencing that fear. It's a powerful magnet that pulls you in, of wanting to know what that's like, and wanting to experience that fear, kind of wanting to see how deep that fear can run. Seeing how close to the flame you can stand without getting burned. Problem with that is, you stand a good chance of getting burned at some point."

Moments of profound fear have a kind of beautiful purity, Anderson said. All of the gray areas of life disappear, and there is only the matter of living or dying. "And the simplicity of that, the crystal clarity of that, is so powerful, so beautiful and it's—it's hard to put that into words, but calling it adrenaline, or chalking it up to being an adrenaline junkie, that's not it at all, that totally misses the point." As they discussed these things, Hetherington encouraged Anderson to accompany him on the second Benghazi trip, but Anderson opted out because he didn't have the necessary funds to go.

Hetheringon returned to Benghazi in April to document what Bouckaert later described as "the interplay" between the fictional fighters—the soldiers they had seen on TV and in movies—and the fighters they were trying to become. He would do it with slightly eccentric equipment. As he explained, merely framing an image involves a certain artifice, and there is a natural tension between the need for honesty and the need for impact. While an honest photo need not be a beautiful photo, the most memorable ones are both, which is why a photographer inevitably resorts to certain contrivances to magnify the power of his subjects. The rebels were merely embracing this dynamic. So he did too.

Even having accepted that, after a long day of covering the fighting near Ajdabiya during the second trip, he had the feeling he was somehow missing the reality of the war. He wondered if the fighters' acute awareness of his presence would make the resulting images more honest or less so. Some of the other photographers he met in Benghazi were producing great work, Hondros in particular. So was Orlinsky. Another American he met there, Michael Christopher Brown, was likewise producing compelling images on his iPhone after having dropped and broken his SLR camera, and he had managed to sell some of his iPhone images to *Fortune* and *National Geographic* magazines. Because Hetherington was more interested in intimate, almost formal portraits, he lamented not being fluent in Arabic, which would have made it easier for him to earn the fighters' trust, to become familiar with them, to develop a deeper understanding of their world. He was meanwhile shying away from competing with his peers. He had his own ideas and knew that a group mentality was in many ways potentially dangerous. Getting a great image could change everything—an individual career, Western interest in the war, even the action of the war itself—yet the overwhelming desire to get that image could result in a kind of myopia and recklessness.

War photographers are inevitably drawn to taking predictable photos, ones that the editors clustered in conference rooms back home are looking for, and the idea of embracing the artifice in his images, whether his own or his subjects', was a different approach even for Hetherington. The equipment he chose for the task was a small video Flip camera and a medium-format film camera coupled with a large flash apparatus typically used for wedding photography. Because he was limited by the number of frames per roll he would have to choose his shots carefully, and he would not see the results until much later, after the film had been processed. As a result, he would be unable to upload his photos for use by the media or photo agencies. In almost every way, he was going against the grain of every other war photographer in Libya.

Several of the photographers he met in Libya during his second trip asked him about his camera kit, and it no doubt seemed strange that he was using equipment more typically used for weddings to record images of violence and death. He reconciled this seeming inconsistency by treating his method as something akin to crime-scene photography—deliberate and methodically framed yet, he hoped, ultimately revealing. During his first trip he had observed that the Libyan war veered between moments of careful posturing and incredibly dangerous encounters, many of them brought about by the rebels' ignorance of combat. The fighters weren't trained soldiers and, as a result, there was a great risk of getting hit by friendly fire or being caught in an unplanned counterattack. Working in such an environment obviously had precious little in common with wedding photography; it was more like photographing a crime scene while the crime was still taking place.

In the town of Brega, Hetherington had watched in alarm as the war turned its focus on him. The rebel lines had collapsed, which prompted the pro-Gaddafi townspeople to come out of their houses and begin shooting at both fighters and photographers. It was a perfect example of the futility, in Libya, of adhering to the familiar war journalist's rule—to determine an acceptable level of danger and take pains not to surpass it. Instead, it was necessary to quickly respond to a series of terrifyingly fluid, constantly morphing dangers. It wasn't always clear where the danger lay, or when it would present itself. Meanwhile, there were few restrictions on where a journalist could go, which greatly expanded the possibilities for making potentially fatal mistakes. It was very serious business, he had told Kamber over dinner that night in Brooklyn.

If he was aware of the erratic dangers, he had not prepared for it as rigorously as had other photographers such as Orlinsky and Hondros.

The American photojournalist Bryan Denton, who met Hethering-ton in Benghazi during his first trip, had loaned him a set of protec-tive gear, including a bulletproof vest, after noting that Hetherington didn't have what Denton considered essential equipment. By then the two, along with the *New York Times* writer-photographer Chris Chivers, had been regularly meeting for coffee and to look over each other's photos, and what struck Denton was not that Hetherington was a daredevil—he wasn't—but that he was "an amazingly kind and engaged individual." He did not fit the stereotype of the callous war photographer. Hetherington's twin attributes of thoughtfulness and daring struck some as like that of T. E. Lawrence's *Lawrence of Arabia,* though he would have blushed to hear it. In any event, Hetherington had returned the bulletproof vest to Denton and had not brought one with him the second time around.

By the time he arrived in Benghazi in early April, the Arab Spring had become a sort of package tour for war journalists and would-be war journalists, starting in Tunisia, with a stopover in Egypt, and now a potentially extended stay in Libya. Hondros, who had covered the Egyptian uprising as well as wars in Afghanistan, Iraq, Kosovo, Sierra Leone, and Liberia, knew Hetherington, and the two had covered some of the same terrain, including in Liberia, where Hondros had produced some of his finest work, earning a Pulitzer Prize nomina-tion in the process. His image of the jubilant soldier on the Monro-via bridge had been reproduced countless times and made the cover of *Photojournalism: The World's Top Photographers,* which featured his and Hetherington's work. The soldier himself, whose name was Joseph Duo, had become a local celebrity as a result, and he had driven around Monrovia with the page from a magazine on which the photo was printed plastered to the windshield of his car.

Hetherington and Hondros were close to the same age—Hetherington was forty and Hondros had just turned forty-two when their paths intersected in Benghazi—and both tended to take more than a passing interest in the subjects of their photographs; Hondros had befriended Duo, visited him in postwar Liberia, and funded his education. Also, like Hetherington, Hondros was a romantic figure in the world of typically hard-bitten war journalists. In addition to being well dressed, he was an opera fan, an avid chess player, and an accomplished pianist. But what set him apart was the intimacy and raw power of his photographs, which at their best managed to be both artistic and newsworthy, a rare combination. His portrait of a young Iraqi girl spattered with the blood of her parents after they had failed to heed warning shots at an American checkpoint in 2005 "carried the full freight of war and its collateral effects," the *New York Times* observed. In addition to the Pulitzer nomination, Hondros in 2006 won the Overseas Press Club of America's Robert Capa Gold Medal award—one of the highest honors in photojournalism—for what was described as the best example of photojournalism requiring exceptional courage and enterprise.

Orlinsky, for her part, was awed to be in the company of such seasoned and renowned photojournalists. She had enjoyed making the trip to Ajdabiya each morning after breakfast at their hotel, during which they talked about photography and life. Considering where they were, it struck Orlinsky that both Hondros and Hetherington talked a lot about not being there. Hondros was focused on his upcoming wedding to Christina Piaia, while Hetherington seemed to be nearing the end of a long career of war photography, talking at length about settling down.

Hetherington, Hondros, and Orlinsky had visited Ajdabiya numerous times, occasionally with other journalists—Brown, Guy Martin, Patrick Wells, and Muneef Halawa—photographing the rebels as they fired rockets toward unseen Gaddafi troops, zooming in on the faces of otherwise average young men who had been thrust into combat. They had visited a hospitalized rebel who, after having been surrounded by Gaddafi troops, had chosen to turn his gun on himself rather than be captured. As everyone snapped pictures of the man in his hospital bed, Hetherington had the unsettling feeling that they were behaving like vultures.

They had also visited the local morgue, where they saw the body of a man who had been executed, his hands tied together. And they had photographed the incinerated corpses of government soldiers who had been killed in an air strike, the odor of which haunted Hetherington afterward, though he felt those images illustrated the raw power of war better than his comparatively formal portraits. As they toured the war zone, Hetherington and the other photographers discussed their subjects, their own approaches to them, and the relative merits of being on the front lines. They had heard that NATO was dropping air strikes east of the city, but for the most part they were waiting for something big to happen within range. At one point they managed to get caught up in a large demonstration, during which Hetherington and Martin, a fellow Brit, climbed atop a fire truck to follow the cheering crowd into Benghazi's main square, but the excitement soon passed. Hetherington went back to shooting portraits of men sitting in the sun, using his fill flash, and wishing that he could see the results. Along the way they talked about the besieged city of Misrata, west of Benghazi on the Mediterranean coast.

There weren't many restaurants still open in Benghazi, but Hetherington, Hondros, and Orlinsky had heard about a place on the waterfront where customers picked their meal from a display of fresh shrimp and fish. The restaurant "was a nice kind of respite from everything, and reminded you that just a few months before this was a city," Orlinsky recalled. "You could step back to reality." Over dinner, they talked about the war, about photography, and about mutual friends back home. Toward the end of the meal, Martin and Brown joined them. Then they went back to their hotel, which had been taken over by the rebels during the first few weeks of fighting and offered rooms to journalists for free, because the rebels wanted them there.

The next day was quiet. Hetherington visited the hospital to check for casualties and bodies, then traveled to Benghazi's western gate to see who was hanging out. By then, the road to Brega had been closed to the press due to the fighting so he, Hondros, and Orlinsky headed back to town to begin planning a trip to Misrata. Finding Benghazi saturated with media personnel, yet somewhat dull, they saw Misrata as a potential avenue to something more meaningful. On the way back to Benghazi, driving on the loop road around Ajdabiya, they and their driver suddenly encountered a sequence of three mortar explosions very close by. It seemed strange that they might have been killed during a seeming lull in the war. When they reached Benghazi, there was exhilaration in the air, following a rout of Gaddafi troops, and people approached them to thank them for being there. Among the joyful crowds, Hetherington took what he expected would be some good photos, in nice light near the courthouse, though there was no way to be sure, given his inability to review the images as he could have with a digital camera. Later, as he strolled around town, he bought himself a scarf, which would be part of his war ensemble in Misrata.

A few days later, Hetherington returned to the harbor to photograph the arrival from Misrata of a small cruise ship, the *Ionian Spirit*, loaded with migratory workers from India, Bangladesh, Nepal, and Nigeria who had been rescued by a group called the International Organization for Migration, and he inquired about traveling to Misrata aboard the boat. Afterward he called Idil Ibrahim, told her about the siege of Misrata, and said he had decided to go there.

When Sebastian Junger, who was still in New York, heard about the planned Misrata trip he was alarmed, and he e-mailed Hetherington to say, as he later recalled, "Listen, it's really dangerous. Gaddafi does not want journalists in there for obvious reasons." Junger, who had been in Sarajevo during that city's siege in 1993 and 1994, later said, "I know governments don't want that kind of atrocity being broadcast, and that's what was happening in Misrata, and I just said to Tim that they will do anything they can to keep you guys out of there or to punish you for being there. Just be careful. There's only one way out, by boat. Just be really careful." After sending the e-mail Junger said he felt like a mother hen.

Junger knew that photographing young men thrown together in a life-threatening struggle held a particular attraction for Hetherington. But whatever rationale Hetherington used for stepping closer to danger, he was also trying to make a living, and that meant getting the most compelling photographs he could. As Brabazon later observed, "You can have lots of grand, noble thoughts about, you know, pursuing this project or that project, but fundamentally, you're a professional and there to earn cash. Someone has to pay the rent, right?" Despite his assurances to his friends, Hetherington was not one to stay back and shoot quietly behind the scenes, and that was not what his potential publishers or audience wanted either. Misrata represented the most intriguing battlefield in Libya; it was attractively difficult for photographers to get there and it fit into Hetherington's desire to catalog the relationship of young men to war.

As Paradiso pointed out, every culture has its mythologies about great warriors, which inspires young men to prove themselves. In Liberia, as in Libya, that mythology included movies and TV. Liberian teenagers bolstered themselves to fight by visiting video shacks where, even in remote towns, "somebody would find a battery and they'd hook up a VCR and they'd watch Chuck Norris films—or, actually, Steven Seagal was the most popular—you know, this guy ended up everywhere," Paradiso said. "And so their sense of how to fight was derived from these films." Despite Hetherington's careful framing of his previous work in Benghazi, the best place in Libya to explore the relationship between young men and war, whatever their motivations, was not behind the scenes. It was Misrata. There, young men were fighting for their homes, their families, their own lives. So the next day, following their dinner at the fish restaurant, Hetherington, Hondros, Orlinsky, Brown, Martin, and Guillermo Cervera, who was from Spain and traveling on his own, went down to the harbor to inquire again about boat passage to Misrata—something several of them had previously done on their own. They were told that Gaddafi forces were shelling the port there and that fifteen people had been killed and thirty wounded that day, meaning the situation was dire. Still, if they wanted to go, they would be permitted to board on Saturday for a trip that would take about twenty-four hours.

Among their group, Guy Martin, twenty-seven, was enterprising and daring and had proved adept at chasing down stories in conflict zones. When he was barely of drinking age, in 2004, he had slipped into Iraq through Turkey without affiliation with any news organization to photograph the effects of the U.S. invasion, focusing on "softer stories," as he put it, such as the miles-long queues of trucks at the border. He now worked with the Panos agency, as did Hetherington, and had come to Libya by way of Egypt, where he had spent a month documenting the uprising in Cairo's Tahrir Square for the *Wall Street Journal.* Martin had a keen sense of humor and was, he liked to say, "mad into surfing." He had arrived in Benghazi with a college friend and fellow photographer named Ivor Prickett a month after the uprising began as a minor protest over the arrest of a lawyer who represented victims of a prison massacre. On the day the two arrived, the rebels were celebrating the first air strikes by British and American forces around Tripoli, which helped empower the nascent revolt. Afterward, Martin and Prickett had spent almost three weeks following the rebels between Ajdabiya and Sirte, south of Benghazi.

Martin saw Libya as the latest chapter in a bigger project he envisioned about the Arab Spring, and afterward he planned to move on to Syria, Yemen, Morocco, and Algeria. He felt the Arab Spring would define his generation of war photographers, much the way Vietnam had defined a previous generation. A book of photographs from the Vietnam War, given to him by his parents when he was seventeen, had inspired him to become a photographer. Martin had met Hetherington a few times before: briefly, when Martin was working as an intern at a gallery in London where Hetherington, who had just returned from Afghanistan, was staging an exhibition of *Sleeping Soldiers,* and again in Libya, during Hetherington's first trip there, when Martin and Prickett were on the road in the east. "There was this famous rebel charge from Benghazi to Sirte," Martin recalled, "and I was sitting in a car on the side of the road and we started chatting." Hetherington told him he had seen Martin's *Wall Street Journal* photos from Egypt, online, and that in fact he had looked at them every day, "and I thought, no way," Martin said. "Our industry is full of egos, hotheads, photographers who don't give you the time of day, and I was amazed that he recognized my work."

Martin occasionally ran into Hetherington during that first trip to Libya. The rebels, he said, "would take miles and miles of ground, then end up making a mass retreat back to Benghazi. One day some of us decided to stay in the desert that night. I was with Ivor, and we didn't really know what to do. I said, 'Tim, is it safe here?' and he gave us a five-minute talk about the advantages of staying there that night, about the various ordnances being used. It was an amazing reassurance, so we found a place to stay. We stayed on the roof, and we could see tracer bullets in the distance. Tim shared funny stories about Liberia, like when this guy with a huge afro tried to sell him a women's curling iron."

The night that Hetherington, Hondros, Brown, and Orlinsky went to the fish restaurant, Martin and Prickett got a text message from Hondros inviting the two to join them, which is when they first talked about traveling to Misrata. Because Prickett had by then departed for an assignment in eastern Libya, Martin decided to join the group. "I felt such a mutual understanding with Tim and Chris," he said. "We had these intellectual conversations. In general there was a very good and productive group dynamic. We were always phoning, traveling around together, talking through ideas, seeing the same things, talking about the same things. Sometimes the details were far more interesting than going to the front lines. The group was really strong . . . We laughed a lot. We shared the same sense of humor."

Misrata, where fierce street fighting was taking place as a result of a full military siege by the Gaddafi forces, seemed to Martin to be emblematic of the bigger story of the Arab Spring. By then, he said, he was growing tired of Benghazi. "I was no longer seeing things with fresh eyes. I was getting almost cynical about the rebels. I'd been thinking about going back to Cairo, seeing friends, maybe. The Benghazi rebels were always home by teatime. You'd see them on the front lines but come sundown they'd all be standing down by the waterfront for the al Jazeera crew." Later, with Hetherington, the two had discussed how Misrata offered a new dynamic, a new landscape, with new people and a situation that was a more truthful reflection of a rebel fighting army, something more indicative of what a revolution should be.

Martin, who could see the *Ionian Spirit* from his hotel window, had previously inquired about traveling on the boat to Misrata along with a group of American print reporters he had met up with in Benghazi. The boat was leaving for Misrata the next day, "so we had an evening and the next morning to figure out if we wanted to go," he said. "I never had this sense that it was an ungodly suicide mission."

There was a hospital operating in Misrata; reporters for the *New York Times* had been there and come back, he said. He gave Hetherington a call and found that he had already obtained the necessary permission to travel to Misrata but had also been looking at other boats. Hetherington returned to the *Ionian Spirit* that evening with Hondros, saw the injured being unloaded, and talked with the people in charge.

Martin said he found it interesting that Hetherington had chosen to travel with Hondros, because it seemed to him that they were polar opposites. Hondros, he said, was all about hard, breaking news, "and there was Tim with his slow camera. But everyone was swapping ideas, talking about what was important to photography, and what wasn't." Despite their varied backgrounds, and the inevitable competition for the next big shot, the group had much in common. Like Martin, Brown and Cervera were avid surfers, and Brown and Hetherington both worked—though not simultaneously—with Bouckaert, in Hetherington's case during his first trip to Libya, when he was hired by Human Rights Watch to reproduce photographic archives; reproductions of the originals, which spanned the Gaddafi and King Idris eras, were later featured in an exhibition at the London Festival of Photography.

Brown, like Martin, had been in Libya since soon after the revolution began, though at the time he had not expected a full-scale war and later said that had he known what lay ahead he probably would not have stuck around. Putting his life at risk for a photograph, he afterward concluded, was "stupid," though he conceded that being on the front lines was a rush. He had planned to stay only a few weeks but had gotten caught up in the action. During an attack he had been shot in the leg, though the wound was not serious.

At thirty-three, Brown was about midway between the youngest and the oldest in the group. Like Hetherington, he had chosen to break from the photographic norm and was documenting the war exclusively with his iPhone, using the trendy Hipstamatic app, which transforms images into a square format and, through software filters, gives them higher contrast and velvety color saturation. The aesthetic paths that Brown and Hetherington were following had diverged, but both relied more on presentation than strict documentation. Hetherington was striving for a formal, classical presentation while Brown's use of Hipstamatic resulted in images with a stylized, enhanced feel.

Guillermo Cervera was more mainstream by comparison. A charming, enigmatic forty-two-year-old from Madrid, he alternated between a conventional 35mm digital camera and his iPhone. He also had been in Libya for a while, and he had grown weary of shooting what he felt were the same recurring scenes. When he first saw Hetherington and Hondros he'd noted that they were new arrivals, and they had approached to talk just as missiles began passing overhead. Cervera noticed Hetherington's medium-format film camera and, because he liked classical photography, asked, "Oh, is this a Mamiya?" Hetherington responded with his characteristic grin, which charmed Cervera. At the time, Cervera was ready for a change. He was unsure if Misrata was a good idea, in that it carried the war's unpredictable risks to a new level, but concluded that it would at least be a change of pace.

Cervera had come to photography indirectly, after his father caught him looking at his private stash of *Playboy* magazines when he was a boy. In response, his father had tried to interest him in his collection of *National Geographic* magazines, which, with their occasional photos of nude natives, have long provided a kind of pseudoporn for legions of pubescent boys. Cervera was, he recalled, "amazed with the pictures" and soon decided that he wanted to be a photographer. In response, his father again tried to steer him in what he considered to be a more appropriate direction, sending him to the United States to study aerospace engineering. But after living in upstate New York for five years Cervera, then twenty-four years old, returned to Spain, where he ran into a friend at a party who proposed a trip to Bosnia to photograph the war there. Intrigued, Cervera had packed his Olympus camera along with a cache of film and the two had set off. He was soon hooked on war photography and afterward he traveled to Rwanda, arriving a week after a notorious massacre. What he saw on these trips shocked him, and he decided to give up war photography almost as abruptly as he had begun. Returning to Spain, he opened a photo shop, which he ran for more than a decade. Then, in 2007, he closed his shop and, on an impulse, returned to war photography, traveling to Chad, Sudan, Sri Lanka, Afghanistan, Pakistan, Egypt, and Libya. Since then, he had been working freelance for various European newspapers, while in his off-time he photographed his favorite pastime, surfing.

Like everyone in the group, Cervera was curious to see Misrata, and Hetherington, in particular, had a hunch that it would be an intense and productive experience. Hetherington expected Misrata would bring some revelations about the "feedback loop," as he described it, how the culturally powerful imagery of war sparked in young men an overpowering desire to take up arms, to insert themselves into the scenes. So on Saturday, April 16, the six returned to the Benghazi port and boarded the *Ionian Spirit,* a small Greek-flagged cruiser that had been pressed into service ferrying refugees, injured civilians, journalists, and supplies. The leader of the rescue operation, Jeremy Haslam, told the photographers that they would have to disembark in Misrata even if the port was being shelled, that he was going to lower the bridge, unload quickly, and no one would be allowed to reboard before the boat departed. "You have no other options," Martin recalled Haslam saying. "This is the decision you've made. There could be rockets coming into the port." The photographers, Martin said, "just stood there and nodded, but I was thinking, That sounds really scary, actually. I wouldn't have been on that boat if it weren't for the people I was with."

The boat did not leave until late afternoon. "At the last minute they got a satellite call saying they needed medical supplies," Martin said, so the five photographers found a room on the boat and returned to town to buy about twenty pounds of tuna and almonds, as well as medical supplies. By the time the boat left they had eaten half of their supplies already, he said. Once under way, the group talked about photography and about Egypt. Martin had been there at the start of the uprising, and Chris had seen the end. There was a feeling that they were watching history unfold, he said. Also on board were perhaps a dozen other journalists, which Hetherington had winced to see, because he did not like working in a crowd of photographers and reporters. He reconciled himself that this was an inevitable consequence of the magnitude of the moment.

Despite the crowd of photographers, Orlinsky was drawn to Misrata because of what she described as "this media black hole." Few people knew much about what was going on inside the city, but the news that managed to filter through was attractively intense. She had observed the arrival of rescue boats bringing refugees and the dead and injured from Misrata, including hundreds of children, which told her that what was happening there was crucial, and extremely dangerous. From all appearances, Misrata was the front line of front lines.

Before departing, Brown had e-mailed the Brazilian photographer André Liohn, who had followed the Arab Spring from Tunisia to Bahrain and Egypt and who had been in Misrata since early April, shooting pictures for the International Committee of the Red Cross. Liohn had briefly met Hetherington in Ajdabiya, though he had not yet known his name. At the time, Liohn was hiding in the dunes during a very disorganized rebel maneuver, and he'd seen Hetherington approaching, on foot, exposed in the middle of an open road. "Where is the front?" Hetherington had asked, and Liohn, who was somewhat incredulous that Hetherington and his small entourage seemed mindless of the danger, gave him directions.

By e-mail Liohn offered Brown advice about traveling to Misrata, and about what to expect once they arrived. The situation, he warned, was very bad. By then, several Libyan journalists had been killed or injured in the war, and Anton Hammerl, a London-based photographer of Austrian and South African citizenship, had disappeared after setting out with three other reporters in a taxi driving from Benghazi to Brega. Hammerl's group had been walking along a road when they came under fire from government troops and took refuge in a grove of trees. One of the reporters, James Foley, had shouted to Hammerl to ask if he was okay. Hammerl had answered no. Soon after, government soldiers in trucks descended upon the area and began beating the journalists. Hammerl bled to death, though his friends kept his death secret during their six weeks of captivity to avoid provoking their captors, because the Libyan government was publicly claiming he was still alive. As Hetherington and the other photographers prepared to depart on the *Ionian Spirit,* Hammerl's fate was still unknown.

Everyone knew that Misrata was going to be off the charts. In Benghazi the fighting had stretched over vast distances, enabling fighters, as well as journalists, to calibrate their risks relative to the front. In Misrata, the fighting was very close, the rebels had their backs to the sea, and it was clear that the Gaddafi forces would stop at nothing to annihilate them. There was street-to-street—sometimes room-to-room—fighting, and it would be impossible to know, when rounding a corner, whether one might encounter rebels or Gaddafi soldiers or both.

The trip to Misrata was itself fraught with peril. Boats traversing the Mediterranean between Benghazi and Misrata were vulnerable to air strikes by pro-Gaddafi troops as well as to floating mines, which made it even more important to choose the right captain and the best route. The photographers had passed over the first two boats they found in the Benghazi port because they seemed unreliable, and they were relieved to happen upon the *Ionian Spirit,* which was scheduled to return to Benghazi with a thousand or more Nigerian migrant workers who had been abandoned by their employers and were marooned at the Misrata port.

As she lay in her berth that Saturday night, Orlinsky reassured herself that the *Ionian Spirit* had safely transported numerous journalists, and that the trip itself would be over in twenty-four hours or so. Still, nothing was guaranteed, either aboard the boat or after they arrived in port.

10
ZEROING IN:
BENGHAZI TO MISRATA

The *Ionian Spirit* was luxurious when compared with most of the boats used to smuggle journalists, rebels, and medical personnel from Benghazi to Misrata. André Liohn had traveled aboard a small fishing boat that also carried medical supplies and a cache of weapons on a trip that took about sixty hours. The boat had continuously rolled on heavy seas, had been waylaid by a suspicious NATO boat crew, and had been forced to drop anchor for several hours after receiving word that Gaddafi navy boats were in the area. Liohn made the passage about a week before Hetherington and his group, after he had been rebuffed by numerous fishermen whom he had approached for a ride. The first, he said, had laughed at him when he asked if they would take him to Misrata, but a few days later he'd seen a very small fishing boat being loaded with weapons, assumed it was destined for Misrata, or, if not, had reasoned, "I know this boat is going to do *something*." He approached to a safe distance and then, speaking in Arabic, asked to be allowed closer. Granted permission, he then told the crew, "You cannot stop me to go there because Gaddafi is the one who stops journalists." He meant to shame them into taking him, and it worked.

Few people would have gone to such pains to finagle their way aboard a small, unknown fishing boat, during a war, to travel in heavy seas to a place that thousands of people were trying to flee, but Liohn was determined—some would say hardheaded. He could be cautious when necessary and was aware of the dangers of the trip, and of going to Misrata, but these fell within his acceptable limits. Once underway in the swelling seas, Liohn almost immediately got seasick and stayed that way. "The boat was very small, very heavy, the weather was very bad," he recalled. "I was sick all the time and all the time we heard rumors that Gaddafi helicopters would come and sink us." Over the course of two days, he regretted "every single minute in that boat," he said. But it got him to Misrata, which was where he wanted to be.

The *Ionian Spirit* would make the trip in a little over a third of the time. Soon after the boat sailed out of the Benghazi port, Hetherington snapped a portrait of Martin with his old-fashioned camera. Martin looks happy, expectant, though the mood on the boat, Cervera recalled, was "kind of weird." Everyone was excited to be headed for the action, knowing that it would bring the potential for great photos, but they were also scared, not only because they would be entering a besieged city through a port that might be under bombardment, but because no one knew what the ultimate outcome would be. They were casting their lot with the rebels and if the Gaddafi army won control of Misrata they could be arrested or killed. Considering all that, the *Ionian Spirit*'s comparative luxury offered a moment of respite. The photographers caught up on much-needed rest, read, talked, and looked over one another's photos. Hetherington, who was reading a book about the life of the poet and musician Patti Smith, hadn't brought a laptop and often sat down with the other photographers and helped them edit their photographs. The photographers shared berths, and most ended up sleeping an hour or so by themselves on the deck. Martin shared a berth with Brown, Cervera, and Orlinsky, the latter of whom almost immediately became "horribly seasick," Martin said. Hetherington and Hondros had a berth to themselves. At one point during the trip they all gathered in the galley to make around a thousand cheese sandwiches for the refugees who, along with ICU patients, would be boarding the boat in Misrata for the trip back to Benghazi.

Starting out, Orlinsky saw the trip as a minivacation. She enjoyed chatting with the other photojournalists and reporters onboard and tried to make the most of the downtime. Soon, as the boat rolled on the waves and she got seasick, she mostly kept to herself, trying to pump herself up for what lay ahead. In her vulnerable state she ended up doing the opposite, imagining all sorts of frightening scenarios awaiting them in Misrata. As she put it, she psyched herself out. Adding to the stress was the fact that she was one of the few aboard who was on assignment, and so she was worried about meeting her deadline. She would have only about twenty-four hours to shoot in Misrata before she had to file her first pictures for the Paris newspaper *Le Monde*. Recognizing her dismay, both Hetherington and Hondros tried to reassure her, telling her everything would be okay.

It was late the next day when the passengers got their first view of the Misrata port. Beyond a man-made breakwater, along an otherwise unbroken stretch of tawny-colored sand, tall cranes loomed above docks lined with warehouses and shipping containers. The outskirts of the city itself, partially hidden behind tall, palm-studded dunes, looked deceptively calm, aside from telltale wisps of smoke in the distance. Some of the reporters tried to make contact by satellite phone with people they knew were in the city, hoping for some assurance that they would be picked up promptly and not left at the mercy of incoming rockets or, perhaps, a stampede of desperate refugees. The captain waited for three hours in the open sea because the Gaddafi forces were shelling the port, a routine occurrence each time a ship arrived. Though the rebels controlled the port and adjacent sections of the city, pro-Gaddafi spies were in place to signal the firing to begin. Typically, there was a lag of about fifteen minutes. Sometimes the mortars exploded harmlessly in the sea or fell short and killed civilians cowering in their homes, while terrorizing the thousands of refugees camped nearby. Now, in the distance, the mortars passed across a purplish sky at sunset, though, Martin said, "by the time we got close it was really, really quiet. I made some pictures of the sunset, like a tourist."

When Liohn had arrived, a week or so before, the port was already closed to commerce, and all that awaited the fishing boat were a few vehicles and rebels who immediately started firing their guns into the air, threatening the fishing boat to see how its crew would respond. The crew had slowed the boat and begun firing back, also into the air, signaling their friendly intentions, after which they were allowed to dock. The crew then began unloading the shipment of guns and ammo and Liohn had disembarked.

Now, as the *Ionian Spirit* lingered offshore, bobbing from side to side, Misrata looked serene but for the faint traces of smoke in the distance. Orlinsky had spoken with her friend Bryan Denton, the photographer who had loaned Hetherington the bulletproof vest back in Benghazi and who had photographed the siege of Misrata for the *New York Times,* and he had tried to give her the lay of the land. In addition to the mortar fire, she was leery of the prospect of thousands of desperate African migrant workers trying to get on the boat as her group disembarked.

When the more readily identifiable *Ionian Spirit* approached the port, a little after 7:30 p.m., the crew hoisted the rebel flag. It was still light, though night would fall by the time they finally reached the long series of docks. There were no lights on, so the only illumination came from a bright full moon. About twenty minutes later the boat was tied off and the gangway lowered. A couple of TV news crews chose not to stay, having apparently worked out an agreement with Jeremy Haslam to return to Benghazi on the boat, despite his previous warning that everyone would have to disembark; they simply shot a few quick scenes at the port, got their Misrata bylines, and reboarded the boat.

As the rest of the passengers disembarked, Hetherington and the others scanned the docks for someone to greet them but, as Martin recalled, his group found no one was there to meet them. Then a group of rebels and Red Cross representatives—Orlinsky dubbed them the Misrata welcoming committee—appeared out of the darkness, just as a tragic parade of refugees began streaming onto the dock, including migrant workers, injured people, and busloads of women and children loaded down with their possessions. In response to the surge of refugees, the nervous photographers began doing what photographers do: taking pictures and video. For Cervera, it was like a scene from a *Mad Max* movie, with murmuring crowds of raggedly dressed figures hurrying about the docks and alleyways in the moonlight. Cervera was frightened, unsure where his group was headed or if the mortar fire would resume. No one even knew where they would spend the night.

Martin said he was unable to help find a ride because he spoke poor Arabic, and "it took an age to figure this out. I was a little uncomfortable in the middle of this huge, open space. I started to get a bad feeling." A few men approached them, offering to drive them into the city, and though they were friendly Martin did not want to take them up on the offer. "Guillermo and Michael were trying to network, to get their own driver, to go to another part of the city," he said. "So we're talking for a half hour about who to get in the car with."

The Misrata rebels, aware that journalists were their best hope for getting outside aid, had established a media network of bodyguards, drivers, fixers, local journalists, and tech guys, and soon Cervera heard someone say, "Okay, let's go, we found a place." Reda Muntasir, a man of early middle age with curly, gelled hair, hurried them into his vehicle and drove them to a nearby hangar. He seemed to have appeared randomly, but Mohammed al-Zawwam, the rebel photographer who had accompanied the group from Benghazi, had contacted him from the boat. There were far too many journalists crowded together inside the hangar for Hetherington's taste, but soon the print reporters went their own way and the six photographers got into a four-door pickup truck with two drivers who worked for the rebel media center: Ahmed Muntasir, Reda Muntasir's nephew, a twenty-one-year-old fighter who was working as a journalists' driver, and a second driver, a burly man who spoke broken English and said "fuck" a lot, named Mohammed al-Zain. Hetherington, Hondros, Martin, and Brown climbed into the cab, with Cervera and Orlinsky in the bed, and they headed off down the darkened road. Their destination was a safe house owned by a local businessman, Bengasim el-Karshini, which was being used to lodge journalists.

El-Karshini's house was large, in an upscale neighborhood of walled compounds transected by sandy streets without names. The routes leading to the house were blocked by a succession of checkpoints and closely monitored by residents who had taken in friends and family members from more vulnerable sections of the city. Once there, the photographers passed through a gate into a spacious, tiled courtyard. To their left was a patio containing a large store of weapons and ammunition. Through the doorway they entered a long hallway, off of which, in the former living room, was the rebels' local command center, complete with satellite uplinks. Beyond that was a series of rooms strewn with mattresses and crowded with rebels, journalists, and all their accoutrement—duffel bags, sleeping bags, cameras, and bulletproof vests.

In addition to Libyan rebels there were six or so journalists staying at the house, whom Martin would later describe as "a small French contingent—an older French guy, a well-built cameraman, a geeky radio guy, possibly one woman." Later it would be hard to be sure who was who, because their arrival was so chaotic. Reda Muntasir said the number of journalists staying at the safe house sometimes swelled to as many as twenty-five, for a total of about forty occupants, including the rebels.

Hetherington, Hondros, Cervera, Brown, Martin, and Orlinsky cast about for space to put their things, and everyone except Hondros found a mattress on the floor. Hondros took the last available sofa. The scene, Martin said, "weirded me out. On the stairs there was a young Libyan guy, fifteen or sixteen, very thin, covered with mud, wearing only army pants, no shoes, with this curly mop of hair, who was being shouted at by people in the house. He was a Gaddafi sniper, supposedly. It was the first time I'd seen the enemy, ever, alive. I thought, Am I going to have to sleep next to him? . . . We were not allowed to take pictures. I don't know what ever happened to him. Even Ahmed was standing over him, coercing him to talk."

One of the photographers, who had been in Misrata for a few days, showed them videos of the fighting on a laptop. It was, Martin observed, "horrific, noisy house-to-house fighting." Not long after, the bombing resumed, rattling the windows of the safe house. "Benghazi started to seem like Club Med by comparison," Martin said, but the Libyan rebels took pains to make them feel welcome. For much of the war, Misrata's plight had been ignored by all but the Arab media, and the rebels were glad for the attention from the West. For the people of Misrata, it was unfathomable that the outside world did not seem to care. The hope was that the journalists would report what was happening and that it would lead to increased NATO support.

Misrata was, like most Mediterranean ports, an ancient city, established around the seventh century as a terminus of Saharan caravans. It had been built around an oasis a few miles inland, a geographic feature that often baffled visitors, who wondered why the city was so close to the turquoise waters of the Mediterranean yet, aside from the port, seemed to ignore it. The region around Misrata had been part of the Roman Empire—the ruins of Leptis Magna, west of the city, were a popular tourist attraction at one time—and the city fell under Ottoman rule from the sixteenth century until World War I, after which Libya became an Italian colony. The Italians had eventually been driven out, after which Libya was ruled by King Idris until the 1969 coup by Muammar Gaddafi. On February 17, 2011, during the Arab uprisings, small demonstrations began taking place in Misrata, and subsequent arrests by Libyan police fueled public discontent. Larger demonstrations followed, prompting government forces to fire upon the civilians, killing many (the total is subject to debate; some sources say as many as seventy). Gaddafi's army arrived on February 24, only to be repelled by a hastily organized rebel force, then returned on March 20 with tanks and artillery and began besieging the city. By the time the Western photographers arrived more than a thousand civilians had been killed and three times that many injured. The tide had started to turn as a result of NATO air strikes and the smuggling of weapons to the rebels, but the battle was far from over.

The photographers slept fitfully on their first night in the safe house, not only because of the bombing in the distance but because, as Martin said, "Guillermo snored horrifically, and there was a mosquito there, and Tim was the only one who had packed a mosquito net." Hetherington, he said, had "like, a little Narnia tent. He said he learned his lesson in Liberia. You feel like it's your own little area, nothing can harm you."

The next day, they loaded into a pickup truck and drove to the al-Hekma hospital, a small, formerly private hospital that had become Misrata's primary medical facility after the city's other functioning hospital was bombed by the Gaddafi troops. Al-Hekma, whose emergency room was a triage tent set up in the parking lot, would become a pivotal site for everyone in the coming days. While the others toured the hospital, Orlinsky set off with al-Zain to photograph refugees at the port for *Le Monde,* hoping she could meet her deadline.

At al-Hekma the photographers picked their way through hallways crowded with the injured, some with bullet or shrapnel wounds, others missing arms and legs. Hetherington was particularly moved by the presence of so many injured children, including some with gunshot wounds to the head. He also came upon a Gaddafi soldier who had been badly beaten and who the rebels would keep alive for further interrogation. At first the medical staff did not allow them to take pictures of the soldier but they eventually relented. The photographers also snapped pictures of scores of injured people on gurneys and hospital beds, as well as medical staff and others hurrying down hallways and in and out of the double front doors, which received so much traffic that they stood open twenty-four hours a day. Along the way, someone showed Hetherington a dead fighter lying in a side room, a scene that evoked a funerary portrait of an ancient pharaoh. In his photos, the man is wrapped in black, white, and gray fabrics, his head partially covered by a scarf as he lies on a gray tiled floor in the corner of a room. A white rope is tied around the man's waist to keep his arms in place. Hetherington took several photos but always from a distance; he didn't get too close.

After the hospital, the group returned to the hangar at the port, then got their first glimpse of the front on Tripoli Street, where they encountered full urban warfare, with street-to-street fighting and numerous snipers in the taller buildings. Then it was back to the port, where they again saw the masses of refugees, along with numerous Libyan families who complained that they were not being allowed to leave. It was an eventful first day, and the atmosphere at the safe house that night was animated. "Much to talk about, much to think about," as Ahmed Muntasir later observed, with a smile. Orlinsky, for her part, wasn't feeling the happy vibe. She was uncomfortable at the safe house, having started off the night before with a bad impression, made worse by the fact that she had arrived tired, sick, and unnerved by what they had encountered at the port. She was also grumpy to be sharing a room with nine men, and it occurred to her that the safe house contained the rebels' command center, which made it a potential bombing target. "But they took good care of the journalists," she said. As had been the case at the hotel in Benghazi, the rebels were doing everything they could to ensure the photographers got what they'd come to Misrata for.

11

THE SIEGE OF MISRATA

When Majdi Lusta arrived on the front line on March 20, 2011, the rebels faced an enemy equipped with automatic weapons, machine guns, long-range rifles, mortars, RPGs, artillery, and tanks. Guns were rare among Misrata residents, so Lusta, a thirty-two-year-old computer engineer who had gotten married a month before, and who didn't own a gun, carried a heavy steel rod. The alternative, he said, was to go to war empty-handed. "Who would do that?" he asked.

Mahmud el-Haddad, an anesthetist who worked at al-Hekma, observed, "No one in Misrata was trained to fight in a war. Nobody has a gun. Everybody is trying to find a weapon, and when they do, sometimes they don't even know what the weapons are."

The results were occasionally disastrous, with many rebels killed or injured by friendly fire, but as Ibrahim Safar, a forty-four-year-old radio announcer who also joined the rebels, said, "We had no choice but to fight. The Gaddafi troops had come to kill us and our families. It was evil. Evil had come here, to our homes."

Computer engineers, journalists, lawyers, students, shopkeepers, truck drivers, mechanics, dock workers, businessmen, and

unemployed laborers became soldiers overnight, arming themselves
with anything they could get their hands on. Though Lusta never had
to wield his steel rod, he was prepared to do so if necessary. For the
first ten days he supported the lucky few who did have guns, carrying
ammunition, food, and water, hoping for an enemy soldier to be killed
whose weapon could be retrieved, which finally happened in early
April, when the rebels blew up a white Mitsubishi truck, killing three
soldiers and scoring four guns. Lusta, a young man with an intense
gaze and the build of a football lineman, retrieved an FN machine
gun from the truck. "I used it immediately," he said. He commenced
shooting from a bombed-out wedding gown store at vehicles containing Gaddafi soldiers and at the windows of a nearby high-rise being
used as a snipers' nest. He was unsure if he killed anyone. "Always we
shoot and hide," he said.

The rebels developed a strategy of hiding along side streets and
emerging to attack government forces traveling the main thoroughfares, then quickly retreating. Though many of the fighters were killed
in the process so, too, were many Gaddafi soldiers, which meant more
arms for the rebels, enabling them to kill more Gaddafi soldiers and
get more guns. Meanwhile, fishermen were smuggling weapons and
ammunition into Misrata through the port.

Finding themselves besieged by a well-armed force that would
stop at nothing to win, the people of Misrata rose to the occasion,
Lusta said. "I feel scared the first day, but once I started fighting, everything changed," he said. "I felt very sad when I lost my first friend. But
then, that's what happens."

El-Haddad was studying to become an anesthesiologist when the
war broke out, and he spent the next five months living and working
at al-Hekma hospital. The city's central hospital had been closed for
renovations and was soon occupied by Gaddafi forces. The next hospital in line had been bombed, which left al-Hekma and a few smaller

clinics to care for the injured in a city of 300,000. El-Haddad worked both inside al-Hekma and with ambulances on the front lines, where he treated the injured, who then returned to the fight or were transported back to the hospital if their injuries were serious. When the first missiles began streaking across the night sky as he stood outside al-Hekma, el-Haddad said, "I was so afraid I felt myself verging on panic. I thought, I am going to die. I have no other place to go." But he was bolstered by the courage, or resolve, of others around him, he said. His fear spurred him on. "I saw so much bravery," he said. "The most famous fighter in Misrata was a man named Mohammed el-Halbous. He was the most brave guy." El-Halbous, a truck driver who was later killed, learned by observation to wait for the moment when a Gaddafi tank crew were reloading their weapon, then to step in front and fire his RPG from twenty or thirty yards away. "He hides, shoots, and takes off," el-Haddad said. "Other people follow his example. They destroy many tanks this way."

Reda Muntasir, who managed the media center and frequently drove journalists down streets that were alternately occupied by rebel and Gaddafi forces, said that in the early stages of the fighting some people panicked, others were paralyzed. But even terror has a life span. "Fear is the first time. Not the next time," he said.

Those with specialized skills, such as drivers, welders, translators, and doctors and nurses, adapted them for the cause. Women, children, and the elderly—the "hidden fighters," as Lusta called them—found supporting roles, volunteering at the triage center, donating blood, cooking and transporting meals to the fighters on the front lines, inspiring them with shouts of "Allahu Akbar," praying for them in the mosques. Women often sent the fighters sweets, along with notes of encouragement.

In an era when military engagements are typically fought over vast distances, using computer-assisted weaponry, and when the closest most people come to war is what they see on TV, the battlefield in Misrata was measured in city blocks and, in some cases, the interior rooms of individual buildings. Though a few residents fled early on, and some sought rescue alongside migrant workers at the docks, for the majority there was no escaping the war. Local mechanics welded steel plates to pickup trucks, cut off the roofs and sometimes the windshields to allow unobstructed firing, and outfitted them with captured artillery. Engineers made adjustments to prevent the converted vehicles from flipping over when their weapons were fired or from being too unwieldy to drive. Welders fabricated homemade mortars out of steel pipes and operated makeshift weapons repair shops. Electricians climbed transmission towers, under sniper fire, to switch routings after the Gaddafi forces disabled power supplies. Fishermen with experience using explosives to kill fish at sea became munitions experts, rigging booby traps to kill Gaddafi soldiers. Teenagers learned how to drive ambulances. Most of them—the fighters and the hidden fighters—were operating in or near their own neighborhoods and so were on familiar ground. Sometimes their only fortifications were cinder blocks stacked atop desks and office chairs.

Though there had been signs that the siege was coming, no one could have been fully prepared for the resulting onslaught—round-the-clock bombing and sniper fire, with electricity and cell phone service shut off, as food and medical supplies dwindled. Overnight, everyone's lives were transformed. "It became like a dream," said Ahmed Muntasir, the quiet, sleepy-eyed driver who helped shuttle journalists through the city's overlapping war zones. One day people were running errands, checking e-mail, loading trucks and ships at the port, ringing up purchases in stores, listening to the war news on their radio or watching it unfold on TV or the Internet, and the next they were careening through streets they had known all their lives as bombs fell, frantically trying to find their children, their husbands and wives, their mothers and fathers and sisters and brothers and friends, wondering which way the fighting would go, which avenues would be shut off to them, whom they could count on and for what. They quickly found a common purpose, which was to survive. Old debts, disputes, differences of opinion fell by the wayside, alongside the shattered facades of buildings, broken glass, shrapnel, spent bullets, and possessions dropped on the run.

For families trapped in their homes, the potential for a direct mortar hit was the greatest fear. Children couldn't go outside to play because the shelling was almost constant and there was no way to know where the bombs would land. At best, they might play games together in houses or schools that were occupied by numerous families. Looming over the center of Misrata, the city's tallest structure was a nine-story concrete tower known as the insurance building, which became the deadliest among the Gaddafi snipers' nests. Hundreds of government soldiers, many of them trained snipers, picked off rebels, ambulance drivers, even women and children from behind its shattered windows. The tower became a terrible landmark, visible from throughout the city, but snipers were encamped in the upper stories of buildings everywhere, aided by scopes, radios, and night-vision goggles, killing pedestrians and drivers night and day with Kalashnikovs and long-range rifles.

Abdullah Gazal, a forty-seven-year-old writer and mechanical engineer who had been imprisoned and tortured by Gaddafi after publishing a novel about Libya's war with Chad, said the streets were strange and mostly empty during the siege. One neighborhood boy, he said, nine years old, was killed by a sniper shot to the head as he stood in the street waving a rebel flag. Gazal counted 480 missiles in one night, after which his mother, who was eighty-five, asked him to sell her gold bracelets to buy guns and food for the fighters. "A lot of old women did this," he said.

Initially, movement was paralyzed by the snipers, but as patterns began to emerge observers, including Ibrahim Safar, pinpointed their locations and enabled the rebels to fire upon their positions. As he raced through the city, delivering communications or supplies, Safar would floor the accelerator of his white Hyundai when he passed through the snipers' fields of fire. His car was hit twice but never disabled.

Prior to the siege, the army units that had been stationed in Misrata had left abruptly, and Safar met with friends that night, knowing the government forces would return. The consensus was that they needed a local radio channel and to make plans for banding together with citizens in other cities in the coming fight. They also needed to coordinate with doctors and nurses at the remaining hospitals and prepare for the inevitable bloodshed. For the next two weeks Safar, a journalist and a radio host, helped develop the radio program, soliciting feedback from residents, along with donations of time, money, medical supplies, and other needed equipment. The radio station had been set up two decades before by Gaddafi as part of a national network, much like a public radio station but bent on disseminating propaganda. It was a mechanism for controlling people's access to news, Safar said. Now it was being used against Gaddafi.

Two weeks later, the Gaddafi forces returned to the eastern side of Misrata, but they encountered local resistance and left after only a few hours. The battle was a way of testing the rebels, for whom it was likewise an important exercise. Safar, who was there, observed that during combat there is "a lot of noise but the mind is clear. You see things differently. You pay attention, you're very sensitive to things . . . we know the real war is coming very soon." That night, Safar met again with fellow fighters, and with government soldiers who had defected, and told them, "What you did today you can't learn in the academy." They had shown the courage to stand their ground in the face of an overwhelming force, he said. The Gaddafi forces returned two weeks later and dug in at the airport, on the west side of town, which is when the round-the-clock shelling began. When the soldiers entered the city on the main thoroughfares and ring roads, the rebels engaged them from side streets, pushing them toward the city center. Because the rebels still had few guns, they attacked with Molotov cocktails, hunting rifles and pistols, sticks, steel rods, and knives. "After that we understand what we have," Safar said. "At this moment we understood that war is here." Beyond the Gaddafi-held areas, the rebels began setting up checkpoints around the ring roads and along major arteries, fashioning roadblocks from sand berms and lengths of heavy mooring line brought from the port. They also began organizing themselves.

In addition to besieging the city from three sides and mining the port, the Gaddafi forces kidnapped young men, used trapped families as human shields, and put spies in place, including at the al-Hekma hospital, where they logged the names of wounded fighters for use in reprisals against their families. "They'd kidnap young people by promising them weapons, then torture them and make them go on TV saying they'd taken drugs, raped women, that they were linked to al-Qaeda," Safar said. "It was a kind of dirty media," designed to stifle support for the rebels, at home and abroad, he said, and it was one more reason the fighters welcomed the foreign journalists, so the world would know what was really happening. The Gaddafi forces also began busing in people from other cities who supported the army and releasing them into Misrata.

Safar spent the first days of the siege at the radio station, and each night he drove around rebel-held areas in his car, speaking with fighters at the checkpoints, which were the best clearinghouses for gathering and distributing messages. The plan, he said, was evolving. "Another day, another plan, because we don't know," he said. His primary role among the fighters was as a strategist, though his defining moment came later, when he was helping rescue a hostage family and was caught in an ambush during which he was shot seven times.

Safar and his friends initially met on the second floor of a house and surveyed the streets with binoculars, gathering intel. They remained in the house all day, eating stale bread and wishing NATO would start making air strikes against Gaddafi forces, as they had done in and around Benghazi. "It was very sad for us," he said. "All the world watches Benghazi, not Misrata. I feel the world has forgotten Misrata. The people are very scared. The schools are full of people, the hospitals are full of the injured. The first week was very bad. You need lots of courage. Lots of people are paralyzed and can't act." The consensus among the rebels was that they needed to attack the Gaddafi forces along Tripoli Street. They decided to attack quickly and run away, "just to send a message: we are here," Safar said.

Fighters in other locations, without communications—there was no radio or cell phone service at the time—came up with the same basic plan, he said. His group meanwhile began looking for FN rifles. They had one machine gun but it wasn't suitable for sniping, and they didn't have enough money to buy the weapons they needed on the street. "I don't have money to buy a Kalashnikov," he said. "I only had two thousand dinars, and it cost three thousand. And anyway, then I'd have no money at all, and I needed money for batteries and food. There was no one to ask for money. Everyone was in the same situation."

At the time, Gaddafi troops controlled about half of Misrata, but the fighters continued to assail them, and began to entrench themselves at the harbor, where mortars and, later, long-range rockets were taking their toll on the refugees awaiting rescue there. Ships hastily discharged their cargoes of medical supplies, then took on refugees and ICU patients bound for Benghazi, often under rocket fire.

Lack of communication between rebel groups was a big problem, and because Safar's family was trapped in a Gaddafi-occupied zone he eventually set out on his own to check on them. He traveled through the sand dunes toward the Coastal Road, then saw a checkpoint up ahead that he assumed to be manned by Gaddafi soldiers and turned back. He later learned the men at the checkpoint were actually rebel fighters in disguise.

Downtown Misrata was the worst part of the city at the time, but as the siege wore on the most intense fighting moved westward, along the linear battleground of Tripoli Street, which stretched from the city center to the long bridge over the Coastal Road, in the direction of the airport and Tripoli, the capital. The rebels eventually managed to clear the downtown area, as they put it, by isolating the snipers in the high-rises, and in particular the insurance building, also known as the Tamim building. At first they vied with Gaddafi troops block by block so that, had it had been possible to travel down one of the streets in the city center, one would have passed a rebel enclave on one side and a Gaddafi army position on the other; later on the same day the dynamics would have changed. The rebels knew the city better than the Gaddafi troops because most of them had grown up there, and they managed to travel around by dodging sniper fire or knocking "rat holes" in the interior walls of buildings in order to move from one to the next. Over time they succeeded in isolating the snipers in the insurance building through a daring maneuver: cutting off their lines of supply with a system of ingenious roadblocks, a method they later used throughout Misrata. Semi trucks pulling ship containers filled with sand would be driven as close as possible to the street that the rebels wanted to block, parked perpendicular on a smaller, better-protected side street, facing backward, then put in reverse, at which point the driver would bail out, allowing the truck to creep under its own power across the street until it rammed a building on the far side and stopped, at which point a marksman would shoot out its tires. If need be, a second truck and ship container would follow, to complete the blockage. As el-Haddad pointed out, the idea was simple and relied on readily available materials: "We have ship containers, and we have sand." When the Gaddafi troops tried to remove the obstacles with bulldozers, rebel snipers opened fire. "Bulldozers are a piece of cake," el-Haddad said. When the soldiers tried to plow through the barricades with tanks, the rebels disabled them with RPGs. Soon the snipers ran out of ammunition and food and water and either fled or died in the building, which by then was riddled with rebel mortar and machine-gun fire. By mid-April, when Hetherington and his group of photographers arrived, the rebels had hit their stride, though the city was still a lethal battleground and the insurance building was still in snipers' hands. The rebels had transformed downtown Misrata into a maze by blocking off streets with shipping containers, and in areas where tractor-trailers weren't a viable option they had built sand berms with bulldozers armored by local welders with protective steel plates.

Misrata was now at the forefront of the revolution, and the Gaddafi army was determined to stop its westward progress there. Yet in many ways the siege transcended the Libyan war. The people of Misrata had more at stake than the revolution, and more in common with the formerly besieged residents of Sarajevo, Leningrad, and Troy than those of Benghazi or Tripoli. Their lives had been transformed overnight, and the group imperatives that affect soldiers in any war were felt by the entire population. Like it or not, they shared a clarity of purpose that most people live their entire lives without experiencing.

As the Gaddafi troops slowly retreated to the west, they dug in along Tripoli Street, in the vicinity of the original main hospital and the vegetable market (where they hid tanks in a covered concrete warehouse that later took a direct hit from a NATO air strike) and around the former furniture store known as al-Beyt Beytik. They also continued shelling the city from the airport and from towns south of

Misrata, with mortars and, later, Grad rockets, while snipers in the remaining strongholds targeted rebels, civilians, and ambulances. In webcam videos posted by rebels and civilians during the siege, the city looks abandoned, yet cars sporadically emerge from side streets as people seize the moment to flee from one location to another. The vibrations from mortar shell explosions set off car alarms. Now and then the metallic cracking of sniper fire is heard and buildings, sidewalks, and piles of rubble erupt in tiny, deadly puffs of dust. Liohn, one of the first Western photographer to arrive in Misrata, said there were hours when the action was nonstop, and others when it died down, yet it was impossible to predict when a new canto was about to begin.

Once they arrived, the journalists were also hemmed in, working with limited information. Photographer Bryan Denton, a tall Californian who turned twenty-eight while covering the siege, recalled that his fight-or-flight response was soon completely shot, "and I was the closest I've ever been to all-out panic—it took a lot to keep my composure. What compounded the fear most was the realization that many of the things I'd taken for granted while embedded with U.S. troops, like a robust medevac chain, advanced communications, and situational awareness tools, and all the other goodies that I'd grown accustomed to, were absent. Our access was total and completely unfettered, which I think is why most of us braved it through those days . . . The pictures, if you could muster the courage, were amazingly dramatic, but for the most part, and this became a theme throughout the Libyan conflict, we were working in the blind, and basing decisions with very real deadly consequences on very little information, if any at all."

By mid-April the momentum appeared to be shifting to the rebels, though the outcome of the fighting along Tripoli Street was far from certain, and it was still very dangerous to move around because of the snipers. The bombing showed no signs of letting up and NATO air strikes, though crucial to the outcome, were sporadic. "Strangely enough, I sleep well at night," Safar said. "Because our aim is very clear now. I trust myself and my friends." Particularly for younger fighters, there was something seductive about being thrust into conflict alongside their brothers and friends. Despite the fear, they felt a kind of perverse excitement in seeing their familiar neighborhoods transformed into dramatic battlefields, a feeling that many of them would later miss. But there was a high cost to pay. One man observed that more than a year later he was still unable to make himself delete the phone number of his brother who was killed during the siege, and that his mother continued to prepare a portion of the evening meal for him as if he were still alive. She always protested that she had done this without thinking but, he said, if she did not prepare his portion, "She just feels that she betray him, like he was nothing but a guest for a while, and then he left. I feel the same way when I attempt to delete his number."

12
THE FRONT LINE,
APRIL, 2011

If the momentum had shifted in favor of the rebels, the front line along Tripoli Street was growing more intense as the battlefield became more concentrated, centering on the nearby vegetable market and the area around al-Beyt Beytik, not far from the bridge over the Coastal Road. For the photographers encamped at el-Karshini's house, the narrow battlefield presented great photo opportunities, whether their focus was on breaking news or on more intimate portraits of the rebels.

During their first full day in Misrata, the photographers were driven around by a succession of drivers, whoever was available at the time, though finding a ride was sometimes difficult because the rebels, including their media drivers, were seriously overtaxed. Occasionally Reda Muntasir, stepped in to help with the driving duties. In addition to managing the safe house Muntasir, who had been in the marble business before the war and been briefly imprisoned by the Gaddafi government the preceding February, also helped organize arms shipments from Benghazi. His main job was to make sure the journalists had what they needed—food, drivers, translators, contacts, a place to

166

sleep, medical attention, soap, whatever, within the obvious limits. In addition to the food prepared by a chef hired by Muntasir, who stayed in the house, Muntasir's wife brought the journalists meals she had prepared at home. With so many journalists from varied backgrounds, speaking different languages, all with their own agendas, Muntasir was forever revising plans in response to shifts in the fighting or the photographers' interests. It was an inexact system, and the photographers sometimes found themselves scrambling for a ride or waiting in frustration until a driver returned.

Among the other drivers was Mohammed al-Zain, thirty-seven, a hyperkinetic, athletic former truck driver with piercing eyes, a shaved head, and goatee who chain-smoked and would later give up working at the media center to become a fighter on the front lines. Also driving were the famously charismatic Omar Guti, at nineteen the youngest, who also drove an ambulance; Kaleefa bin Soud, a popular, energetic twenty-one-year-old who meanwhile fought on the front lines and stood guard outside the safe house at night; Mohammed el-Naas, forty-four, who also worked as a translator; and Muntasir's nephew Ahmed, who would set off with the photographers on their second day with a CD of old Bee Gees tunes playing on the stereo in his truck—their introduction to the Misrata front was accompanied by "How Deep Is Your Love."

In a house full of photojournalists and rebels, Hetherington thought of himself as being on a slightly different mission. Martin, likewise, did not see himself as a conventional war photographer and shared Hetherington's fascination with the volatile relationship between young men and war. That was what had first attracted him to the Egyptian uprising. Among the photographers, Hetherington was a favorite of al-Zain's. "He's very polite, he smiles, he listens," al-Zain said. "Some of the journalists I don't like. There was a guy for al Jazeera English, he was a fucking bad guy," he said. "He doesn't talk to me. He has an Australian bodyguard. He always wants to stay in a safe area." Then there was "one old woman who was a fucking professional, a professional journalist, a fat white woman. But Tim talk to you, he smile."

Though Hetherington stood out, the fact that he saw himself as being on a slightly different aesthetic mission was largely irrelevant in the context of the siege. Nearly all the photographers had the same aim: to get as close to the action as possible without getting killed.

Like many of the Libyans who worked and lived at the media center el-Naas, who had a doctorate in biochemistry, enjoyed the company of the journalists who stayed there, who came from Argentina, England, France, Germany, Spain and the United States, alongside reporters and cameramen from al Jazeera and the BBC. El-Naas saw Hetherington as the most gregarious and driven among the newly arrived journalists. "He was always saying time is crucial," he said. Hondros, by contrast, tended to be quiet. "He works on his laptop, never speaks unless you ask something," el-Naas said.

El-Naas had come to work at the safe house around the time Hetherington and the others arrived, inspired to join the rebels after seeing a large group of Misrata residents, including several hospital workers, trying to flee the city. He realized that if Misrata was going to hold out against the Gaddafi forces the rebels would need the support of world opinion, and to get it they would need journalists who could publicize what was going on. It was a commonly held view among the media-savvy rebels. As Hetherington and Martin had noticed in Benghazi, the rebels understood PR and had their own TV channel. After the Gaddafi forces cut cell phone and Internet service, they received news by radio and satellite connections from al Jazeera and media outlets in the United States, the UK, Malta, and Italy. The safe house itself was designed like a two-story villa, with a walled courtyard out front. Though it was located in the best-protected part of Misrata, el-Naas noted that "safe" was a relative term. Mortars and missiles aimed by the Gaddafi forces at the port sometimes fell short and exploded in the neighborhood, and one such strike had recently killed two people in a nearby house.

Each day, the photographers visited sites around the city and returned to the media center at around 9 p.m. Those who had assignments, including Hondros and Orlinsky, filed their photos over the satellite uplink, after which everyone had dinner, worked on their laptops or compared photos, then turned in around midnight, though there were always people up, conducting interviews or filing photos and stories across time zones. Initially, Hetherington satisfied himself with making what were essentially war-zone portraits. As time passed, and the action heated up, he would shoot more video. Ahmed Muntasir drove them to the Mtiaz Hotel, where they took pictures from the roof, then close to the infamous vegetable market, a major staging area for the Gaddafi troops. Muntasir said the group seemed comfortable traveling through dangerous zones. "Everyone panics sometimes in a war, but when you see other people around you, you feel safe," he said. "I take them as close to the [Gaddafi] troops as possible so they can capture them with the camera." As he drove, Muntasir also reported the geographic coordinates of the Gaddafi forces back to the rebel command.

Seeing the battlefield of Tripoli Street "shocked all of us," Martin said. At one end of the street were the rebels, at the other the Gaddafi forces. "It was so close," he said. "There was this scene we all photographed, on a corner on Tripoli Street, where the rebels had put a mirror on a piece of wood to see what was going on [around the corner]." Eventually the group decided to move on, but Cervera didn't want to leave, Martin said. "It was about solidarity, safety in numbers, but he didn't seem to be into that," he said. In Cervera's version of the episode that followed, he went around the corner to relieve himself and found that the next street was full of rebels, had met one of them, talked for ten minutes or so, and when he returned found that his group had left. Cervera said he went back to the rebel he'd been talking to, who was a fighter during the day and worked in the hospital at night, and asked if he could take him to a safer zone, where he might find a ride back to the journalists' house. The rebel agreed. Cervera took photos of the rebel as they walked; he was handsome and wore stylish Ray-Bans and occasionally struck poses for him. He asked Cervera to e-mail him the photos. The rebel led Cervera through a series of alleys and side streets, telling him to run when they passed through sniper zones. Cervera photographed graffiti on bullet-pocked walls and other rebels along the way. Around sunset, they encountered a firefight and took a detour that led them to a safer street, where they found Ahmed Muntasir and Mohammed al-Zawwam waiting by the truck; they had come back for him. Muntasir had taken the rest of the photographers to see a rebel snipers' position. "We made pictures of dudes firing through holes," Martin said. "Then we went to the port, where there were hundreds and hundreds of migrant workers in this amazing golden sunlight."

On the way back, Martin said, they noticed a huge plume of smoke in the distance. Al-Zain was driving them then, along what was known as the Heavy Road, which led to the port. Al-Zain recalled hearing a bomb explode, after which they saw "fucking big black smoke, and Tim wanted to go there. I say, 'Gaddafi will send more in two minutes.' He tell me, 'No,' and he wants to go. So we go. He stay only ten meters from a fucking big fire."

Martin described it as "an Armageddon-type scene," with roiling fire beneath a deep blue evening sky. In his view, the problem with being so close wasn't that it was dangerous but that the scene was more impressive from a distance. After photographing the fire, the group returned to the safe house, and Martin contacted Panos, his agency, to see if anyone needed anything. "Tim," he said, "did his thing, looking over our shoulders at our work." They read the news on the Internet and e-mailed a friend of Brown's back in the States to taunt him with exciting news of their day, comparing Misrata to Stalingrad and the Crimea, each sentence more grandiose than the previous one.

The next morning, al-Zain said, he and Hetherington talked about the front lines while making coffee. "All the time he smile, but he don't scare of bullet," al-Zain said. Al-Zain was mindful that the journalists seemed prone to taking risks and felt he had to constantly rein them in. Despite Hetherington's previous assurances to his friends back home, he "always want to get too close to the front line," al-Zain said. Once, when Hetherington urged al-Zain to get closer to the insurance building, "I say no," al-Zain recalled. "He have one answer: 'This is what I come for.'" Al-Zain recalled that he had the same debate with Hetherington "more than ten times," after suggesting they travel safer routes. Occasionally, he said, he had to speed through intersections under sniper fire. "All the time he's writing," he said.

Mahmud el-Haddad, the anesthetist who met them on their first day at the hospital, said everyone was fascinated by the photographers, and grateful for their coverage of the siege, but baffled by their motivations. "I asked a Spanish photographer, 'Why are you here, really, risking your life?'" el-Haddad recalled. "'I am from here, but you choose to come to a very bad place. Every place you go there is conflict. Afghanistan, Tunisia, Egypt, Libya. Do you believe in something?'" He said the Spanish photographer told him, "I like the feeling of adrenaline." Others whom el-Haddad spoke with told him they felt a responsibility to share what was happening with people around the world. He said another photographer told him that war photographers were paid the same as sports photographers. "'How's that?' I asked. 'You're risking your life and he is having fun?' But I have to say, I love these guys," he said. El-Haddad, who learned English by watching subtitled American movies, concluded, "It's like the movie *Fight Club*.

At the beginning, Edward Norton is always suffering from insomnia, so he goes to a shrink. The psychiatrist tells him to talk to people who were really suffering, who have cancer, who are dying. So he attends conferences where people discuss their suffering. 'What is the meaning of life?' you know. I think, in the end, the photographers want to tell everybody else other people's stories."

El-Haddad observed that some journalists came to Misrata to take what they needed and move on, but others felt a responsibility to convey with their work the magnitude of what was happening. He said it's possible to live life surrounded by illusions, but during a war "you see people's true character, what's strong inside. You learn what truly matters." Hetherington had told one interviewer back in the United States that through his work he was trying to explain the world to the world, but el-Haddad said that he, like many of the other photographers, "was maybe also trying to find himself. Maybe it is also about proving that your own life is valuable. You know, everybody at some time thinks, 'I am the most clever guy *in the world*.' It's not a bad thing."

The second day had started frustratingly for the photographers, Martin said. "We missed the first lift, couldn't find Ahmed, who was the only one who spoke good English. Katie had her own thing to do, and Chris was pissed about that. The idea was to stay together. He felt kind of protective of her." They ended up finding a driver who took them to a different hospital, which was much smaller and less modern than al-Hekma. "It was hellish, very chaotic," Martin said. After an hour or so they went back to the safe house and heard about the death of one of the fighters who stayed there, Kaleefa bin Soud. The staff of the media center was hit hard by his death, with everyone in a sort of daze, Martin said.

The people living in the media center were like a family, observed Reda Muntasir. "Kaleefa was the first to be killed from the house. At that time, he was a driver in the morning, and at night he guards the house or goes to the checkpoint with his friends, near the front line." Listening to his uncle talk about bin Soud, Ahmed added, "He was hyperactive." Al-Zain described bin Soud as "like my son." After a pause, he added, "Life is fucking expensive."

As el-Naas later talked about bin Soud, whom he described as the most popular fighter in the house, he began quietly to cry. Regaining his composure, he said, "He was the most energetic person I've seen. For three or four days he sleeps only two or three hours, takes duty at night to guard the house, and during the day he drives the journalists around. Very intelligent." After his death, he said, "Everyone was disoriented. Sad, very, very sad, not focused. I ask Tim, 'Where do you want to go?' He said, 'Your friend is my friend. We're going to go with you to the grave.'" With el-Naas, the photographers set out for bin Soud's funeral but, owing to the hasty burial, missed it. There was another funeral immediately after, which they photographed.

Hetherington, Hondros, and Martin had previously shot another funeral together, in Benghazi. As Martin noted, "Every six hours there was a funeral." At the Benghazi funeral, Hetherington had climbed up on the dais, next to the imam who was leading the ceremony, and motioned for Martin to join him there. "We were perhaps looking for similar things," Martin recalled. "I wasn't on assignment. I could take more time. We could stay in that scene a bit longer. Chris was leaning against a post, ready to go." Hetherington and Hondros had shot that first funeral differently, he said. "It was all these guys, twenty to thirty years old, and Chris had seen it all before."

Now, at what they first thought was bin Soud's funeral, which took place in a cemetery, "the scene itself was incredible," Martin said. "The sounds of huge Grad rockets [exploding] very close, but nobody flinched, they just stayed focused on the funeral. There were a lot of young men, which I often found myself drawn to, like the Russian Cossacks in the Caucasus." There were perhaps one hundred mourners, all male, and the ceremony was officiated by a man who did not seem to be a cleric, who gave "a rather angry sermon, with lots of gesticulating, that lasted fifteen or twenty minutes," Martin said. Afterward, the rebel was buried in a section of the cemetery that was full of fresh graves. Hetherington's photos show men digging new graves with shovels and a young man leaning against a tombstone, crying.

After the funeral, the photographers returned to Tripoli Street. "The light was still good," Martin said, "and we went down the side streets, through rat holes to Tripoli Street. There was one scene where this father and a kid wanted us to photograph them holding up bombs. Chris and I said we're not going to take it. We didn't want to be a part of it. Tim did. Walking back, we saw a doctor who was with an ambulance in a garage who pulled out a packet, supposedly containing cocaine or Viagra, that he said had been pulled off a mercenary. It felt staged, a bit weird." In the rarefied, highly publicized war zone, Martin wondered, "How do you separate fact from fiction?"

Back at the safe house that night, "Chris didn't want to go out, nor Tim," Martin said. But he, Brown, and Cervera did. "Al-Zain was going back to the port," he said. "This time Libyans were trying to flee, and they definitely didn't want their pictures taken. There were probably five hundred men, women, and children, and they pushed through the metal gates and made a crazy run-through—a dash for the boats. We met Katie there. It was an incredible scene. There was a small ferry waiting to take the Bangladeshi and Nigerian workers, and the Libyans were running on. The captain started lifting the bridge and put the boat in drive, and people were jumping into the water. There were suitcases in the water. It was nuts. Then the boat sailed off into the night. When we got back, Tim and Chris were like, 'Where have you been?'"

By now, Hetherington made no pretense of being focused on shooting portraits behind the lines. He was caught up in the group's yearning for action. As the photographers made their rounds, they observed that many of the fighters and private citizens were likewise documenting the siege with video cameras and cell phones. Ahmed Shlak, who had helped create the media center as a way to gain international attention and document the revolution, was among ten rebel photographers, and he said that with so many people with cameras, "I think every minute of this revolution is filmed."

Among the rebel photographers was Abdulkader Fassouk, a slight man of twenty-six who smiled and laughed easily and whose filming earned him a terrific scar running down the middle of his neck, with a corresponding exit wound on the back of his shoulder. Fassouk, who been shot twice in previous episodes, was filming on the front lines when he was hit at close range by a round from a Kalashnikov, the result of friendly fire from a rebel who was trying to get his gun unjammed. Judging from Fassouk's scar, it seemed impossible that he could have survived, and his brother later observed, "It was a kind of magic." Not surprisingly, that episode was also photographed and filmed. Liohn also filmed Fassouk's arrival at the hospital where, later that day, a mortar round killed one of the doctors. At the time, Fassouk was bleeding profusely from his wounds, which his cousin had tried to stanch with his head scarf. Fassouk remained conscious until being sedated but then was in a coma for a week.

Liohn, who stayed at al-Hekma throughout the siege, observed that while Western journalists feverishly sought the most newsworthy photos from the front lines, the people of Misrata, like their counterparts elsewhere in the tumultuous Arab Spring, were "telling their own stories to the world. They went to war with almost as many cameras as weapons, and their mobile phone pics are far stronger than ours. They're free and personal, they correspond to their culture but also go beyond their culture. They documented the war very well from both sides."

Like Hetherington, Martin didn't refer to himself as a photojournalist, didn't see himself as "someone who photographs news, like the *New York Times* in Afghanistan. That's generational, before my time," he said. "I have to be invested in a story, to feel deeply connected to it, not chasing dudes with guns. That's not really my thing." He had come to the Arab Spring by way of Cairo, and although he had an assignment for the *Wall Street Journal* he was more attracted to what he saw as "a story of these young people taking charge. They were people my age, using new technology to spread something, to drive a revolution. That was something I could relate to."

After Egypt, Martin agonized over whether to go to Libya, he said. "I didn't want to go without a flak jacket and helmet. At the time Bahrain was a massive story. Oman. I had to think carefully about what I wanted to achieve . . . Egypt had really moved me. I felt privileged to cover that revolution . . . Then the time came, it was clear NATO would get involved [in Libya], and British intervention was a big deal. So I drove from Cairo to the border, with Ivor and our Egyptian fixer, and on the other side we hooked up with other photographers."

Because Martin had an aim similar to Hetherington's, there are few combat scenes in his archive of Libya photos. "There were so many journalists taking the same pictures," he said. "I studied long-term documentary photography, and photographers who invest years in their work give so much to a story. They don't just go to the front lines. They give a different view. That was really important to me—to give as full a record as possible." By the time he got to Libya, "I was in so far," he said. "I was going to see it through to the end. I never felt I had to prove anything . . . There are other ways to tell stories without a flak jacket."

Still, like Hetherington, he felt the inexorable pull of the front line. On the morning of their third full day in Misrata, the photographers planned to return to the most hotly contested area of Tripoli Street, which was full of snipers and within easy striking distance of the mortars being fired by Gaddafi's troops from near the vegetable market and at the airport. Anchoring what was then the most dangerous block of Tripoli Street was the furniture store, with apartments and offices above, the al-Beyt Beytik, which translates, "My house, your house." The building would dominate their next day.

As the group turned in for the night, Hetherington tweeted, "In besieged Libyan city of Misrata. Indiscriminate shelling by Qaddafi forces. No sign of NATO."

13

IN THE EYE OF THE STORY

In a walled alleyway near al-Beyt Beytik, out of sight of the snipers who occupied the building's upper floors, Hussein Aboturkia and Mahmud el-Haddad waited beside an ambulance. Aboturkia, the driver, was twenty-six, with long, dark hair that he wore in a ponytail and a magnificent black beard that was as thick as fur. Aboturkia had a tendency to brood, and he sometimes unnerved people with his unwavering, dark-eyed stare. He was legendary among Misrata's ambulance drivers, as four of his vehicles had been destroyed by mortar attacks, during two of which he was seriously wounded.

El-Haddad was also twenty-six but, unlike Aboturkia, was very animated, with a voice that rose in sudden crescendo when he became excited. He was outgoing, prone to joking around, and before the war had enjoyed watching American movies and old episodes of *Friends,* reading Charles Dickens, and listening to pop music by Celine Dion and Linkin Park. He had accompanied Aboturkia, as he often did, to treat the injured that day. Both men lived at al-Hekma during the siege. El-Haddad was meanwhile studying for his medical exam, and he typically studied or worked eighteen hours a day. He welcomed the chance to escape the unceasing chaos of the hospital for the different chaos of the war zone and liked to say that he sometimes went to the front lines to relax. "Seriously, on the front line there's some nature, birds and trees, and people talking," he said. "Sometimes there's a bomb but, for example, at one place there was a Ping-Pong table. I played there, on the front line."

Everyone expected bloodshed along the last blocks of Tripoli Street before the bridge over the Coastal Road, which were dominated by a high-rise apartment building and al-Beyt Beytik. There had been a firefight in the area the previous day and night, when the rebels managed to drive the snipers from both buildings, then failed to secure them during the night, enabling the snipers to return. The snipers had not even removed their sleeping bags from the uppermost rooms, through the walls of which they had knocked large, ragged holes to shoot through, or from the rooftop terraces, where mattresses lay amid thousands of spent bullet casings. From their perches the snipers could pick off anyone who dared to emerge onto Tripoli Street, or who passed within range along side streets or on the four-lane bypass known as the Coastal Road. They had been doing this for forty days.

Aboturkia's nearest brush with death—his own, at least—had come when he was transporting a wounded rebel near the Tripoli Street front line. A mortar exploded near the rear of his ambulance, blowing out its windows and tires, lacerating his right leg, and perforating the bulletproof vest loaned to him by Liohn, who was working on a video project for the International Red Cross about medical care during the siege. Liohn had been concerned about Aboturkia venturing into dangerous zones without protective gear in a clearly marked ambulance, and rightly so. That day, Aboturkia was riding with another doctor when they heard heavy gunfire ahead. The doctor protested that he had no intention of going farther and demanded that Aboturkia stop. He got out of the ambulance and Aboturkia, hearing the gunfire and

179

knowing there would be injured people there, continued on and came upon a rebel who was badly wounded in both legs. He got out of the ambulance, hurriedly removed the gurney through the rear doors, and managed to get the man onto it, then manhandled both back inside. As he began to drive away the bomb went off beside the ambulance and, glancing down, he saw that his own right leg was bleeding badly, so he quickly made a tourniquet with his scarf and tied it around his leg. The wounded rebel in the back was also further injured by the bomb blast, and because the ambulance would not move Aboturkia had no choice but to get out. He pulled the gurney out of the back doors, hefted the man over his shoulder, and hobbled as fast as he could toward cover. Because of his own injuries he didn't make it very far before he had to put the injured rebel down.

The man, who could not walk, began dragging himself forward with his arms, in the middle of the road, presenting a perfect target for sniper fire. Aboturkia limped ahead and took refuge in a doorway. As he waited there, the wounded fighter shouted that he could crawl no farther and stopped in the middle of the open road. Aboturkia told him he would try to get help and hurried, as best he could, back to the intersection where the doctor had abandoned the ambulance and where he had seen what was referred to as a Chinese car, one of a fleet of white pickup trucks that the rebels had commandeered from the port, all of which they had spray-painted black to make them less visible at night. The Chinese car was parked by the door to a house, so Aboturkia banged on the door. When a man answered Aboturkia told him he needed help rescuing the injured rebel. There was already an injured fighter in the house so the four of them—Aboturkia, the doctor, the man who had answered the door, and the second injured fighter—piled into the Chinese car, drove back to the rebel who was still lying in the road, alive, loaded him up, and raced to al-Hekma. The rebel in the road survived; Aboturkia would never hear what happened to the other one.

Back at the hospital, after being treated for his leg wound, Aboturkia found shrapnel in Liohn's vest and realized it had protected him from a potentially fatal chest wound. In a subsequent episode, the vest was again riddled with shrapnel; Liohn told him to keep it. In the second attack, Aboturkia suffered only some cuts on his fingers. In Liohn's view, Aboturkia was one of the two most important ambulance drivers, the other being the teenaged Omar Guti, who was famously nervous, yet brave, and would later give up ambulance driving after his vehicle was destroyed in a mortar attack.

Aboturkia had been a truck driver before the war and decided to drive ambulances after seeing that no one else wanted to do it. "It's disappointing to see injured fighters brought in by truck or Chinese car," he later observed. In the beginning, because there were few weapons to be had, he saw driving an ambulance as a more important mission than ferrying supplies. It was also extremely dangerous, because the Gaddafi soldiers targeted ambulances and their drivers, who went to the front unarmed. Soon, all the fighters on the front lines knew Aboturkia, which was important; an ambulance driver who wasn't recognized could be shot as a suspected pro-Gaddafi soldier, because the government soldiers sometimes disguised themselves that way. Once Aboturkia began driving, el-Haddad decided to accompany him. In the beginning there were only five ambulances, but others began to arrive by boat from Benghazi until there were more than twenty. Aboturkia's first emergency vehicle was a regular car but it was destroyed almost immediately, during the initial, short-lived invasion of Misrata, prior to the siege.

Aboturkia didn't normally spend a lot of time waiting with the ambulance. There were many fronts during the siege, which required him to stay on the move. He would listen to the radio to determine where the most intense fighting was and then go there. Because he'd been the first ambulance driver, he was identified as No. 1 in the radio dispatches. His second serious injury came when the ambulance was targeted by a sniper. He was in a convoy of vehicles outfitted with machine guns and had two doctors with him. When they reached their destination, some of the fighters went inside a house to check for Gaddafi soldiers, to see if it was safe for Aboturkia to park beside it. Soon heavy firing commenced and the operator of one of the machine guns was shot in the leg by a sniper. As they loaded him into the ambulance, Aboturkia was also shot, in the leg that was still healing from the mortar explosion that had destroyed his ambulance three weeks earlier. This time, he attempted to drag himself into the ambulance, and when he had his hand on the handle of the driver's door a sniper's bullet shattered the windshield. The bullet passed through the headrest of the driver's seat and hit the injured gunner in back in his other leg. "I was so scared," Aboturkia said. "It was so precise." If he had been in the driver's seat he would have been shot in the head.

The injured rebel, now shot in both legs, began to scream, "Get me out of here!" Aboturkia glanced at the doctors, who had taken cover and waited in silence. Aboturkia saw a fighter manning a cannon, a man he had previously saved "like, six times," he said, so he shouted for help. The cannoneer left his gun and climbed into the driver's seat. When he saw the shattered windshield, he asked Aboturkia, "When did this happen?" Aboturkia, who had managed to get into the passenger seat, replied, "Just now." The fighters provided covering fire to get the ambulance out, and the cannoneer drove them to al-Hekma; the cannoneer was later killed. Two of Aboturkia's fellow ambulance drivers were also killed during the fighting, as well as a teenage boy who rode with the drivers and helped with the injured.

Liohn was initially so frightened by the intensity of the fighting that he didn't leave al-Hekma during his first week in Misrata. At one point, the Gaddafi forces had come within one hundred yards of the hospital, along a parallel street. Liohn observed that it was not unusual to meet people in the morning who returned to the hospital, dead, in the afternoon. "I was afraid," he said. "I say, I'm not going out." He eventually found himself drawn to the drama of the ambulances and began riding with Aboturkia, at first to photograph people who were being used by Gaddafi troops as human shields, positioned in the line of fire to prevent NATO air strikes that would result in civilian casualties. After that, he began riding in an ambulance with Guti, who had taken up driving because he was afraid to fight, not realizing that driving an ambulance was even more dangerous. There was a certain stigma attached to not fighting, and the rebels had told Guti, "Okay, you don't want to fight? Here, we have an ambulance. You can drive it."

To everyone's surprise, Guti "became the man for the hard job," Liohn said. So when he wasn't covering the influx of wounded people to al-Hekma, Liohn began alternating between riding with Guti and riding with Aboturkia. His most frightening moment during the siege came one night while he was driving with Aboturkia. "The Gaddafi soldiers were shooting tracers," he said, in an effort to attract reinforcments, "so you could see the bullets." Aboturkia had to cross a wide, open street and intently watched the tracers to look for an opening. The tracers were like a storm of miniature meteors, any one of which could have killed them. "We were driving without the lights," Liohn said. "I was so afraid." But they had made it across.

Then, on the morning of April 20, Aboturkia and el-Haddad drove to Tripoli Street. Liohn was already there, having spent the night in an ambulance with Guti in a garage not far from an apartment building occupied by Gaddafi troops. A firefight at the building the day before had lasted until around midnight, then resumed around four in the morning. The rebels were trying to push the Gaddafi troops westward, toward the Coastal Road, and Liohn and Guti had not slept much. Guti, characteristically, was very nervous, and everyone was trying to calm him down, Liohn said.

183

Given that all of Misrata was a battlefield, the myriad dangers faced by the ambulance drivers were, in fact, relative. Liohn had met one driver who took his young child with him on his ambulance runs, even to the front lines, which initially struck Liohn as insane. But as the journalist Chris Chivers pointed out, people were in danger of dying even if they stayed in their homes, and by bringing his child with him to the front the man at least would be able to know what was happening to him. Rebels at checkpoints also sometimes took their children, even toddlers, with them to their posts.

The ambulance provided a unique perspective on the war, Liohn said. Because it provided a main line to the action, wherever it was, it afforded a photographer a rare vantage point, both on the war and on emergency medical services. It also led to a discovery, after el-Haddad, riding with one of the ambulance drivers, noticed a different kind of shrapnel lying on the ground. El-Haddad often inspected bomb debris, out of curiosity, and in this case he noticed pieces that were of a different shape, with unfamiliar markings. When he got back to the hospital he described what he had seen to Liohn, who suspected he had discovered the remnants of a cluster bomb, a weapon that had been outlawed in various international treaties. Liohn then called a representative of Human Rights Watch and put el-Haddad on the phone to tell him what he had seen. After confirming that what el-Haddad had seen was a cluster bomb, Liohn caught a lift in an ambulance to meet a Human Rights Watch investigator who arrived by boat, and their investigation concluded that the Gaddafi troops were using cluster bombs manufactured in Spain. Soon after cluster bombs had been banned, the Spanish government had sold them to Libya rather than destroy them, and Misrata represented the first known incidence of their use against civilians trapped inside a city.

Both Liohn and el-Haddad stayed in the hospital compound, which was powered by a generator after the Gaddafi forces cut electricity to Misrata. Liohn had gone straight to al-Hekma after arriving at the port, and on his first night he had slept on the floor of the hospital's basement, before being assigned an apartment in a building on the grounds. One day he was playing in a grassy area nearby with three children who also lived there, which made him think about his own kids. He heard gunfire and bombs nearby, yet the children were calm, so he remained calm. It was a moment of respite from the war. "And then, these kids were playing a little bit outside the house in the compound, and a minute later, I enter in the house, a mortar land and kill the kids, and I too could have been killed," he said. He felt guilty for not encouraging the children to go inside. One of the girls had survived for a while but died inside the hospital. The deaths of the three children rattled him.

El-Haddad said that for the length of the siege the staff typically worked eighteen-hour shifts with little or no food, then slept two or three hours before returning to work. Sometimes the doctors chose not to use anesthetics because they were in short supply, though they never ran out. Neither did the hospital experience blood shortages, despite the constant need for transfusions. All that was necessary, when supplies got low, was to spread the word and people would line up to donate.

There was no protection from the fighting for the hospital staff, as the ambulance drivers' deaths illustrated. One of the staff physicians, a native Libyan anesthesiologist named Aly Aldarat, who had left his wife and two children in Germany to travel to Misrata, where he was put in charge of resuscitation at al-Hekma, was driving to a front-line field hospital when he was captured, imprisoned, and executed by Gaddafi troops. Other doctors had been mortally injured at the front lines because they stayed too long. Then there were the perennial patients, living on borrowed time, such as the young man who had lost his brother and father to the war and who kept returning to al-Hekma, injured, and each time returned to the front line, until he, too, was killed.

Liohn often shot video of the al-Hekma staff receiving the wounded in the triage tent, taking pains to stay out of their way, and interviewing them when things were relatively quiet. But his best video was shot when he accompanied ambulances to the front. In one, shot during a firefight, he follows a group of rebels attempting to save a mortally injured comrade who called for help after being hit during an assault of cornered loyalist forces, who were attempting to escape from their holdout at Misrata Central Hospital. Liohn's terrifying footage begins as he crouches within a brushy area, with bullets flying all around, then shows the rebels preparing to fire a truck-mounted M40 gun into a walled compound where a group of Gaddafi soldiers are holed up. When the M40 fires, the round explodes against the compound wall, sending shrapnel and other debris back toward the rebels themselves, who are too close.

As Chivers, who later posted Liohn's video on the *New York Times* website, observed, the M40, an American-made weapon that was by then largely out of service around the world, was among the heavy weapons the rebels had captured from former Gaddafi arsenals, and one they were not adequately trained to use. The explosion sent a violent shock wave, laden with shrapnel, in the rebels' direction, some of which hit the man Liohn filmed, who was now lying on the ground with one hand aloft as he called for help. The man, whose name, Liohn later learned, was Hamid Shwaili, was hit by shrapnel in his femoral artery, and began bleeding out. At that point, rebels at a nearby building fired machine guns into the compound as Shwaili's friends, with Liohn filming close behind, dragged him into an alley, to what appears to have been a small garage, where doctors—including el-Haddad—tried to administer immediate aid. El-Haddad, dressed in his blue hospital scrubs, appears in the video to be the one most aware of what needs to be done, and after checking Shwaili's vital signs and attempting to stanch the bleeding he helps load him into an ambulance. Shwaili died soon after.

During the course of his filming, within the garage itself, Liohn was grazed by a bullet in the back of his neck, which knocked him to the ground, causing his footage to reel. As Chivers wrote, "you see Mr. Liohn's feet and then, about five seconds later, hear him growl in pain. And he growled again later, too, trying to keep his bearing and composure as he worked. He kept shooting throughout." Afterward, Liohn tracked down Shwaili's family and friends to find out who he was. He had been an unemployed mechanic, caught up in the fight to defend the formerly quiet streets of his home. Five rebels were killed in the assault, but the Gaddafi forces were eventually routed.

This was the world that Aboturkia, el-Haddad, and Guti inhabited for three months, from March to May of 2011. On the morning of April 20, as they waited in the alleyway off Tripoli Street, no one had any idea what would come next but there was no doubt that people would be injured, and that some of them would die.

14

TRIPOLI STREET

"We could not get our shit together in the morning," Guy Martin recalled of April 20, 2011. "We got up early, then sat on our asses waiting for someone to give us a lift. Katie was off doing her own thing. Then this Che Guevara–looking guy—tall, good-looking, well built, very tanned, wearing a red beret—showed up and told us they'd freed Tripoli Street during the night."

The photographers, who had not previously met the man, were skeptical of his claim because they had been on Tripoli Street the evening before and the area was still hotly contested. But they needed a ride, so Martin, Brown, Cervera, Hetherington, and Hondros piled into his truck and he drove them to the front line. Once there, he stopped in the middle of Tripoli Street, at the spot where the rebels had looked around the corner with a mirror the previous day, and told the group to get out. It was around 9:30 a.m. "The rebels are firing into a building with flames coming out of it," Martin said. "There's a guy on his knees firing into the basement. Bullets are flying. You can hear the whistle of incoming rounds. My whole thought is it's so exposed. We ran toward the first building, and halfway down Tripoli Street a guy gets down on his hands and knees, right between my knees, and fires into this burning building."

Shooting photos as they moved forward, toward the source of the action, the photographers were amazed by what they saw. "It was apocalyptic," Martin recalled. "Rebels in the street, smoke filling the sky." The fighters had brought in two semis attached to shipping containers to block Tripoli Street and consolidate the ground they'd taken, and diggers were filling the containers with sand. "I thought, My God, the enemy are pretty close," Martin said. "I'm standing next to Tim and I see a guy on the brow of a hill, on his hands and knees, crawling away. There was no way to know, was it a rebel or a Gaddafi dude?"

Cervera had been elated when the rebel offered to take them to Tripoli Street, excited that he was finally "going to see the real thing." Now, seeing the real thing meant being uncomfortably exposed as the rebels fired endless rounds, as well as RPGs, into a burning building, with Gaddafi snipers inside. "It was a kind of crazy situation," Cervera said.

The previous night, NATO forces had bombed nearby Gaddafi strongholds, enabling the rebels to push forward along Tripoli Street, in hopes of routing the remaining snipers. When Cervera and Brown entered one of the burning buildings, after it had been secured by the rebels, they found four or five dead Gaddafi snipers on the rooftop terrace, "and the rebels were very happy, showing off to the camera with the gun, like, 'We killed them,' or whatever," Cervera said.

At that point, Cervera and Brown were ahead of the other photographers, who did not see them enter the smoldering building. In the heat of the action, they were beginning to lose track of one another. While Cervera and Brown were inside the building the rest of the group passed, and when they came out mortars began to fall. They ran forward to catch up with the others. The action was feverish and confusing. Later accounts of the battle would often conflict—sometimes wildly so—as a result of the confusion and the inevitable desire of some of the witnesses to adapt their recollections to the perceptions of others or in the interest of their own portrayal. There is particular disagreement over what happened next, which was a sort of play within a play—a fight between two photographers, Cervera and Liohn.

Liohn and Guti had spent the night in the garage behind the contested apartment building. After the night battle over the building, and the surprise return of the snipers in the early morning hours, the action had again become centered there. By now the rebels had gained significant ground, claiming the street as far as al-Beyt Beytik, though the contested apartment building—partially burned—still contained Gaddafi snipers, as did al-Beyt Beytik.

Liohn was behind a wall, near the burned building, where he had taken shelter alongside Guti. Initially, he said, he was glad to see the other photographers arrive. He recalled meeting Martin in Cairo during the Egyptian uprising. But when he saw Cervera walking near the corner of the burned building, at a spot where a rebel had been shot and killed only an hour before, Liohn shouted at him to move away. In Liohn's version of the story, he was trying to warn Cervera of the danger; in Cervera's version, Liohn was miffed that he had intruded into his frame and was demanding that he move out of the way. In response, Cervera strode toward Liohn and confronted him.

"He came walking and putted his nose in my nose, telling me never to tell him what to do again, and I told him to fuck himself hard and I knocked his nose with my head," Liohn said. "I'm not a pacifist," he added, "and after months controlling my anger, he was the perfect chance to put all out."

In Martin's account of the fight, he was standing beside Hondros when, "inexplicably, with bullets coming from the building, and from other directions, André makes a beeline for Guillermo and gets into a scrap with him."

Martin had encountered Liohn in eastern Libya, when he saw him arguing with a hotel clerk about his bill, pounding his fist on the desk and cursing the man, at which point Martin decided he was someone to avoid. Now, seeing Liohn head-butt Cervera, Martin stepped in to separate them. He pushed Liohn back, saying, "'Chill out.' I'm a surfer," he later said, "and I tried to give him some *brah*." Liohn later conceded that he was annoyed that the other photographers had been in Misrata for only a few days yet were behaving "like they were experts." Cervera's counterpoint was that Liohn was angry that the group had intruded into the domain he had previously had to himself and went after him because he was the smallest and weakest in the group. This much was clear: the tension of the moment was making its way down to a very personal level.

After the altercation, the photographers ran the remaining gauntlet of Tripoli Street and arrived at al-Beyt Beytik, a three-story concrete building, beyond which stood the bridge over the Coastal Road and the uncontested domain of the Gaddafi forces. Al-Beyt Beytik still contained an unknown number of snipers, and as the photographers approached they saw rebels firing into the building. Then, they heard the rebel commander Salah Hadin Badi, who was standing nearby, talking about preparing to undertake a rescue of a family that had been trapped in their nearby home for two months. The Gaddafi soldiers had been forcing the family to work and cook for them, and Badi wanted to take advantage of the rebels' newly held position to rescue them. Hearing about what promised to be a great photo op, all of the photographers wanted to go. Liohn made arrangements to ride to the rescue site with Guti, while the other photographers hurried across Tripoli Street on foot, accompanying a group of rebels down side streets to the hostage family's house. Once they arrived on the hostage family's street, Liohn realized the Gaddafi troops were "very, very close. They were in a parallel street, on the other side of the houses, because there was the road between the city and the airport, and they were there, at that road."

Hetherington filmed as Badi, the rebel commander, attempted to coerce the family to go with them. The family was terrified and initially refused to leave. The Gaddafi troops had begun lobbing mortars into the neighborhood, which were exploding nearby, and the mother in particular was paralyzed by fear. In an inspired move, Badi picked up the youngest child and carried her to a waiting vehicle, which prompted the other family members to follow. Liohn got into the ambulance with Guti and they sped away.

Martin watched the ambulance disappear, then realized, "Suddenly, there's nobody around me. I heard a huge explosion, maybe fifty meters away, and I start running for all I'm worth. I didn't know where anyone was. I ran for my life. There was one explosion after another, and one guy fired so close to my right ear I was deafened. I ran and ran and ran. Then a truck pulls up, stops on my left side, someone says, 'You might want to get into this truck.' I launched myself into the truck. I had my head in someone's crotch, with my legs sticking out [the door]." The people in the backseat of the truck were Hetherington and Hondros. Badi was behind the wheel. By the time they reached Tripoli Street the firing had stopped. Badi let the photographers out near the foot of the bridge over the Coastal Road, and they walked back to al-Beyt Beytik, which had now become "the focal point" of the fighting, Martin said. After the shooting they had earlier observed, into and out of al-Beyt Beytik, "We couldn't figure out how anyone was still in there, but that's when the battle for that building started."

The ambulance carrying Liohn and the rescued family, which Guti was driving, had passed the bridge under fire and barely missed being hit by an RPG. Once they made it to al-Hekma, Aboturkia was told over the radio that an ambulance would be needed at al-Beyt Beytik, because the rebels were about to enter the building, so he, Liohn, and el-Haddad headed back there. The other photographers were already there, along with a Spanish radio reporter and her Libyan fixer, hiding from the shooting. Liohn recalled seeing numerous dead bodies of Gaddafi soldiers in the street. Ahmed Shlak, the rebel photographer and videographer, was filming from the opposite side of Tripoli Street.

The final assault on al-Beyt Beytik was "very disorganized," Cervera said, and took place both inside and outside the building. It appeared that four or five Gaddafi snipers were holed up in various rooms and they were beyond desperate—they were trapped and knew they were going to be killed. The rebels entered the first floor of the building, with Cervera, Martin, Hetherington, Hondros, Brown, and Liohn behind. Only Martin and Hondros wore flak jackets and helmets. As they crept from room to room and ascended the shadowy stairwell, they heard occasional gunfire, not sure if it was coming from rebels or Gaddafi snipers. There was no way to know who or what they might encounter around each corner. The rebels were using a piece of mirror to peer around the corners, after which they would fire into the rooms. As Hetherington filmed, Cervera mentioned how amazing it was to be there, and Hetherington agreed. Having unfettered access to the absolute front line of battle was definitely "not normal," Hetherington later said. Liohn went a step further in his assessment. He was shocked, he said, that the photographers seemed intent in getting not only as close as possible to the action, but in some cases out in front of the rebels. Almost immediately after they entered the building, one of the rebels nearby was shot in the head and fell. Cervera and Hetherington helped carry his body out of the building, and at that moment, Cervera said, he recognized the magnitude of the danger and realized from the look on Hetherington's face that he did too. Why it took them so long to reach that conclusion no doubt had something to do with adrenaline, but afterward Hetherington, in particular, seemed acutely aware of his surroundings, Cervera said.

As the fight progressed, Hetherington rarely used his antiquated still camera, relying almost exclusively on his video Flip cam, with which he managed to get a few stunning portraits of rebels, including one of a chiseled, bearded guy, framed by a ragged bomb blast in an interior wall, holding his gun and listening intently to the fighting in the adjacent rooms. Hetherington's video portrait of the man begins almost as a still photograph—the rebel waits, listening; then his face turns and he glances nervously at Hetherington.

In the stairwell the rebels prepared to set fire to car tires that they would then roll down into a side room to try and smoke the snipers out. When they set the first tire on fire and rolled it in, the flames went out, so they lit another with gasoline. In Hetherington's video we see perhaps a dozen people crowded tightly into the stairwell, some shooting guns into the side room, some filming with iPhones, some just looking on. At one point Hetherington turns the camera toward Martin, who grins. They seem to be enjoying themselves. Hondros alone looks worried. Martin would later say that he has a tendency to smile as a kind of defense mechanism, that on the inside he was "deeply, deeply scared. And every fiber was telling me to not be there." Still, he said, he kept telling himself that he was doing his job as an independent observer, that it was important to be there, and despite his fear "there was truly nowhere else on the planet I would rather have been."

Liohn, on the other hand, realized that the building was full of ammunition, which would explode during a fire, so he hurried down the stairs and was surprised that Cervera, Hetherington, Hondros, and Martin remained behind, shooting video and photographing. Eventually Hetherington and Martin ended up in another side room, in what appeared to be an office, which aside from the broken glass on the floor was strangely untouched by the fighting. A computer sat undisturbed on a desk, and in one corner was a perfectly positioned arrangement of fake flowers in a vase atop a pedestal. Both Hetherington and Martin noticed the flowers and photographed them. "Then someone throws a grenade down the stairs. I don't know if it was the rebels or Gaddafi guys, but there was the distinct sound of a grenade dropping down the stairs, *bap-bap-bap,*" Martin said. "When he hears the grenade sound, Tim turns around and throws himself on top of me, and we fall into the glass."

Martin did not remember hearing the grenade go off. At that point, he said, there was so much going on, and his face was pressed against a pile of files and broken glass on the floor, with Hetherington on top of him. When they got up, they noticed the rebels were rolling burning tires down the stairs and the fire had begun to spread, and Martin thought, "Are you kidding me? I don't want to be trapped in a burning building. So I made my way down the stairwell. Tim and Chris were still up there."

Soon everyone who remained on the upper floors found their exit routes blocked by the flames. In Hetherington's video, we hear him call Cervera's name, after which his footage runs wild, unfocused, through the smoke-filled rooms. Cervera leaped down the stairs, taking several at a time as the flames spread around him. Hondros was the last to make his way down the burning stairway. "I have this amazing image of Chris jumping headfirst through the flames," Martin said. "He did this perfect roll, then stood up, adjusted his helmet, and walked on." Liohn, waiting at the foot of the stairs, also photographed Hondros "falling in the fire," as he put it.

With the stairs now fully engulfed in flames the upper rooms began filling with smoke, and the surviving snipers—now also trapped— continued to shoot blindly through the building. In his video we hear Hetherington say, "We can get out this way?" and his footage veers through the rooms, alighting on a large hole in the wall from a bomb blast that rebels are exiting through. At that point Hetherington stopped filming and followed, escaping the third floor through the hole, descending on a rickety wooden ladder along with a group of rebels.

After descending the ladder, Hetherington shot video of rebels coming down, including the Che Guevara–looking guy in the red beret, then watched as the rebels fired RPGs into the building. As Martin photographed a rebel who was firing his gun into al-Beyt Beytik, seemingly at random, he laughed to see, on his camera's screen, that in one of his photos Cervera's iPhone and his hand had intruded into the frame. He then noticed the ambulance, with Aboturkia and el-Haddad inside.

Soon after, Martin said, he saw Liohn shouting at Cervera from a short distance. "André's suddenly very mad, making these erratic kicks," he said. "He's completely and utterly possessed by Guillermo, about Guillermo using an iPhone. You know, 'Fucking shit, getting in my shot.'"

El-Haddad saw perhaps fifty rebels in front of al-Beyt Beytik, the most he had ever observed in one place during the siege, along with six or seven photographers. As he and Aboturkia waited for what would happen next, he was surprised to see it arise from an unexpected source: Liohn and Cervera. After getting out of the ambulance, el-Haddad stood beside an abandoned car wash, just east of al-Beyt Beytik, and saw Liohn and Cervera on the edge of Tripoli Street, arguing. As he watched, Liohn kicked Cervera in the butt, causing him to drop his iPhone, which skittered across the pavement.

Martin again intervened, as did Brown and el-Haddad, and the two managed to pull Liohn and Cervera apart. Martin noticed Hetherington eyeing the minidrama from a distance, declining to get involved. After Liohn stalked across the street Badi, the commander, showed up, furious. "Salah point at André and said this man should go," el-Haddad recalled. "I said, 'No, you should inquire first. Consider what you think versus what you know.' André had told me this guy wasn't professional, just taking photo with iPhone for his Facebook page, for his self-interest. But Salah was so angry. Maybe he thought he was the commander and everyone should respect him and consult with him."

Liohn later said that Cervera, after the earlier head-butt, had been deliberately trying to sabotage his pictures by moving into the frame. No one was interested in hearing his explanation now, but in the end Badi allowed Liohn to stay. By then the shooting into the building had temporarily died down.

For a while everyone milled around, the photographers searching for new scenes to photograph. El-Haddad, Aboturkia, and Liohn spent some time poking through an abandoned Gaddafi supply truck, which contained uniforms and bulletproof vests, alongside some of the fighters. Hetherington, Martin, Hondros, and Brown crossed to the other side of Tripoli Street, into an open area, and as they lingered there a group of rebels offered them a "picnic lunch" of dates and milk, as Martin would describe it. Soon after, incoming sniper fire began hitting the ground around them. "Chris and I were in the open area having our picnic at the time," Martin said. "I saw Tim sprint across the grassy area to take cover." Hetherington and Martin hid behind a cinder-block wall, Brown got behind a tractor, and Hondros hid behind a tree. The firing went on for only a few minutes, though it "seemed like an eternity," Martin said. During a momentary lull, they decided to run back across Tripoli Street to the cover of the buildings there. "Chris tapped me on the soldier and said, 'Ready to run?' and we ran to a garage," Martin said.

For the next twenty minutes or so the rebels tried to suppress sniper fire from al-Beyt Beytik by shooting into the building. "Different guys would take cover in the garage and step out [to fire]," Martin said. Then they saw a pickup truck speeding backward along Tripoli Street with a heavy artillery piece mounted in back, which stopped across the street from the building. Among the rebels gathered around al-Beyt Beytik, many continued to fire into the building, though others were, as Martin put it, "sitting on their hands in the doorway."

The rebel Majdi Lusta later said two surviving snipers had been discovered by a group of three rebels who had been scouting the dark, sooty rooms and that one of the rebels had been killed.

Cervera watched a group of rebels diagram the floor plan of the building on an exterior wall, after which they began firing RPGs and automatic weapons inside. "They had told the snipers to give up but they didn't," Lusta later said. "So they smoked them out, then killed them with a 160mm cannon." Liohn felt a wave of disgust as he watched Cervera and Brown photographing the scene on their iPhones. "Who is going to take this picture seriously?" he wondered.

To Martin, it seemed impossible that any of the snipers could have survived the previous assaults on the building, and certainly not after the rebel in the back of the truck began unloading rounds into the interior rooms. Once the quiet returned, the rebels—and the photographers too—reentered the ground floor of al-Beyt Beytik. "I remember there was one fighter who was sitting on the stairs, and he was exhausted," el-Haddad recalled. "One of the journalists took a photo of him and then calls his friends over to do the same. The fighter goes along with it, blowing his breath out in frustration."

Hetherington and Liohn made their way to the rooftop terrace, where some of the snipers had been camped. A mattress lay on the floor, along with thousands of spent bullet casings, discarded boots and vests, and human feces and chicken bones. They looked out over a panorama of the city, which appeared strategically impossible to defend, just a sandy plain on the edge of the Mediterranean. Then they saw Gaddafi troops beyond the bridge and realized that the troops could also see them. "Fuck," Liohn said, as he and Hetherington ducked and retreated to the interior of the building.

It was only later that Martin understood how reckless the photographers had been. "I recognized something in myself," he said. "It was like a changing character of me that I didn't like, almost liking the gung ho, fatalistic world of the rebels, although every fiber of my body was telling me it was the most ridiculous thing I could be doing. I felt safe because Tim and Chris were there, but by the time we had got back and I began to process what we'd done that morning, once the bravado and testosterone began to filter out—it was like after surfing big waves in Indonesia, I was trembling with fear. It was a similar physical reaction. I was shaking with fear."

When the other photographers reentered al-Beyt Beytik Martin had remained behind. "I didn't see the others for twenty or thirty minutes, when Michael and Guillermo surfaced," he said. "I never went back into that building."

By now, Liohn had decided it was time to go. As he put it, "Then another person dies, like, shot inside, so okay, it's too dangerous to be here. We should leave. We should leave."

For most people it doubtless would have seemed too dangerous long before then. But these were war photographers, accustomed to taking risks; Liohn had taken his share, including when he ran under machine-gun fire to film the rebels attempting to rescue their friend during the central hospital assault. But Liohn could also be extremely cautious when he felt it was warranted. He had observed that the Gaddafi forces tended to launch new mortar attacks in the early afternoon, in retaliation for whatever assaults the rebels had made in the morning, and then would do so again in the late afternoon. Based on his observations on the front lines and at al-Hekma, where he saw the arrival of the injured, the afternoon assaults resulted in the majority of each day's casualties, which at the time averaged fifteen killed and twenty to forty injured. Experience now told him it was time to leave Tripoli Street. Before leaving Liohn warned Martin, who was sitting on a ledge at the front of al-Beyt Beytik, but after his problem with Cervera "everybody was a bit mad with me," Liohn said, "and I remember Guy saying, 'We have been here all the morning. There's no problem.' I said, 'Okay, you know. Fair enough.' I don't try to convince him. I just leave." He headed back to al-Hekma with Aboturkia and el-Haddad in the ambulance.

El-Haddad said he also expected things would get bad at al-Beyt Beytik later in the afternoon. It made no sense that the Gaddafi troops had not retaliated after the morning's setback, nor after the second assault on the building by the rebels. "So quiet," he said of the aftermath of the assault. "Too quiet. It's the front line. It's strange."

As for why the group didn't heed Liohn's warning, Martin later confirmed what Liohn suspected. "He'd made such an embarrassment and an ass of himself that day, I didn't want to listen to anything he had to say," Martin said. "We were making group decisions that so far had gotten us through. Fuck, I wasn't going to start listening to André. The situation called for the coolest of heads." As it turned out, the photographers also packed up and headed for the safe house not long after the ambulance left, but they made plans to return later in the afternoon. Hetherington was almost out of film and needed to charge his video camera, Hondros was eager to file his photos for Getty Images, everyone was hungry, and Martin was drenched with sweat and wanted to change clothes.

Before leaving, they snapped photos of each other standing beside the abandoned Gaddafi supply truck, then climbed into the back of a rebel vehicle. In the photos, everyone looks cool and happy. Hetherington wears his shades and the plaid scarf he had bought in Benghazi. As Badi drove them to the safe house, the photographers talked excitedly about what had happened that morning, and were flabbergasted by what they had observed, Martin said. "We all felt lucky to have come out of that unscraped. Those guys, as much as they'd been through, they'd never seen anything like it."

After returning to al-Hekma, Liohn filed some of his photos on his Facebook page, feeling a bit demoralized by his experience that morning. He felt bad, and "stupid," he said. "I felt like, 'My God,'—you know? 'Mad—this is mad.'" He phoned Peter Bouckaert at Human Rights Watch, unaware that he was a friend of Hetherington and Brown, and told him he was preparing to leave Misrata "because I don't want to fight for a space with these people."

Once the photographers arrived at the media center, Hondros uploaded his photos to Getty while the others checked e-mail and Martin "got all domestic," as he put it—took a shower and changed into some dry clothes. After his shower, Martin sat on a small couch, downloading and backing up his photos and Skyping with his partner back in Budapest, Polly Fields. Occasionally Hetherington "would literally throw himself down and peer over my computer and comment about what I was doing," Martin said. Without a laptop or a digital camera, Hetherington had time to kill. He did have his iPhone with him, and Michael Brown had, in Martin's words, "made a splash with his," selling Hipstamatic-enhanced iPhone photos to *National Geographic* and other magazines. "Tim was oblivious to the fact that he could have a Hipstamatic app, so we downloaded it for him on his iPhone. He was, like, 'This is great.' He would take similar scenes with his iPhone, in love with his new toy. He loved it."

Back in New York, everyone who saw the photos Hondros filed was amazed. Hetherington's studio mate Chris Anderson, who had covered wars, said that when he saw Hondros's photos his first reaction was, "What the fuck are they doing there?" after which he felt envious, thinking he too would have liked to have been there. "They're in a house. The house is on fire, and there's guys shooting at each other at close range, you know, and I'm thinking, 'Wow, I miss that.'" When he later saw the video footage from the firefight, Anderson was struck by the fact that it "looked like what Hollywood films usually make wars look like, you know? Wars usually don't look like Hollywood films look like."

Though he had planned to rely almost exclusively on his old-fashioned camera, Hetherington was by then shooting far more video. He had made a good number of still photos during the rebel funeral but his still camera was not suited to an indoor firefight, and when the group returned to the safe house he had not finished his last roll—he had five exposures of twenty remaining. His last shot of the morning was on the roof of al-Beyt Beytik. The decision to switch to video was not merely logistical. It had to do with a shift in his approach to covering the Libyan conflict, which would become more pronounced that afternoon. He was moving from his original plan—being, essentially, a war-zone portrait photographer—toward filming the action, which meant being on the front line.

Martin had talked with Hetherington about taking film stills in Libya; his friend Ivor Prickett had been using a film camera, too, and had gotten into "a similar spot of bother in the east because he was running out of film . . . He was trying to find an inner Zen, you know, only push the shutter when it absolutely warrants," Martin said. But war zones do not lend themselves to this kind of contemplation. Until the firefight in al-Beyt Beytik, Martin said, Hetherington "was still going to look for those moments, those almost decisive moments . . . In the back of his head, there were one or two key moments that he reserved his Zen for—that hostage situation and the guy under the tree, which I think are great. The rest of the day was so hectic and violent, and it was so dark in that building he couldn't possibly have photographed it with the camera he was using."

In hindsight, Martin said, they had been lucky that morning, and they might easily have called it a wrap. But after a lunch of bread and tuna, as they talked about what they would do that afternoon, Hetherington became "quite forceful" about going back, he said. "Tim drove the decision to go back to that street. Chris didn't really want to go back. He and I thought about going to the port. Tim was persistent, very forceful, very determined and driven. 'Do you guys realize, we have to go back with the rebel commander, we have to go back and reinforce this relationship.' My heart wasn't in it, but wherever they were going I was going to go." Still, Martin said, "I went back reluctantly. These guys were double my age and had double my experience. I convinced myself it was the right thing to do. I got caught up in something I never thought I would do."

The group's frequent driver, Ahmed Muntasir, who had once narrowly survived a direct hit to his car from a tank that had injured him and killed his cousin, advised them not to go, saying it would be too dangerous to return to Tripoli Street that afternoon. Muntasir felt so strongly that he said he would not drive them there. No matter, Hetherington had already made arrangements with Badi, the commander, to pick him up. Muntasir later said, "Everybody's wondering about this, about why Salah [would] take them there. Maybe he want to show them how tough the front line is."

Cervera was interested in going back. Michael Brown "wasn't very in the mood of going back, neither Chris," Cervera said, but the French journalists were going, so the consensus was, "Okay, let's go there for a few minutes or for one hour," after which they would head to the port, for what had become their familiar fallback position, photographing the poor migrants waiting there to be rescued.

Orlinsky, who had been to the port numerous times, was intrigued with the idea of seeing the front line. After returning to the empty safe house to file her photos, she had waited for the guys to return, interested in hearing what they had done. When they got back and told her about their crazy morning and she looked over their photos, "and they were so pumped up, they were so excited, and especially Tim," she got excited, too, she said. "I'd never seen Tim sweat, and Tim was sweating, and he was just smiling, and he'd gotten really great stuff. But I think it was more, not necessarily that he'd gotten great stuff but that he'd figured out, kind of, what he wanted to do, or he'd found his character, which was this commander of the rebel army." It sounded to Orlinsky like the rebels wanted to showcase their achievements on Tripoli Street, and Hetherington meanwhile wanted to focus on Badi, who soon returned with two trucks, at around 3 p.m.

Badi, a taciturn, fiftyish man, had military training, a rarity among the rebels. He had studied at the Libyan air academy and been captain of a Mirage fighter jet. He would later go to great pains to blunt criticism over his having taken the journalists back to Tripoli Street. In Badi's version, Hetherington said he wanted to go to the most dangerous place in Misrata, then brought his friends along. In any event, when Badi returned with two vehicles, the six photographers, along with four French journalists, piled in. Orlinsky was excited, but scared, as they were about to get under way. "It was comforting seeing Tim," she said. "Tim was sitting up in the front of the other truck with the rebel commander and . . . the way that Tim was talking with him made me feel comfortable, you know. Seeing Chris always just . . . kind of relaxed me and made me feel comfortable, but I was scared going out there. Definitely."

Hetherington typically rode in the front seat because he was so tall, and the drivers liked him and wanted him there, Orlinsky said, but before driving off Badi made her get out. "I don't think he liked me, or maybe he just didn't like the idea of a woman going out, because I was the only woman in the group and he kind of kicked me out of the car and at that point I almost didn't go," she said. Then Badi told her she could get in the other truck, and "I remember standing there in between the two trucks and I almost went back to the house and was like, 'No, you know what, guys, I'm going to go to the port.' But Chris was definitely going, so I went. So I got in the other truck and we drove there."

As they drove, Martin noticed kids running out of houses to see Badi's entourage drive past. Some tried to climb onto the back of his truck and flashed the V sign. "He was saying hello to everyone," Martin said. Hetherington filmed the drive through Badi's cracked windshield. Now and then we see his face in the rearview mirror as the war zone slides past and Badi, in his rakish head scarf, behind the wheel. Hetherington was looking for the theatrics of war, for portraits of fighters, and for action. In Badi, he was getting all three. In hindsight, Martin said, Hetherington was like a different person that afternoon on Tripoli Street. He said he almost didn't recognize him. Hetherington was fixated on getting as close to the front line as possible, and this after telling everyone he didn't need to go to the front to do what he wanted to do in Libya. Orlinsky recalled that he "had this look on his face, agitated and excited and beaming," which bothered her a little.

Badi dropped them off at the foot of the Tripoli Street bridge over the Coastal Road, the far end of which was held by Gaddafi forces and which would provide the only escape route for Gaddafi troops at the vegetable market and the central hospital. It was a bridge to certain death. Being there was "intense," Orlinsky said. A group of other photographers remained near the trucks. Tripoli Street had been devastated by the fighting, and Orlinsky could see rebels sitting in front of bombed-out buildings, and there were burned and blasted cars and trucks in the middle of the street. Some guys were standing around in the street, which Orlinsky took as an encouraging sign, that the danger had passed, but the consensus among the group was that they were too exposed at the foot of the bridge, so they headed back toward al-Beyt Beytik. Cervera had told them about the Gaddafi snipers' bodies on the roof of the first building that day and they wanted to see them.

Orlinsky lagged behind, trying to take it all in. When she came upon a group of rebels sitting on some steps, "they were doing the thing like, 'Take my picture, take my picture,'" she later said. "And I only remember this because I looked at my photos for the first time about a week ago and saw these pictures of these rebels waving right before . . . right before, you know . . . everything."

15

THE MORTAR ATTACK

Earlier in the day, a friend of Majdi Lusta's had asked him to accompany him to his home, which had been ransacked by Gaddafi troops, "to see where they stole the money and gold," as Lusta recalled. By the time he returned to Tripoli Street, the rebels had mostly "cleaned out" al-Beyt Beytik, meaning they had killed the last of the snipers on the block. He got there in time to get trapped on the third floor after the attack with the burning tires and was among those who escaped down the rickety wooden ladder.

Lusta was happy over the victory yet sorry to have missed a big part of the Tripoli Street fight, which he called "the battle to free the traffic lights"—a reference to the effort to eliminate sniper attacks at the major intersections and, beyond that, to drive the Gaddafi forces westward and out of town. April 20 was the third and final day of that battle, and a turning point for the rebels. In the coming days there would be intense fighting elsewhere, but it was beginning to seem as if the remaining Gaddafi troops in Misrata would soon be killed or captured, or else would escape beyond the bridge.

Lusta was among the rebels who were congregated along Tripoli Street as the photographers walked up from the bridge, where Badi had put them out. Badi had then walked out onto the bridge, but no one, including Hetherington, followed. If Hetherington thought he had found the ideal subject for his photos, it would not be evident in the shots he took that afternoon. Nothing much was happening. They later saw Badi, in the median of Tripoli Street, talking to some rebels, but for the most part the fighters were sitting or standing around as the photographers tried to find something to shoot. Those who had experienced close combat knew that boredom often bordered extreme danger, and Cervera would later say the quiet "felt weird."

Martin had a similar feeling. It was, he said, "deathly silent. That weirded me out the most." Quiet front lines often represent the calm before a storm, and they have a tendency to lull people into complacency. There was occasional gunfire in the distance, and perhaps even a mortar explosion, which is why the photographers found the bridge too sketchy. But the ennui of Tripoli Street was not much better.

Up ahead, as the photographers walked on, two shipping containers full of sand that had been placed across Tripoli Street that morning marked the visual boundary of the rebel-held section, and the photographers were beyond it. They were an easily targeted group, and there was no way to be sure that no snipers were within range. Mortars, too, could fly for miles and land in locations whose coordinates had previously been locked in. A spotter located in a nearby building might report the locations of rebels or journalists to the distant mortar crews, and even an imprecise launch could randomly kill whoever had the misfortune to be nearby. Yet there the photographers were, in the open, near the front lines.

In the wars Hetherington and most of the other veteran combat photographers had covered, mortars were common threats. In Afghanistan's Korengal Valley, both sides had been equipped with advanced weaponry but relied heavily upon comparatively simple yet effective mortars. In other wars, fighters often started out with primitive, even ancient weapons, which could be effective in the hands of an enraged fighting force. The bayonet charges during the American Civil War illustrate that the unnerving menace posed by a large group of screaming men with glinting knives affixed to the barrels of empty guns could rout an army with plenty of guns, ammunition, and even cannons. But a person miles away, armed with a mortar, was not likely to be deterred by the threat of hand-to-hand combat. The Misrata rebels would have been annihilated quickly had they not been able to procure better weapons and had not NATO supported them with strategic air strikes.

Mortars represented a wild card for both sides. They could be fabricated in any welding shop, ranging in size from small to large bores, and fired by a single man. In the beginning, the rebels were less skilled than the Gaddafi army at using all weapons, including mortars, with which they had been unfamiliar until the siege, and they were likewise not trained in battlefield triage, which meant that a fighter could be injured in a mortar explosion, or even accidentally shot by one of his friends, and bleed to death from a treatable wound. Simple though it is, few people know how to stanch heavy bleeding: applying a pressure compress to impede the flow until the person can be transported to a hospital, where the arteries and veins can be stitched back together and blood transfused.

Mortars are light, easily maneuvered, and particularly useful for plunging fire, or precision attacks that arc steeply and can fall precipitously within compounds or in homes, buildings, and narrow streets. They are the simplest of weapons, essentially breach-loaded tubes that provide a launching mechanism for self-propelled bombs, which can be keyed into a target using GPS coordinates or honed on targets by trial and error. In either case spotters, equipped with radios and binoculars inside nearby buildings, may be used to improve their accuracy. In Misrata the deadly utility of mortars meant that few parts of the city were safe from them, and those were subject to longer-range rockets. As the photographers milled around Tripoli Street, Cervera wondered if they were inside a vacuum waiting to be filled. It was quiet; what did that mean?

None of the photographers had given serious thought to walking onto the bridge with Badi, but no one was comfortable staying where they were, so Cervera and Brown suggested they walk east along Tripoli Street, toward the city center. At least there would be cover along the way. Brown, in particular, wanted to return to the building that he and Cervera had entered that morning, where the bodies of the snipers lay on the roof. This seemed like a good plan to the others.

As they headed up Tripoli Street, Cervera broke off because he wasn't interested in photographing the snipers' bodies again. Martin walked shoulder to shoulder with Hondros, and along the way the two of them, with Hetherington, took a side trip into a bombed building that was still furnished with a TV and a fine set of leather chairs. Martin snapped a few photos inside the building, which appeared to have been a business that sold farm equipment, but the truth was, "I was just over it by that point," he later said. "There was an occasional crack of gunfire, but nothing alarming, except that it was so damn quiet." Up ahead, they now saw Badi walking in the middle of the boulevard, talking to a group of young rebels. As Martin recalled, "I said to Chris, 'What are we going to do?' We decided we'd stay a half hour and then leave."

In a grassy area adjacent to al-Beyt Beytik, the Gaddafi supply truck left behind when the troops fled captured their interest, just as it had caught the eye of rebels and other photographers earlier in the day. The truck's contents were both a curiosity and a potential source of supplies or souvenirs. In hindsight, it might easily have been a setup, because the Gaddafi troops, though perhaps a mile away, were aware of having left the truck behind and knew exactly where it was. If someone with binoculars had been watching the people picking through the army's abandoned stuff, it would have been both a little galling and an opportunity to specifically retaliate. Yet the slow looting of the truck's merchandise had been going on all day, without incident. "We all kind of stopped at it," Orlinsky recalled, "and it was this really eerie scene of this open truck filled with Gaddafi soldier uniforms, and they were all over the ground, and there was a helmet—a green helmet— with a bullet hole right through the top of it, and I'm pretty sure Tim took a photo of it." After spending a while going through the contents of the truck, which by then had been picked over, and taking photos, everyone except Orlinsky moved on. Orlinsky lingered there, snapping photos. She liked the spot, she said, "because it was behind a corner, and I didn't like being on Tripoli Street." At one point she noticed that the guys were moving farther up the street, at a pretty good clip, so she decided to catch up. She thought, "I've got to catch up with Chris."

Cervera was hanging out by a much-photographed Pepsi billboard, a brilliant, bullet-riddled field of blue set against the equally brilliant blue sky. He thought, "Oh, nice picture. So I stop by and they keep on walking." Nearby, parked on the side of the street in a pickup truck, was a young rebel, Ismael Gumal, who noticed the photographers approaching. Gumal, twenty-nine, a truck driver by trade, was now a fighter who occasionally delivered supplies. He noted that in addition to the familiar tall Brit and the two photographers wearing army helmets, there was a woman in the group this time. They stopped when they reached his truck, and because they didn't share a common language Hetherington communicated with Gumal by gestures, indicating that he offered his congratulations to the rebels for having won that section of Tripoli Street. Everyone smiled. The photographers snapped a few pictures, then moved on. Gumal would later cherish the memory of the encounter, when he and Hetherington had shared a pleasant, happy moment a short time before their paths crossed again in a far more fateful way.

A moment before the mortar came in, Martin and Hondros stopped so Martin could apply sunscreen to Hondros's nose and the back of his neck, because Hondros's fiancée had been after him about getting sunburned. As he applied the sunscreen, Martin told Hondros that he was ready to head to the port, and Hondros responded that he thought this was a good idea. From there, "We make our way out in front of the building, walk another ten feet or so, and then, 'Where's Tim?'" Martin recalled. They turned, and "Then we see him coming from behind, sprinting, like, we're going this way. It's a full sprint, and the moment he caught up with us—I was on the left, Chris an inch from my right shoulder, Tim a foot from him—that's when the explosion came in."

In the seconds before the explosion, as Hetherington ran, his eyes were fixed on Hondros and Martin, who had partly turned to face him. He ran along a sidewalk strewn with rubble and bullet casings as a group of rebels looked on, past the ruined facade of al-Beyt Beytik and the narrow alley in which he had earlier climbed down from the roof on scaffolding painted brilliant sky blue, to the spot, in front of an auto garage with an oil change bay out front, where the explosion occurred.

When the mortar round hit, Cervera was still on the opposite side of the street, where the rebel photographer Ahmed Shlak was also filming. "I heard a noise, a very loud noise of a grenade, or whatever, falling," Cervera said. "I didn't know what it was but it was very loud, and I saw the explosion." Martin later said he had no idea why Hetherington had sprinted toward them. Had he heard the thud of the mortar being launched or seen a spotter in a window? Maybe he was running to take a photo up ahead, Cervera speculated. All Martin knew was that Hetherington had been running with his camera in his left hand, holding the strap to his rucksack with his right to prevent it from bouncing around, and that he was not slowing down as he approached. He didn't speak but the message Martin got was, "We're going this way." It was a few minutes after Martin took his last photo, which carried a time stamp of 4:19:52 p.m.

Cervera saw people running away from the area as a cloud of dust billowed outward and thought, "Oh my God. They were there." At first he thought it was an RPG blast, and he would later report that it was, an error that would be repeated numerous times in subsequent accounts.

Though Cervera's photos of the aftermath show Martin running, holding his side, Martin does not recall getting back on his feet after he was knocked down by the explosion. When he opened his eyes he saw the dust and smoke billowing out across the sidewalk, as if the ground were on fire. Hondros and Hetherington were obscured but Martin remembered what he described as "the rarest of glimpses out of the corner of my right eye—for what would amount to a millisecond, I saw Chris tumble beside me, in a motion that looked like someone was falling forward, [who had] been tripped up, almost the way a gymnast would tumble forward from mid-chest height. That is the only and last memory I have of Chris."

All around him, he said, "rebels were dead or injured, screaming. I did a check—my legs were there, but there was massive pain in my stomach. Then everything went white. I thought, 'I need to find cover,' so I pulled myself into an alcove. There was lots of scaffolding, blue. The pain was increasing, and that horrible dialogue started happening: 'Shit, this is it, I'm dying.' I couldn't say a word. Looking up in the white and the heat I see Mike saying, 'I'm hit.' I remember thinking:

'*You're* hit? *I'm* hit. You look fucking terrific.'" Then, he said, "I began to fall asleep. I woke up in the arms of two rebels."

Brown, who had been a few paces behind the others when the mortar came in, had been hit in the shoulder, chest, wrist and calf. As Cervera ran toward the cloud of smoke, he saw bodies strewn about and Brown and Orlinsky screaming for help, and when he reached them Brown was holding his hand over his shoulder, saying, "Please help me. Help me." Brown would later recall, "I thought I was hit much worse than it turned out. So the only thing going through my head was, 'I have to get out of here, it's not worth it. I mean, just to get a few pictures of guys with guns shooting at each other?'"

Orlinsky had taken a moment to photograph in a nearby alley, which shielded her from the blast. Out on the sidewalk, Hondros was now unconscious, Hetherington was grasping his leg and calling for help, and Brown was holding his chest, saying he had been hit. Cervera saw a small truck emerging from behind a building, as its driver tried to flee. He stopped the car, opened the door, and pushed Orlinsky and Brown inside.

Once inside the car, Orlinsky did not want to leave the others behind. As the driver sped through the sandy streets on the way to al-Hekma, she put pressure on Brown's chest, trying to slow the flow of blood. He had two wounds, one in his chest and a deeper one in his shoulder, and he was having trouble breathing.

Cervera looked around him and saw ten or so bodies on the ground, some dead or unconscious, others calling for help. Hondros was unconscious but Hetherington lay on his back, with his eyes open. They had been blown a few feet away from each other by the blast. Cervera saw that Hetherington was scared. "When he saw me, he told me, 'Guillermo, please help me,' so I [said] to him, 'Don't worry.'" The rebels were now dragging the injured behind the protective wall, then loading them into trucks. "And then I look at my back, I saw a pickup car with two guys. I say, 'Please come very fast!' and they pull back and they . . . help me to put their bodies into the back of the pickup." The guys in the truck were Ismael Gumal and his friend and neighbor Adel Maiel, who had met Hetherington and the other photographers just moments before. After Hetherington and Hondros were loaded into the truck bed, which contained boxes of ammunition, Cervera climbed in beside them. As they drove away he saw the bodies of three rebels still on the ground, some motionless, others writhing in agony. One of them was Majdi Lusta.

Lusta had a serious chest wound that had punctured one of his lungs and caused significant internal bleeding. At the time of the explosion, he had been a few feet from the photographers, peering into a car in which the rebels had killed three Gaddafi soldiers earlier in the day. In hindsight, he would recognize that he had been in an exposed location, visible, perhaps, to spotters and within range of guns and mortars. "We are not really soldiers," he said, in explanation for the lack of foresight. "We're just looking at cars, hav[ing] a coffee. We forget we are surrounded by Gaddafi soldiers. It had been quiet for perhaps four hours." He did not immediately recognize that he was wounded. "I tried to tell myself I was okay, until the blood started coming out of my mouth," he said. "I saw Tim and Chris. Tim [said], 'I'm here. Somebody help me.' I tried to get up and run, but fell."

Badi, who was back near the bridge, heard over his radio that a group of journalists and rebels had been wounded at al-Beyt Beytik. Ibrahim Safar, who had lost a member of his group earlier that day across the street from al-Beyt Beytik, as well as a close friend, a photographer, in a separate sniper attack, also heard on his radio that "some journalists from the U.S.A. were hit." His first thought, he said, was, "Who drove the journalists to that dangerous place?"

The Gaddafi forces usually followed one mortar attack with another, to destroy the ambulances that would respond, so Lusta knew he needed to take cover. But he was too weak to stand, much less walk, and couldn't seem to get enough air into his lungs. As he lay on the ground, his chest bleeding and heaving, he saw a group of rebels dragging injured men behind a wall to protect them. Then a pickup truck screeched to a stop beside him and two rebels jumped out, picked him up by his shoulders and feet, and pushed him into the backseat. There was another injured guy lying in the bed. The truck lurched forward, the driver going as fast as he could along the sidewalk, which was littered with debris, to an alley that emptied into a side street running perpendicular to Tripoli Street in the direction of al-Hekma.

From there they followed "subways," as Lusta called them—a network of narrow, bumpy dirt roads through a residential area—that eventually connected with a series of wide boulevards. The area, Lusta knew, "was quite severe," meaning it was subject to mortar attacks and sniper fire. They went very fast, and as he lay in the backseat Lusta believed he was dying. He thought about his new wife and how unlucky she was. Then—and he doesn't know why or when it occurred to him—he began to feel that he would survive.

Ahead of them, Orlinsky was trying to reassure Brown that he would be okay. When she saw an ambulance going in the same direction she flagged it down and got Brown into it, then went back to the car and told the driver, "You have to go back that way" to help the others. Then she got into the ambulance with Brown. She had not seen Hetherington and Hondros being loaded into a vehicle and wanted to make sure they were, but the driver of the car chose not to go back.

Meanwhile, Martin, who lay bleeding in the alley, holding one hand against his protruding intestines, was staring up at the blue scaffolding set against a vivid blue sky when the pair of rebels grabbed him by his arms and legs and carried him to a waiting pickup, which was already crowded with dead bodies and seriously injured men. "I knew it's not far to al-Hekma," he later said—it was about three kilometers— "and all I have to do is keep my eyes open." Still, he thought, "Why is this taking so long? I'm in a truck full of very badly wounded and dead, and when I was able to speak I said, 'Wrong truck. I'm alive.'" Hearing him, the rebels pulled him out and moved him to another truck, which then sped away.

"Somebody had his arms around my stomach," Martin said. "I'm not sure if it was the same dude from earlier, but he was wearing a red beret. I have a very vivid image of him, this really handsome guy, very tanned, with a camera around his neck, in a red beret, against a perfect blue sky. Every bump we hit was the most painful horrific experience, but he looked phenomenal. It was this incredible image."

As Gumal's truck, with Cervera, Hetherington, and Hondros in back, emerged from the alley, Cervera noticed that Hetherington's blood was rapidly draining from his upper leg and pooling in the bed. There was a lot of blood. Cervera tried to inspect the injury but the shrapnel hole was between his crotch and his hip, too high to apply a tourniquet. All Cervera could do was press against the wound with one hand while holding Hetherington's hand with the other. Hetherington had seemed frightened when Cervera first came across him on the sidewalk, for obvious reasons. "I saw by his side was a guy who lost one leg and you could see him with no leg screaming for help," Cervera said. "And you don't know who is going to take care of you. I said, 'Don't worry, Tim. We go. We are going to the hospital.' So I think he was not scared at that moment."

Hetherington soon appeared to go into shock, Cervera said. "He was this kind of conscious, like, very, like, almost . . . almost out of that situation. I don't know how to explain, like in shock. He couldn't really realize the real situation. He was almost out." He later said he didn't think Hetherington realized he was dying, though considering how many people he had seen bleed to death in the war zones he had covered—and considering the video snippet he had included in *Diary*, of blood gushing as if from a fire hose from the neck of a giraffe that someone had shot on safari, which quickly staggered and died—it is hard to imagine that he did not know. Cervera insisted that there was no panic in his eyes. "He was just in a very bad situation. When you lose blood, you get, like, asleep, you know. I think he was okay because someone he knew was with him . . . I don't think he knew he was dying. I think he knew he could make it to the hospital. I was trying to give him good vibrations—'You're okay, come on! We are going to get to the hospital, Tim. Don't worry!' You know?"

At the point where the alley emerged into a side street, Gumal came upon an ambulance and decided to transfer one of the injured men to it. Because Hondros lay at the back they decided it would be him. Cervera thought that Hondros was already dead. Each time the pickup had hit a bump, tissue had fallen out of his head, he said, but it was quicker to move him from the truck to the ambulance, so that is what they did.

Then, as the rebels were loading Hondros into the ambulance, Cervera took the opportunity to photograph Hetherington, lying in the bed of the truck, with his eyes closed, against the boxes of ammo. Why Cervera did this would later baffle him, and he would feel uncomfortable about it, just as he would about the photos he had taken immediately after the blast. But even more bewildering is what can be seen in the edge of the photo: the arms of two men resting on the side of the truck. It is as if the men are standing around talking, with all the time in the world, looking at Hetherington as he lay dying in the back of the truck. What was taking so long? Why were the men so casually resting their arms against the truck? Hetherington, unlike Hondros, might have been saved, and the fact that he was not transferred to the ambulance would later torment Hetherington's mother, though el-Haddad said that, based on what he heard, the ambulance driver would not have known how to save him. Cervera's photo is most disturbing precisely because of the seeming lack of urgency.

"It took a minute to transfer Chris to the ambulance," Cervera later said. "That picture, the guys leaning on the side to look in the back of the truck, maybe it's a body or an injured guy, but you see it a lot. They think, 'I hope he'll make it,' something like that. They're not surprised." Among Hetherington's own last photos are several of the bloody body of a rebel lying in the bed of a pickup truck, including one in which he purposely included two photographers' hands taking pictures of the scene with iPhones.

At the time Cervera made his photo, Hetherington was still alive, and in the photo he looks surprisingly good, though his right sleeve and pants leg are drenched in blood. And contrary to the disturbing lack of urgency evident in Cervera's photo, Gumal later said he had never felt more urgency in his life. Hetherington's life was in his hands and it was clear he didn't have long.

After getting Hondros into the ambulance, Cervera said, the driver looked at him for guidance, "like, 'What should I do?' I say, 'Run! Run to the hospital. Come on, come on!'" Gumal and his neighbor Maiel then climbed into the front of the pickup, and two rebels whose names Cervera didn't know got into the bed of the truck beside him and Hetherington, who was still conscious, though he was increasingly dizzy. "I took his hand, just to, to make him awake, and say, 'Tim, Tim, come on, don't fall asleep. We are getting to the hospital. Just don't fall asleep.'" Each time Cervera spoke to him, Hetherington opened his eyes, like a person suddenly waking, and asked for help, then drifted away again.

Gumal sped down one narrow street to another, making sudden turns, gunning the engine on the open stretches, zooming past walled compounds where, from the bed of the truck, towering palms and power lines occasionally flashed by overhead, framed by the deep blue sky. At one point Gumal had to swerve to avoid colliding with a car full of rebels that sped across their path, which caused Cervera and the others in the back to lurch from side to side in the bed of the truck. "We almost crash," Cervera said. He tried to hang on with one hand while clutching Hetherington's hand with the other. Hetherington said nothing as he rocked against the ammo boxes. All Gumal could think of was getting to al-Hekma as quickly as possible. In the front seat, Maiel was shouting, "Turn here," "Go there!," and "Go faster, faster!"

Hetherington drifted in and out of consciousness. As his blood drained from the severed femoral artery at the top of his leg he weakened and muttered words that Cervera could not understand. "He was bleeding a lot," Cervera said. "All the blood around—a lot of blood. He was losing control of his mind, and he was too weak to talk." After Hetherington remained quiet for a long time, Cervera said, once more, "Tim, Tim, stay awake," but there was no response. He felt Hetherington's hand grow suddenly cold. He later said he had always thought that a person's body temperature would drop slowly after death, but at that moment, "I felt, really fast, this weird feeling in his hand," he said. "I felt [he was] very cold and he was white, very white, you know? So I just say, 'Oh my God. I hope we arrive soon to the hospital' because I thought he was dead . . . or he was dying. I think he was, he died at that moment."

Cervera stared at the floor of the truck bed. He would later struggle to remember when and where that moment occurred, but he could not be sure; it was somewhere along the dizzying network of sunlit lanes between Tripoli Street and the boulevards leading to al-Hekma. "I guess it was the look on my face," Cervera said, "because the rebel put his hand on my shoulder and said, 'I'm sorry for your friend.'" Cervera remembers thinking, "It's not a game. You think, you don't realize what's going on in these places, because it doesn't hit you straight, you know . . . You take pictures of injured people, of dead people, of explosions, but it's quite different when you feel it in yourself." Hetherington was now a casualty of the war rather than an observer. He had chased the story to the point where it had turned and come after him.

Somewhere up ahead the truck carrying Lusta was following the same route to al-Hekma. As it approached a series of rebel checkpoints, the driver had to slow to take the bypasses designated for emergency vehicles, and at others Lusta could hear him shouting, "Open it, open it, open it!" to the rebels who manned the ropes. "It was years for me," Lusta later said.

Finally they came to a roundabout and veered left onto a boulevard, then another roundabout, another left onto al-Hekma Street, and there was the narrow turn between the palms to the hospital, into the lot where the triage tent awaited. The truck screeched to a stop at the front of the tent. "The last thing I remember," Lusta said, "they opened my chest and put a tube in, and I slept."

16
AL-HEKMA

By the time Orlinsky arrived at al-Hekma, she felt compelled to return to Tripoli Street to make sure Hetherington and Hondros had been evacuated, so she found an ambulance that was heading back there and got in, which, as she later recalled, "was just really stupid," not only because it was dangerous but because they passed the other ambulance and truck transporting Hetherington and Hondros to al-Hekma, going the other way. Once she got to Tripoli Street, she encountered a group of rebels who had not been there when the mortar came in, and who were trying to figure out what had happened. After showing the rebels where the mortar hit, she went back to al-Hekma.

She arrived to find a maelstrom inside the tent, which was crowded with people, some in surgical gowns and caps, some in street clothes. It was very loud. Mohammed al-Zawwam, the rebel photographer who had accompanied the photographers on the boat from Benghazi and was staying with them at the safe house, moved through the tent filming everything with his video camera. Some of the injured were quiet. Others wailed. Hetherington lay on a gurney, not far from Brown and Martin. Hondros was inside the hospital.

When Gumal arrived, the parking lot was already full of cars, most of which had brought people from the blast on Tripoli Street. "We were one of the last to get there," Cervera said. At that moment, Liohn was inside the hospital, chatting online with his girlfriend, who was back home in Italy. He noticed a sudden gush of activity outside, which was not uncommon at a hospital that sometimes received as many as one hundred trauma cases a day, and as many as forty in a single hour, and he was trying to placate his girlfriend, who was angry at him for putting himself at risk. He had not yet heard the news about the mortar attack, but he told his girlfriend that he had to go out and see what had happened. He could hear a woman screaming, which, even at al-Hekma, was not normal.

Entering the tent he encountered a frenzy of activity, most of it centering on a patient who he was shocked to recognize was Hetherington. The doctors and nurses were trying to revive him but he was very pale. Then Liohn saw Brown and Martin, and he asked Brown if he was okay, but he just said, "Don't tell my mother, don't tell my mother, don't tell my mother." Liohn then went to Martin's bedside. Martin was very calm and did not mention that part of his intestine was protruding from his abdomen, so Liohn didn't mention it either. Others who were there that day would recall the awkwardness they felt, trying to ignore Martin's terrifying injury as he joked around, saying things like, "It's a scorcher today!"

When Liohn saw Cervera, he said he asked if he was okay, and Cervera said he was. Not surprisingly, Cervera would later give a different account of the exchange, saying Liohn's comment was, "I told you you shouldn't have been there." Liohn also observed that al-Zawwam was getting in the way of the doctors as he filmed, and true to form he walked over, kicked him in the leg, and told him to give the doctors some space. Liohn was filming as well, because he was there to cover medical treatment for the Red Cross, though he said he took pains to stay out of the way. Many people who were not involved in treating them were trying to get close enough to see the photographers, and al-Zawwam's footage seems as invasive as Hetherington's filming of Rougle's body on Abas Ghar had seemed to Raeon.

Cervera stood off to the side, watching the doctors and nurses taking turns trying to resuscitate Hetherington. Then he went to speak with Martin and told him, "Chris is not looking good, but Tim, he is going to be fine." Martin later said he was no longer in pain, that he didn't feel anything at all. He didn't feel an end-of-life flash or think of the sorrow his family would feel if he died. "Just calm and content," he later said. Then he saw a whiteness, and the next thing he knew he woke up. He doesn't remember where he awoke, or when, but it was more than a day later, in a hospital room.

By that point Orlinsky was distraught: "I had no more tears left. I had no more feeling, so I couldn't even fathom if anything were to happen to Guy." People were telling her she should leave, go back to the safe house, that there was nothing she could do at al-Hekma, "so I said, Okay, I'll go back to the house for a couple of hours and come back, and I went back to the house, and then immediately I was like, 'I don't want to spend another second in this place.' There were rebels coming in and out of the house and I was so angry at them . . . I just directed all of my anger towards them, towards the commander who took us there, towards everyone. I was really angry and wanted to not be around them ever, ever again." She packed her things and returned to al-Hekma.

As he stood in the tent, Cervera glanced down and saw that his jeans were bloody and that blood had pooled inside his sneakers. By then Gumal had brought Hetherington's camera and bag from the truck bed, before driving across the parking lot to a hydrant to wash the blood away. Gumal then returned to the front line, assuming Hetherington would survive. From Hetherington's pocket the staff retrieved his Moleskin journal, the pages of which were stained with his blood.

So many paths were intersecting in the tent, stories that encompassed New York, Hollywood, London, Madrid, Paris, Rome, Cairo, and Tripoli as well as out-of-the-way places in Afghanistan, Brazil, Liberia, the United States, and the UK. "It was remarkable to think about," el-Haddad said. "How all of these people come to be here, in this place, on that day." El-Haddad, who had returned to al-Hekma from Tripoli Street with Liohn and Aboturkia a few hours before, had heard about the attack and had immediately left with an ambulance, but the driver had been unsure of the exact location, much less the best route to get there, and had gotten lost. As he'd talked with the dispatcher at al-Hekma on the radio, the driver was told that by then there was no one left at the site of the attack and he should return to the hospital.

In addition to the four photographers, several rebels were killed or injured in the mortar blast that took Hetherington's and Hondros's lives, though el-Haddad would later have great difficulty finding out exactly who all of them were, as there was no reliable clearinghouse of records. Among the men who were taken into al-Hekma that afternoon was Majdi Lusta, who was soon transferred to an operating room in the main hospital. Several rebels were pronounced dead on arrival at the hospital, and their bodies now lay on the floor just inside the entrance to the hospital, covered with sheets, because there was nowhere else to put them.

As Liohn later noted, with some disgust, most of the Western news accounts of Hetherington's and Hondros's deaths would focus exclusively upon them, perhaps mentioning that two other photographers had been injured in the attack, without naming them. The Western media rarely mentioned that any Libyans were injured or killed in the attack. El-Haddad would eventually come up with the names of four who died, but when he tried to locate the families of the men, more than a year later, he found that the list he had was incorrect.

The doctors worked on Hetherington for perhaps fifteen minutes, to no avail. One of them later observed that Hetherington's injury would have been easy to repair had he arrived at the hospital sooner, or had someone known how to properly apply compression to a ruptured femoral artery in the field.

When she arrived at al-Hekma the second time, Orlinsky tried to convince herself that things weren't as bad as they seemed, that Hetherington and Hondros would survive. Then she was told that Hetherington had died and that Hondros was on life support. She went into the ICU room where Hondros lay and held his hand for a while. Also there was Nicole Tung, a twenty-four-year-old photographer who was working for Human Rights Watch. Soon, Orlinsky said, "they kicked us all out." She was told that Brown was going to be okay, but that Martin was actually worse than anyone had realized. He had been hit by shrapnel in his leg, pelvis, and abdomen and had massive internal bleeding.

Cervera didn't know what to do. Could he have saved Hetherington? Could he have somehow stanched the flow of blood rather than simply holding his hand? Should he have insisted that Hetherington be placed in the ambulance, rather than Hondros, who he had been sure would not survive? As he deliberated upon these questions, people began quizzing him about exactly what had happened. He told them he thought the explosion came from an RPG, though a later investigation would conclude that it was a mortar. When he was summoned to the hospital director's office, Cervera asked al-Zawwam to accompany him because "He was kind of a friend of us, he was staying at the same house. . . . So they put me in the room where the manager of the hospital was working and they start asking me questions, weird questions . . . and he wanted me to sign a paper testifying what was going on. But they were making the questions and the answers. It was kind of manipulation. Like to get a sign of a journalist testifying whatever. So I felt weird, and [al-Zawwam] told me, 'Let's go. This is not clear. These people are not acting well, you know?' When he said that to me, they tried to beat him. And finally we end up beating each other in that room to get away. It was very weird, you know. It was like four guys trying to beat him. I push them and we run away of the room of the hospital. So I don't know. It's a war. Nobody's good or bad in this kind of situation. I think that they are trying to do their best to take Gaddafi out, but sometimes I don't think they use the right methods." He said he felt he was being coerced to say that the Gaddafi forces had deliberately targeted the Western journalists, to frame the story that way, and he had no way of knowing if that was true. "Is it fair or not, using Tim's death for that?" he asked. Later, Cervera also visited the room where Hondros lay in a coma. Then he left the hospital.

El-Haddad said that if Hondros had been officially admitted to the hospital the doctors would not have removed him from life support, because it would violate Muslim teachings. But prior to his admittance the Italian doctors were in charge. The word in the hospital was that it was just a matter of time until they would have no choice but to pull the plug on Hondros, Liohn said, so he went back to his room in an apartment building on the hospital grounds. "I don't know what to do," he said. "I talk to Peter [Bouckaert, at Human Rights Watch], say, 'Man, the photographers who were here today, they just came to the hospital. They're dead. You know, the ones that I was complaining about, they just came in. They are dead, man. Shit.'"

After he got off the phone with Bouckaert, Liohn returned to the hospital. Hondros was still on life support but the other bodies had been moved to the former pediatrics room, the only room with an air conditioner, which was going full blast. Because there was no morgue, hospital procedure required that bodies be buried quickly. Liohn said, "The doctor asked me, 'What are we going to do with this? You know, we have to contact people. Who were they? Who they work for?' I say I don't know. I don't know. Because Guy and Mike I knew." He didn't know who Hetherington and Hondros were working for or who should be notified of their deaths. To enlist help in notifying the next of kin, he said, Liohn posted a notice of the deaths on Facebook, for which he would later be vilified, because it seemed such an impersonal way for their families and friends to find out. He also wrote that Brown and Martin were still in surgery.

The question, then, was how to evacuate Hetherington's body—and, soon, presumably, Hondros's. Liohn and Bouckaert organized the evacuations through Human Rights Watch and the International Organization for Migration, which had a boat arriving at the port that day, the *Ionian Spirit*.

Liohn said it wasn't clear who made the decision but he had seen two Italian doctors arguing about whether to remove Hondros from life support. The disagreement was not over whether it was warranted but whether it was appropriate, considering that al-Hekma rarely did so. During the siege, the hospital staff might push patients out the door before they were fully recovered, to make room for more, but they did not like to give up on anyone. The opposing argument was that Hondros would not survive, and there was now an opportunity, which might not be available afterward, to ship his body home. When Liohn returned half an hour later he was told that the decision had been made. Hondros had been removed from life support. The staff then set about washing his body, saying prayers, and drawing up the death certificate.

After Hetherington's body was transported to the port, Nicole Tung, who was working with both Human Rights Watch and the IOM, caught a ride there to make sure it was loaded onto the boat.

While there, she was told that Hondros's body—he had been technically alive when she last saw him—was also on its way.

Liohn accompanied Hondros's body in the ambulance, but when they reached the port the guards were suspicious and refused to allow Liohn to enter. The situation was "very tense," he said, and disorganized. The boat was waiting, with more than a thousand migrant refugees aboard, "so here we are," he said, "asking a boat with thousands of people inside to wait for us, right? I mean, we are putting risk—the destiny of thousands of people right now, to somehow help a person who we respect, but who we know how his destiny ends." So Liohn got out and the ambulance driver proceeded to the ship without him.

Later that night, Ismael Gumal returned to al-Hekma to see how Hetherington and Hondros were doing and was told "they passed away." By then, Brown was recuperating in his room and Martin was midway through a difficult, eight-hour surgery, during which he twice went into cardiac arrest. Before the surgery was over Martin would receive thirty-eight units of blood, more than three times the amount a body naturally holds, but he survived. So did Majdi Lusta.

17

"THAT TOWN"

The *Ionian Spirit* sailed out of the Misrata port under starry skies, headed back to Benghazi. The boat had remained in port only long enough to offload five hundred tons of food, medical supplies, and bottled water and to take on a human cargo—several seriously injured Libyans who were being transported to hospitals in Benghazi, a thousand or more migratory workers who'd been trapped in Misrata, a group of volunteer doctors who set up a temporary ICU in staterooms, and Hetherington's and Hondros's bodies. Hetherington and Hondros, who had made the 240-mile journey from Benghazi to Misrata on the same boat five days before, were headed for their final resting places in England and the United States.

Other journalists meanwhile disembarked in Misrata, including Marie Colvin, an American reporter working for the UK's *Sunday Times* who stood out because of her black eye patch—she had lost an eye during a firefight in Sri Lanka in 2001; she'd come to cover the siege, which was far from over. The *Ionian Spirit* was part of a flotilla of ships, fishing trawlers, and tugboats from Greece, Libya, Malta, and Turkey that served as Misrata's lifeline, hired by international aid organizations to transport refugees and supplies and by rebels who used them to ferry guns and ammunition. In many cases, journalists hitched a ride.

Jeremy Haslam, head of the IOM, had anxiously held the *Ionian Spirit* at the dock that night, under the threat of resumed shelling, waiting for the bodies to arrive. A high wind chilled the April night as the boat finally departed. The next day, hundreds of people greeted the boat in Benghazi with banners that read "UK & US we grieve for your loss."

Cervera had already left aboard a small fishing boat headed for Malta, which was turned back by NATO forces because it carried illegal immigrants. As a result, he ended up in Benghazi as well. After spending a cold night on the deck of the boat, sleeping under fishing nets, Cervera hired a car at the Benghazi port to drive him to Cairo, and from there he flew to Spain. He said he wasn't sure why he was so quick to leave. He was confused, perhaps in shock, he thought.

After Liohn's Facebook post, news of the photographers' deaths had spread quickly. When Junger heard that Hetherington and Hondros had been injured by a bomb in Misrata, he searched for Hetherington's name online, and came upon Liohn's message. So began an endless round of heartrending phone calls.

As the *Ionian Spirit* made its way to Benghazi, word of Hetherington's death was being tweeted, posted, e-mailed, and delivered in person or by phone, around the world, and particularly among the people who had known him in the United States, the UK, Afghanistan, Liberia, and across Europe and Africa. James Marparyan, Hetherington's former driver in Monrovia, received a call during dinner from a man whose name he didn't catch, who was in New York City and "sounded white," and told him Hetherington had been killed. "It was like a dream," Marparyan said. "I dropped the spoon down." When Black Diamond got her call, she began to sob, which upset the young children who stayed with her in her home because they had never seen her cry.

In the middle of a long day and night of communal and personal shock, Junger managed to write a poignant account of Hetherington's death that ran the next day on Vanity Fair Online. Addressing Hetherington, he wrote,

Tim, man, what can I say? For the first few hours the stories were confused enough that I could imagine maybe none of them were true, but they finally settled into one brief, brutal narrative: while covering rebel forces in the city of Misrata, Libya, you got hit by a piece of shrapnel and bled to death on the way to the clinic. You couldn't have known this, but your fellow photographer Chris Hondros would die later that evening.

I'm picturing you and your three wounded colleagues in the back of a pickup truck. There are young men with bandannas on their heads and guns in their hands and everyone is screaming and the driver is jamming his overloaded vehicle through the destroyed streets of that city, trying to get you all to the clinic in time.

He didn't. I've never even heard of Misrata before, but for your whole life it was there on a map for you to find and ponder and finally go to. All of us in the profession—the war profession, for lack of a better name—know about that town. It's there waiting for all of us. But you went to yours, and it claimed you.

Turning to Hetherington's vision for his work, Junger wrote,

Let's talk about that. It's what you wanted to communicate to the world about this story—about every story. Maybe Misrata wasn't worth dying for—surely that thought must have crossed your mind in those last moments—but what about all the Misratas of the world? What about Liberia and Darfur and Sri Lanka and all those terrible, ugly stories that you brought such humanity to? That you helped bring the world's attention to?

After the war in Liberia you rented a house in the capital and lived there for years. Years. Who does that? No one I know except you, my dear friend. That's part of Misrata, too. That's also part of what you died for: the decision to live a life that was thrown open to all the beauty and misery and ugliness and joy in the world.

Brown, Martin, and Orlinsky were still in Misrata. Within a few days, Brown was out of danger, but Martin was beginning a long, arduous recovery from his injuries. Orlinsky's friends in Misrata tried to convince her to evacuate to Benghazi, but she stayed for a few days, not wanting to leave without knowing that Martin was going to be all right. After Brown was discharged and Martin was moved from the ICU to a hospital room, Orlinsky tried, unsuccessfully, to organize a medevac evacuation for him. Then, reassured by an Italian doctor who was working as a volunteer at al-Hekma that he would accompany Martin when he was able to leave, Orlinsky decided it was time to go. Because of everything that had happened, she said, "I didn't want to stay in Misrata . . . I couldn't sleep and I couldn't eat and I didn't want to, because it felt like I could keep everything like a dream." She spent most of her final days in Misrata at al-Hekma, which she said was "just purely living hell, and there's just people coming in, bodies and injured people coming in and out all day long. I knew it wasn't good for me to stay there because I was starting to go crazy, and . . . nobody needed some crazy girl there." In the end, she boarded a UNICEF boat bound for Malta with Brown, who was weak and needed assistance.

Orlinsky's friends and family back home were not yet aware that she had been in Misrata. In the media accounts of Hetherington's and Hondros's deaths, "they listed four photographers and they didn't know that Guillermo and I had been there," she said. "I mean, part of that is because, I think, when I arrived back to the hospital, I said, 'My parents don't know I'm in Misrata, all right?' I was, like, shouting, 'My parents don't know I'm here, I don't want them to find out!' because, in my kind of crazy state of logic, I thought somehow they would never know, so I would never have to scare them and have them know that I'd been so close."

Among the group at al-Beyt Beytik at the time of the attack, the photographers knew only that two rebels had been killed during the firefight that morning. Though they had photographed them and in some cases helped carry their bodies out, none who survived knew their names. Salah Badi later identified one of the dead rebels as a man named Mohammed Karshini. However, no Karshini was listed among the killed that day in the Misrata war museum, nor in the official registry of killed and missing. The number of rebels killed during the firefight and mortar attack ranged from three to seven, in addition to thirteen wounded. It's possible some died later of their wounds, and in any event no one was keeping reliable records at the time. One rebel, Mohammed Smew, whose body was discovered in al-Beyt Beytik on April 20, had in fact been dead for two days.

In addition to the incomplete records, the problem of identifying the dead—even now—is compounded by the multiple methods of transliteration of Arabic names to English, and the fact that some families are wary of discussing with a stranger their relatives' roles in the uprising. The Misrata war museum includes photos of the known dead and missing, including Hetherington and Hondros, while excluding Gaddafi soldiers and mercenaries. Among the rebels were five who reportedly died on April 20, 2011: Ibrahim Mohammed Hamdan; Ali Mohammed al Jaly; Mohammed Ali Shetwan; Abrahim Abdoalssalan Aburawi; and Mohammed Mohammed Eshtewi (the latter a variation on the spelling of Smew). In any event, the deaths of Hetherington and Hondros gave the story its traction; in Liberia, in Sierra Leone, in Darfur, in Afghanistan, and now in Libya, thousands had lived and died without being named in news accounts. It wasn't possible to name them all. Yet in Hetherington's view it was wrong to overlook them, to relegate them to numbers. He was bothered by the tendency of Westerners to consider the unnamed victims as bit players, even in death, and made a point of naming names whenever he could, such as in *Darfur Bleeds,* in which the names of the victims are read aloud. No one in the West would likely recognize any of the Mohammeds who died on April 20, 2011—the very repetition of the names invites a non-Arab reader to scan the list without registering much, but each one brought a lifetime of experiences to al-Beyt Beytik that day, and the love of family and friends who were devastated by their deaths, just as Hetherington's and Hondros's families and friends were. As it was, the families and friends alone knew their names, and they were quickly buried, owing to the lack of ice to preserve the bodies, as well as local tradition, which calls for quick interment.

Four days after the attack Martin was stable enough to be evacuated by boat to Malta. On his last night at al-Hekma, he was told that Hetherington and Hondros had died. When he embarked for Malta, he was accompanied by four Italian doctors, in case he suffered complications en route. His mother, Karen Martin, and his girlfriend Polly Fields met him at the dock in Malta, and from there they flew to London, where he would recuperate at his parents' house for several months before returning to Budapest, where he and Fields lived. He would not speak publicly about the details of what had happened for more than a year.

As Hetherington's friends and family grappled with the loss and began planning his funeral and memorial service, there began the inevitable process of reviewing his life. The public persona of Hetherington, Junger said, was "this tall, handsome, articulate British guy who was also very brave, and a war reporter, and incredibly smart and really funny, and had a heart. That's sort of the whole package, right? What else do you want in a person . . . " Yet in Junger's view Hetherington was far more than that. He was a talented, driven photographer, writer, and filmmaker whose interest in war was in some ways tangential, who was more circumspect than most of his peers. Hetherington, he said, "questioned his own decision to cover something that ugly, and whether that made him ugly inside. We're journalists, making a living, and in some ways, we're feeding off the war." In the end, Hetherington wanted to "bring the truth of war back home, not as an argument against war, not as an argument for war. Just as an argument for truth and for reality." Junger said in the *New York Times*, "Tim wanted to change the world, but he also wanted the world to change him."

As a close friend, Junger could not help ruminating about what Hetherington might have experienced at the end. Was he afraid? Was he in pain? After having re-created the scene in his mind countless times, he pictured Hetherington thinking, "Damn it! That was so stupid. I didn't need to be here." In Junger's imagined scenario, Hetherington would have recognized that "This is just another stupid frontline street in another stupid war, and for all of the grand rhetoric about how these tragedies need to be covered—and they do need to be covered, I didn't need to be out here in this spot right now, where a bunch of young guys are shooting at a bunch of other young guys. Like, that particular piece of information is not crucial to understanding the tragedy of war, necessarily, and here I am, and I'm paying my life for it."

"I think a lot of war photographers, war journalists, have spent a lot of time thinking about that moment, when you know you've made that mistake and it's done," Hetherington's studio mate Chris Anderson told Junger during a subsequent interview for his documentary about Hetherington. As he tried to imagine what was going through

Hetherington's mind, considering how experienced he was, "I think he knew exactly what was happening," Anderson said.

Abdulkader Fassouk, the rebel journalist in Misrata who was shot in the neck at close range with an automatic weapon and very nearly bled to death, recalled thinking rationally right up to the point where he lost consciousness, after which he had dreamed of the people he knew who had died. Ibrahim Safar, who likewise nearly died in an ambush while rescuing a hostage family two days after Hetherington and Hondros were killed, was hit seven times by bullets and shrapnel, in the head, back, stomach, and legs, and later recalled feeling acute anger over not being able to see who shot him. As he lay on the ground, bleeding profusely, he said he could feel his soul leaving his body, which he described as a sucking sensation. After he fell into a coma, he said, he had "magic dreams . . . like when you see white clouds from a plane, dreamy and white."

Whatever Hetherington thought or felt at the end, it didn't last long—fifteen or twenty minutes passed before he lost consciousness and entered a state from which few return.

In a 2010 interview Hetherington had said, "I can count on a single hand the times where I'm in a situation where I think I'm gonna be killed, and gone much further—not just killed, like, 'Aw, I could've been shot,' but really a situation where you think, like, 'This is it. I've gone too far now. My family's going to be so angry with me, they're going to be so upset. What have I done?'"

Anderson told Junger he imagined Hetherington riding to the Misrata front that day "being thrilled, full of excitement, not just for the danger, but this feeling that you're getting to witness what no one else is getting to witness. You're going to lay your eyes on something that no one else is getting to see, or just a handful of people are getting to witness." Such feelings are seductive—and, obviously, very dangerous, Anderson said, because they can override the natural instinct to avoid danger. Hetherington did not need to go to the front line on Tripoli Street to explore the lives of people under duress but "he got sucked in," Anderson said. After the blast, he said, he imagined Hetherington thinking, "'That this' is it. I've made the final mistake,' you know? And all of those questions that you should have been asking yourself beforehand, all of a sudden you're asking yourself now, like, 'Why did I do this? Why am I here right now? Why did I have to come here? I shouldn't have been here. If I could just take—if I could just rewind ten minutes. One day. I wouldn't be here . . . ' Knowing that that moment was coming, and this was going to be the end, in some shitty little patch of dirt in a place that's not your home. And feeling so incredibly alone."

Rewinding was a familiar action for Hetherington as a filmmaker, but he also saw the symbolism in doing so. In his short film *Diary*, cars occasionally travel backward, and as Junger observed the short film is in some ways an homage to Kurt Vonnegut's novel *Slaughterhouse-Five*, in which he describes war as a movie that could be reversed: "American planes, full of holes and wounded men and corpses, took off backwards from an airfield in England. Over France, a few German fighter planes flew at them backwards, sucked bullets and shell fragments from some of the planes and crewmen. They did the same for wrecked American bombers on the ground, and those planes flew up backwards to join the formation." The bombers in turn sucked the flames from burning German cities; afterward the bombs were shipped back to the United States, where factory workers dismantled them and the components were buried in remote locations, "so they would never hurt anybody ever again." In the end, "The American fliers turned in their uniforms, became high school kids. And Hitler turned into a baby . . ."

It was an attractive idea, and Hetherington had considered filming a war movie in reverse. But the only moments of his life and death that could be rewound were in his video footage and films. The closest he would come to going back was aboard the boat, and then on a succession of planes, which transported his body back to where his life had begun.

Magali Charrier, who edited *Diary*, later remembered, "Somehow the work resonated very differently when I heard Tim had been killed. It's almost like how I felt we'd made a . . . a tribute to him, in advance to his death. It was almost like he'd paid tribute to his career and to his work before this happened to him."

At one point in *Diary*, we see his reflection in a hotel room window. Then we see him lying in bed, talking on the phone. There are scenes of conflict and violence juxtaposed with moments in a London tea shop that, through his lens, are as disorienting as the makeshift rebel hospital in Monrovia. Hetherington's longtime friend Stephen Mayes said *Diary* was essentially a manifesto for his future work—his first attempt to "reshape journalism, through a mix of the objective and the personal, narrative with stream-of-consciousness. In a way, *Diary* showed where he was going, but part of the tragedy is that he didn't know where he was going. The work he produced was not what he wanted to be remembered by . . . In terms of his legacy, all we have is an idea. He was exploring, trying to work it all out."

Hetherington's defining characteristic, Mayes said, was curiosity. "Everybody felt touched by him because he was curious about them. It was never about Tim." It was about opening minds, and exploration, more than the images themselves, he said. "It was about this perpetual dialogue. It was a process. *Diary* points the way."

Near the end of *Diary*, as Hetherington lies twisted in white sheets in a hotel room, talking to an interviewer on the phone, he tries to explain his work, but finds it difficult. "I . . . there is a bit of a situation in a war, or catastrophe, and I go there to make pictures, to try to understand what is happening there, for myself. I don't really, um, you know . . . " he begins, then falters. How can he explain what it all means, particularly to an interviewer who, it seems, has suggested that his images portray the hopelessness of the world? "If there's no, if you think about in the pictures that there is no hope, then I'm . . . I'm, you know . . ." His voice trails off.

From there, the film segues to a group of young women pleading with rebels on a roadside in Liberia. There is no audio. They plead in silence. Hetherington zooms in on the girls' faces; they're pretty, searching, focused, scared. At first the rebels—one is Black Diamond—listen impatiently, but eventually their faces reveal what looks like empathy. They say something we cannot hear, then send the young women down the road. The girls glance back at us, at Hetherington's lens, as if looking for something, then continue on.

The film then returns to the ceiling fan from the opening scene, which slowly oscillates above the bed with white sheets, in a room where Hetherington once stayed. The fan gently stirs the gauzy mosquito netting overhead, clicking quietly. Hetherington's camera remains fixed on the fan and the gently billowing fabric. It's beautiful, soothing, abstract. The scene fades to black.

Roaming the world, filming and photographing so much violence and depravity, and at the same time so much generosity and tenderness, Hetherington occasionally turned his camera on himself, as a way of introducing his video footage, tagging it for the archives with his name, date, and location or, as was the case with *Diary,* to allow his own journey to overlap with the stories of the people he was there to reveal. Once, in the ash field of a volcano in the Pacific island nation of Vanuatu, he says, "Here I am, in the fucking volcano." In another, he wanders the rooms of a hotel suite, filming the kitchen, the bathroom, the bedroom, down to minor details, for no apparent reason other than to create a record of one of the places he had been. When he pans across a mirror, he sees his own image reflected back at him, holding the camera, and for a brief moment he films himself filming himself, and says, simply, "Here I am."

AFTERWORD

In July 2012, a little more than a year after the siege of Misrata ended with the routing of the Gaddafi troops from the airport, I traveled there to find out firsthand what had happened before, during, and after the mortar attack. Among the people I met was Mahmud el-Haddad. Roaming the city together, we stopped at a bird market next door to his brother's telephone concession. There, Mahmud noticed a telling detail inside the exotic dove cages. "Look at this," he said, smiling. "The doves are nesting in ammunition boxes." True enough, the females were nesting in empty ammo crates. As Mahmud peered into the cages, the males stood and fluffed their feathers, breasts puffed out in tiny displays of aggression. It was hard not to see symbolism: the emblem of peace nesting in an ammo box. But what did it symbolize? That the war was past, or that it was now a part of everyday life?

By then Libya was no longer technically at war but it would be a stretch to say the country was at peace. It was, Mahmud said, "the chaos period," such as likewise existed in postrevolutionary France, postwar Germany, and countless other countries emerging from violent conflict. Libya was largely controlled by local militias whose agendas were sometimes diametrically opposed. Pro-Gaddafi forces still roamed the desert regions and even cities on the coast. Kidnappings still occurred and the national government, which occasionally detained private citizens and journalists on trumped-up charges, could do little to rein in the militias. In a nation where there had been few guns in private hands before the war, almost everyone had one now; Mahmud said that at one time AK-47s were going for $10 apiece. Huge stockpiles of ammunition remained.

No one's house was being bombed but other places were. In Benghazi, there had been an armed attack on a British diplomatic convoy, and the Red Cross in August decided to pull out of Libya after its headquarters in Misrata was bombed for the second time. If human nature is most clearly evident in times of war, Libya in 2012 illustrated its tendency to remain in flux. By the time I arrived the attacks had all been minor; no one was killed. In a way, they were tiny displays of aggression. But war was reluctant to let go.

On July 7, 2012, Libya held its first national election since 1954, which meant that almost no one in the country had ever voted before. In the days before the election, boys dressed in the local equivalent of Boy Scout uniforms handed out posters at roundabouts detailing the voting process. The day of the election, Abdulkader Fassouk, the rebel photographer, was kidnapped along with another cameraman, Yusef Badi, while covering the voting for Misrata TV. The two were kidnapped in the desert town of Bani Walid, which had supported Gaddafi and which had an old rivalry with Misrata. The militia immediately organized and planned to attack Bani Walid unless Fassouk and Badi were released. The leaders of Bani Walid vowed not to release them unless a group of Gaddafi soldiers were released from jail in Misrata. As tensions mounted, Mahmud prepared to accompany the militia in an ambulance to the expected battle with Bani Walid. This initial crisis was averted after the Misrata militia agreed to release a few pro-Gaddafi prisoners who were not clearly involved in wartime crimes, but not before another group of men from the Misrata militia were kidnapped in Bani Walid, one of whom would later die of wounds allegedly inflicted upon him during his torture.

Then, on September 11, 2012, a mob attacked the American consulate in Benghazi, killing four Americans, including the ambassador to Libya, Christopher Stevens, a champion of the rebels. Large crowds of Benghazi residents turned out afterward to express their opposition to and grief over the killings. The feeling among many Libyans was that a welcome guest had been betrayed. All it took, unfortunately, was a small group who still wanted to kill. Not long after that, the injured Misrata militiaman who had been captured in Bani Walid, Omran Shaaban, credited with pulling Gaddafi from a drainage pipe during his capture, died in France a few weeks following his release from Bani Walid, which was negotiated by the president of the national congress. Soon there was growing sentiment to attack Bani Walid, and Libyan forces and the Misrata militia did so in October, displacing thousands and resulting in multiple fatalities on both sides. Simultaneously, Human Rights Watch released a report alleging that the Misrata militia had executed 66 war prisoners around the time of Gaddafi's killing. Though Bani Walid eventually fell, the potential exists for further fighting, even a civil war. The hope—at least among my friends in Misrata—is that justice will take its course under the auspices of what is essentially a new yet uncertain nation.

Meanwhile, in the United States and the UK, several foundations were set up in the names of Tim and Chris Hondros to further the work the two were engaged in. Human Rights Watch and World Press created a grant program, in Tim's name, to support a photographer each year who is working on a project with a human rights theme. According to the grant's guidelines, the selection committee looks for qualities that defined Tim's career: work that operates on multiple platforms and in a variety of formats, crosses boundaries between breaking news and long-term investigation, and demonstrates a moral commitment to the lives and stories of photographic subjects. Among the jury members are Tim's friends Chris Anderson and James Brabazon.

After deciding to give up war reporting, as a direct result of Hetherington's death, Sebastian Junger established a program to train war journalists in basic triage, in hopes of preventing unnecessary deaths among their ranks in conflict zones. The foundation, called Reporters Instructed in Saving Colleagues, or RISC, offers three days of free training to qualified journalists, paid for through private donations, including from news organizations for which Tim and Chris Hondros worked. To publicly document Tim's work and its impact on the people he had portrayed in his photographs and films, Sebastian spent the summer of 2012 putting the finishing touches on his documentary film about him, which came to be called *Which Way Is the Front Line from Here?* The idea for the documentary had come to him when many of the photographers who had been in Misrata arrived in New York City for Tim's memorial service. Sebastian decided to ask each of them exactly what had happened and to videotape their answers, "and then I thought that if I videotape them, I should make a movie, both about his death and his amazing life."

Tim was an artist and a humanitarian, but in the end, war defined him, and killed him. He and Chris Hondros died while satisfying the world's hunger for violent news. Subsequent journalists' deaths in Syria, and others to come, can be traced to the same yearnings for news about human conflict as well as to the fleeting, obsessive voyeurism of the twenty-four-hour news cycle, Internet websites, and Facebook and Twitter. The public wants to know what's trending, regardless of the cost, which has the odd effect of making the entire enterprise at once more dangerous, more revealing, and more ephemeral.

Sieges are about forced isolation, yet how and why the photographers died in Misrata speaks to a new moment in history when nothing, not even the life of a city under siege, is truly isolated any-more. The price paid for such knowledge is high. The Committee to Protect Journalists reported that forty-seven journalists were killed in 2011, and fifty in the first nine months of 2012, including the Ameri-can reporter Marie Colvin, the French photographer Rémi Ochlik, and the Japanese reporter Mika Yamamoto, all killed in Syria—the next violent setting of the Arab Spring. Some of the deaths were the result of occupational hazards but others seem to have resulted from deliberate targeting by hostile governments and forces.

Among the many meaningful postscripts to Tim's life was an e-mail the *Newsweek* editor Jamie Wellford received from him on April 29, 2011, nine days after he died. It was sent on April 20, the day of his death, "but for whatever reason spent a week in digital pur-gatory," Wellford wrote in an article that accompanied a slide show of Tim's final photos on the magazine's website the Daily Beast. Tim had apparently written it while at the journalists' safe house, between the morning firefight at al-Beyt Beytik and the mortar attack that afternoon.

"Hey man, just checking in," Tim wrote. "Crazy day today. Full on city fight. It's an incredible story . . . and hardly anyone here."

AUTHOR'S NOTE

Tim Hetherington's professional history covers a lot of territory and encompasses events of great importance to people of very diverse backgrounds, so it's not surprising that some factual details are in dispute, or at least subject to different recollections and interpretations. Those include dates, the order of pivotal events, and the spelling of names. I've tried my best to document and cross-reference everything, but names, which would seem to be the easiest to verify, posed a challenge, especially those that are transliterated from Arabic.

I have attempted to corroborate everything recounted here through related interviews, published accounts, and other sources. I have also drawn extensively from transcripts of Sebastian Junger's interviews for his documentary film, which he very generously shared with me, as well as from his book *War* and from James Brabazon's memoir *My Friend the Mercenary*. I conducted my interviews face to face, primarily in New York City and Misrata, and over the phone, via Skype, and through e-mail. I also drew from my own experiences in Monrovia, Liberia and from my personal conversations with Tim. Quotes from all interviews are verbatim, when accompanied by quotation marks, with the exception of some that were quoted by other published sources, which I am not in a position to verify, and of others that have been edited in small ways, such as by the deletion of repetitive filler words ("um" and "like"), conversational breaks that are needlessly disruptive in print. In cases where extensive quotes have been excerpted or otherwise fragmented, I have identified the gaps through the use of ellipses.

Some people chose not to be interviewed because they felt their memories were too personal, because it seemed that everyone wanted a piece of Tim, or because they were weary of talking about it. I made every effort to include anyone who had something meaningful or otherwise important to say, and wanted to say it.

It's not possible to fully capture someone's life in a few hundred pages. It's like attempting to capture the full meaning of a war in a one-hour film. But it is possible to frame the salient details in a way that allows the story as a whole to be honestly told. This book is my recounting of one part of Tim's life, his professional career, and it is necessarily an edited version based on subjective criteria. I hope my interpretation is fair and, most of all, accurate, because it will be a record of a remarkable man and his remarkable journey that encompasses the lives of many others he met along the way.

ACKNOWLEDGMENTS

Anywhere you go in the world, you encounter people who are helpful for whatever reason—because they're helpful by nature, because of who you are or appear to be, or because of what you or your efforts represent to them. You'll also find people who dislike you, even hate you, for the same reasons. Sometimes there's guesswork involved in figuring out who is who, but at other times it's as obvious as it would be in a combat zone. Because Tim's story covers so much territory, touching so many people's lives and so many sensitive or otherwise highly significant issues, writing this book required the help of a great many people. I am grateful, therefore, to those who shared what they could about what matters after having experienced highly stressful circumstances. Most of all, I am grateful to Sebastian Junger, without whom this book could not have been written. Sebastian introduced me to Tim, encouraged me to write the book after Tim died, and helped me in every way he possibly could.

In Libya, specifically, I'm grateful to several people who helped with my research and looked out for me, including Mahmud el-Haddad; Mohammed bin Lamin; André Liohn; and Ahmed Shlak. Mohammed deserves special thanks for putting me up in his flat in Misrata, which enabled me to feel at home in an unfamiliar and potentially daunting place. Mahmud earned my undying affection by driving me around, introducing me to his friends and family as well as to useful sources, letting me bounce ideas off of him, and trying mightily, in the middle of Ramadan, to track down the names of the rebels who were killed at al-Beyt Beytik that day. He also showed me that the world, though it may turn upside down, is full of promise; that a new friend for life may await you just around the corner or, in his case, on the roof of a bombed-out building. I am grateful to André for helping me plan my trip to Libya, for introducing me to Mohammed, Mahmud, and Ahmed, for generally playing the devil's advocate, and for sharing his stories. I am also indebted to Ali Frifer for compiling information about the siege of Misrata.

I am grateful to a great many people who shared their experiences, insights, and information about the various chapters of Tim's professional life and the circumstances surrounding his death, much of which was extremely painful for them to relate: Chris Anderson, Olivier Bercault, Peter Bouckaert, James Brabazon, Chris Chivers, Michael Christopher Brown, David Buchbinder, Guillermo Cervera, Bryan Denton, Corinne Dufka, Judith Hetherington, Majdi Lusta, James Marparyan (who said that if anyone needs a lift in Monrovia, his local number is 0659-3256), Brendan O'Byrne, Katie Orlinsky, Daniela Petrova, Mike Kamber, and Danielle Jackson (especially for sharing what they've compiled about Tim's work at the Bronx Documentary Center, enabling me to reconstruct an accurate chronology of his last days). I'm grateful to Guy Martin and Ibrahim Safar for recounting their memories publicly for the first time, to James Brabazon for his endless help and guidance, and to Dante Paradiso for sharing his taped interviews with Tim. Then there are those who helped fill in the blanks through referrals: Bouckaert, Katie Gilbert, Rachel Anderson, Amanda Rogers, Rana Jawad, Finnbar O'Reilly, Mohammed al-Zawwam, Mohamed el-Naas, Benjamin Spatz, and John Scott-Railton.

I'm grateful to my literary agent, Patty Moosbrugger, who helped me work through many iterations of the proposal for this book and enthusiastically represented it; to Morgan Entrekin at Grove Atlantic, who is everything a writer fantasizes a publisher to be, and who got what this book is about; to my editor Peter Blackstock, who is a pleasure to work with, in every way; to associate publisher Judy Hottensen, director of publicity Deb Seager, and senior publicist Jodie Hockensmith, all at Grove Atlantic; to my fact-checker, April Simpson; and to my publicist, Scott Manning.

Finally, I'm grateful to friends and family who encouraged and supported me, put me up during my travels, fed my dog, fretted over me while I was gone, and respected the no-fly zone during the time I was sequestered at home, writing the book: Marcia and David Abbott; Daniel Allmon; Luke and Missy Bartkiewicz; Jessica Crawford; Irem Durdag; Stu Davey; Mike Davey; Robbyn Footlick; Lee and Dick Harding; Paul and Libby Hartfield; Les and Corinne Hegwood; Ryan Nave; Tritta Neveleff and Hamp Shive; John McLeod; Ozgur Oral; Neil and Catherine Payne; Judy and John Seymour; Pam and Buzz Shoemaker; Andy and Jimmye Sweat; Chris Walker; Scottie and Melissa Harmon.

I have only a few regrets related to the publication of the book, beyond its underlying tragedy: that I could not talk to Tim about it, that I could not find out more about the rebels who died at al-Beyt Beytik that day, and that I was unable to devote more attention to Chris Hondros, whose life is worthy of a book of its own.